IF YOU'RE NOT IN BED BY 10, COME HOME!

Martin Bengtsson

Published in 2005
by Maverick House Publishers,
Main Street, Dunshaughlin, Co. Meath
www.maverickhouse.com
email: info@maverickhouse.com

ISBN 0-9548707-2-7

10 9 8 7 6 5 4 3 2 1

The paper used in this book comes from wood pulp of managed
forests. For every tree felled, at least one tree is planted, thereby
renewing natural resources.

Printed and bound by Nørhaven Paperback A/S, Denmark

DEDICATION

I'd like to dedicate this book to the most honest and trustworthy journalist that I've ever met in Fleet Street. He followed my nefarious career throughout, and inspired me to write this tome. The late Gerry Brown, sadly missed.

I'd also like to thank John Mulcahy, a chum of mine here in Ireland, who's kept me on the straight and narrow since I've lived here.

Also thanks to Bren Barnett. This guy's about to become very famous as an actor.

My biggest thanks, however, go to my ex-tolerant wives.

Note: The names that appear in *italics* in the book have been changed to protect the person's true identity. All vessel names are fictitious and should not be confused with vessels of a similar name.

Conform and be dull.

    - J. Frank Doble

PROLOGUE

Some of the following events may seem far-fetched. Not so. Let me assure you that I'm an adventurer with an almost unbelievable story to tell. It just so happens that it's true. Having been surrounded by intrigue, subterfuge and occasional mayhem, I've been involved in military and commercial espionage, gunrunning, piracy, and general smuggling. I've been part of an assassination hit squad, a personal bodyguard to the Saudi royal family and others, and a stunt man on 16 films (including a number of the classic Spaghetti Westerns). I've been an explosives technician, a leader of expeditions across the Sahara desert and throughout Africa (hot), a ski instructor in Austria (bloody cold)— and I've taken part in numerous equally satisfying enterprises.

I've held three different identities and many alternative addresses, had a number of wives—

including two of my own—and have been forced to kill in self-defence (happily none of the ladies). My employers have included the Mafia, the CIA, British Intelligence, and the Foreign Office.

Very likely I would not have embarked upon this book had it not been for a chance comment at a recent lunch party, when, seated opposite a military chum of long standing, I'd commented that all was not as it seemed with the silver cutlery, some of the pieces being stamped 'stainless, Korea'. His reply prompted me to undertake the task.

'Stainless career, eh? That's more than yours has been, old boy. There's most certainly a book or two within your nefarious past.'

Not one of my exploits was precipitated by any political bias, patriotic sentiment or allegiance to a particular cause. I can honestly say that I did them for the money.

It's not a way of life that I would recommend without a ferocious aptitude for self-preservation, in the knowledge that it's not a rehearsal. It hasn't all been plain sailing and, with few exceptions, those that I've become involved with have usually crapped on me—so much so that on a number of occasions in the past I've seriously considered changing my name to Armitage Shanks.

Having always lived at the margins of the law, society, convention—and most of all, luck—my life has been a broad canvas, some of which, regrettably, I'm unable to change even by painting over it. The result, I fear, would allow the darker elements to ghost through the palimpsest to reveal an indelible mark.

To anyone who might contemplate emulating any of my past, I'm sure that I'm well qualified to offer a word of advice.

Don't.

I

Newhaven harbour, Sussex. 1951.

It all began when one sunny morning at the beginning of February, I walked to the end of pier 14 and threw the briefcase I was carrying as far out into the river as I could manage. It dropped in with a satisfying splash and sank into oblivion, taking with it any suggestion of establishment that might still have clung to me. I watched as its eddy drifted away on the ebbing tide.

I was free. I was still only a teenager but I felt a sense of freedom for the first time in years.

Before me, at the foot of the jetty ladder, lay the gateway to my new life—the trawler *Myzpah*. Built in 1896, this stylish vessel looked totally traditional, adding to the romantic aura of past days of sail in which I'd longed to feature.

I gazed down at her for a few long moments before going aboard, taking in as much as I could, enjoying her allure. At the same time I tried to work out for what purpose some of her equipment might be used, in the hope of appearing less green if asked to do something with it later.

She was, of course, a fine wooden ship. She smelled strongly of a mixture of tarred nets that hung drying from her foremast and, as one might expect, fish. Her pine deck was scrubbed and bleached almost white as a result of receiving constant attention from millions of gallons from the English Channel throughout her 56-year calling.

Apart from an intermittent tapping sound coming from somewhere inside the ship, there was no other sign of life.

It was time to introduce myself, but stepping on board the first time was going to be a moment to savour, and a moment for reflection.

2

As an only child, the product of a doting mother, Molly, and a tolerant father, Victor, I was very spoilt, but at the same time given every opportunity to grow up basically normal. The fact that I didn't must therefore be my own fault.

The formative years of my upbringing were quite strict, but we were, I suppose, a slightly unconventional family in some ways. From the age of about four my parents encouraged me to call them by their Christian names. This was considered rather eccentric by some of their less bohemian friends—and by others as an artful tactic for disowning me if I misbehaved in public, by giving the impression that I was the progeny of someone else.

I was weaned on Guinness, Mozart and Monet, the former being the elixir to which my 106-year-old paternal grandmother attributed her longevity.

She had the good sense to tell the world so when interviewed by a national television company at the celebration of her 100th birthday, thus guaranteeing copious quantities of that beverage arriving promptly each 20 June thereafter, courtesy of the brewers.

The musical influence stemmed from the frequent *soirées* held at Grandma Bengtsson's large Sussex home, where we spent long pre-war summer holidays.

Molly, a talented and competent pianist, could sight-read and interpret almost any score. Vic, on the other hand, was a very pleasing violinist but lacked any formal tuition. If questioned regarding this he would pass it off, saying that he learnt the 'fiddle' while playing jazz in the bars and bordellos in Havana, where he'd resided for a couple of years.

I was encouraged to sing and shyness wasn't permitted, not that there was a lot to start with. I longed for the day when my voice would break, in the hope that it would become a tenor. It didn't. I'm a bass baritone.

Vic not only played violin extremely well, but he was more than passable on cello and piano. Molly also sang beautifully. She had a lovely coloratura soprano voice. Vic used to call her his 'Bohemian Girl' because, although she had a wide repertoire, one of his favourite pieces was *I Dreamt I Dwelt in Marble Halls*. Now, whenever I hear that, or *Meditation* by Massenet or *The Swan* from the *Carnival of the Animals*, I can still vividly see them both.

The music wasn't all highbrow and in no way over-theatrical. It was simply magic, but then these were magical times. I was always allowed to stay up for all these gatherings, and sometimes even given a little alcohol.

Sometimes these evenings would go on until dawn, when Grandma would rustle up a huge breakfast for all. Nobody sat down, as it would be a perched or walk-about job, and always contained porridge, eggs, bacon and fish.

The ensemble was usually completed by an assortment of visiting minstrels, and the resident eccentric cellist aunt.

There was a trunk that stood under the window of a room not called the music room, but the one that housed the piano. It was packed with sheet music that ranged from Gilbert and Sullivan to Verdi, and Chopin to Glenn Miller.

These were pre-television days, and I assumed that all families and households behaved like we did. If we were invited out anywhere, I always wondered why nobody played or sang. It never occurred to me then that other people considered us unusual or totally odd.

Vic also provided the art ingredient, being a truly wonderful painter. In fact he possessed an alarming range of interests, so varied they required indexation, some being rather less serious.

His lessons in lifemanship, on how to escape the consequences of a series of wrong decisions, were numerous and sometimes a little frivolous. For example, 'When avoiding the bank manager, always stay on the side of the road nearest to his window. It's called "narrowing the field of vision" and shortens the time that one is visible ... Always be one step ahead of the devil and the judiciary ... Remember that women are like antique tables—the thinner the legs, the more they cost.'

And his advice when I first started going out with girlfriends, 'if you're not in bed by ten o'clock, come home', carried the extra warning that to avoid catching a chill, one should never get out of a warm bed and go home.

3

Born in 1933, I was just of school age when war broke out in 1939. I can remember quite clearly the parents listening to the announcement of the declaration of war. We heard the broadcast on a large brown Cossor wireless set. It had three horizontal black bars down each side of the front of a fretwork speaker that was in the design of the rising sun.

Molly cried at the end of the bulletin, and when I asked her why, she said that there was going to be a big war. I can remember her smiling briefly when I enquired if we would be able to see it from our balcony.

We were now living in Folkestone in a large suite in the fashionable Hotel Metropole, having moved from London. From this balcony there was a panoramic view of the sea, and on fine days the French coast was clearly visible. At night the light from Cap Gris Nez lighthouse flashed across the 21 miles.

After the 11 a.m. announcement, the three of us went out there. It must have rained during the night as there were some puddles, which caused my tricycle to leave wet tyre marks all over the surface. Molly and Vic stood in silence, no doubt musing that having left London to avoid the risk of prospective bombing, they could now actually see the land upon which the enemy were.

Up until the pronouncement of hostilities, there was an uncertain tranquil spell. A sombre time for everybody, perhaps even more so for Molly and Vic, they being of foreign descent. News bulletins became paramount, and afterwards, furtive conversations would take place out of my earshot.

The army commandeered the remainder of the hotel and on some evenings the officers would dine with us, the discussion centring during the whole repast on the immediate future. Vic, I'm sure, gleaned more relevant intelligence from these social events than the BBC were privy to at the time.

I didn't understand the mood, and although they were anxious, Molly and Vic tried hard not to show it, and life continued almost in normality. My dog Punch, Molly and I made daily visits to the beach.

If you were to ask me what I was doing a month ago, or perhaps during the past week, I probably couldn't tell you. But certain happenings of little significance I can recall in vivid detail. The wet tyre tracks on the balcony, the walks to the beach, and a number of other things that I shall come to later.

Of course, one always remembers little gems about parents.

If Molly was out shopping or away for a week, she would always leave a light switched on at home. I ventured one day to ask why, suspecting that the purpose was to confuse potential burglars. It wasn't. She explained that with all the electricity in the wires, the one light left switched on relieved some of the pressure, like a safety valve.

I didn't argue.

Vic's foibles were quite numerous too.

One very annoying habit—and this took place only in the presence of company—was quite deliberately to use a wrong word or a made-up one. Objects, according to him, were never very large—they were ginormous. There was never a specific reason for anything, but a persific one. People who were fond of the French were Francofools (though possibly there was some logic behind this one).

Despite their eccentricities, we were to make two prudent moves now that the war had actually commenced—firstly to Peacehaven in Sussex to avoid the shelling, and finally to Rottingdean to escape from the in-laws. Rottingdean being a respectable six and a half miles away gave credence to Vic's theory that owing to the advent of petrol rationing, and given that any distance above five miles over unmade roads was disagreeable to walk, they might all be kept at bay.

By now the beaches were mined and sealed off with barbed wire along the whole south coast as a first line of defence against any invasion attempt by Hitler. Although we couldn't actually visit it, the view of the sea, which was to have such an influence on me later, was uninterrupted from our latest home.

My bedroom was in fact a conservatory—a fully insulated one, and was fitted out very comfortably with a bookcase and desk and a multi-purpose table. My radio worked well out there—in fact, better than the in-house one.

I think that the reason for my partial isolation was twofold. Firstly, it was a protection from collateral damage to the main house in the event of over-enthusiasm with several chemistry sets—presents that unwitting grandparents had provided—both from the point of view of explosion, and from the risk of contamination and pervasive smells.

Secondly, the door to this room led directly into the kitchen, and Molly knew that if anything would get me up at a reasonable hour it was the scent of food.

Many a time I'd been awoken to the sound of burnt toast. Not the smell, but the delicate scraping sound as Molly attempted to remove the charred surface. I advised her on several occasions that to carry out this procedure convincingly, she might try holding the cremated offering not vertically but horizontally, and scrape the underside to prevent the blackened crumbs from lodging in the pores of the slice. God only knows what a 'nuked' breakfast would have been like if microwave cookers had been invented by this time.

My 'den' had windows on three sides, and if I forgot to close them all at night, I frequently had to share my breakfast with a number of wild birds. Vic's only comment regarding the windows was to remember what is sometimes said about dwelling in such places:

'People who live in glass houses shouldn't have it off with the lights on.'

Molly insisted that the glass was plastered all over with sticky tape in case a bomb was to fall close by. There was, of course, a much greater risk of the windows being blown outwards, because of the previously mentioned chemistry sets.

We were to live in this house for the next eight years, and it was from here that I unconsciously programmed my strange slant on life. Well, not so much strange— possibly different.

Soon after our arrival in Rottingdean, the army turned up and commandeered the bottom of our garden. They levelled this sector of jungle and built a large circular concrete base. Molly was not at all happy about this and no amount of consoling by Vic, along the lines that it would almost certainly be an observation post, would calm her. When, some days later, Bofors anti-aircraft guns along with a couple of hundred sandbags and a searchlight appeared, she became totally convinced that Hillside, Ashdown Avenue was now the number one target for the Luftwaffe.

The arrival of this weaponry instantly created a brand new hobby for me—that of aircraft identification. I would spend hours with the chaps on the battery scanning the sky, hoping that a foe might appear. Molly only allowed this pastime as it enabled her to keep tabs on my whereabouts, which hitherto had been virtually impossible, but this was on the strictest understanding that in the event of an air raid warning I should run into the house and crawl into Vic's newly contrived under-the-stairs shelter.

This was an amazing structure, fabricated from steel tubes, reinforced concrete, and some slightly modified telephone poles. Most probably it would have withstood a direct hit. However, as the unlikelihood of ever needing it became more apparent, it gradually returned to its previous function. In all probability, we owned the strongest broom cupboard in the world.

Shortly after the outbreak of the war, Vic was declared an alien, being of mixed Swedish and German nationality. As an alternative to internment throughout its duration he was offered 'specialised war work', which he took. The powers that be, in their wisdom, gave him a job developing secret mine-detecting equipment. If he'd had any leanings towards the fifth column or intentions of spying, he'd have been in his element. He didn't, of course, so this had no effect on the outcome of the conflict.

The hostilities, however, also gave Vic an extra diversion called 'fire watching'. This twice-a-week chore consisted of sitting on top of one of the highest lumps of local architecture from eight in the evening until six the following morning getting slowly but steadily pissed, whilst diligently looking for smoke.

Erudite fathers don't necessarily make the best mentors, but as far as Vic was concerned, he taught me more about life in general than I was to learn throughout my entire schooling. Although he was philosophical towards the shortcomings of most, he really couldn't stand failures. One of the paramount bits of advice he instilled in me—something that I would most certainly have to live up to—was that I ought to be different, and not run of the mill.

To a young boy the war was very exciting and not at all frightening, and although the flight-path for enemy planes and V-1 flying bombs on their way to major cities passed directly over our area, the only real danger to us coastal dwellers was one of these protagonists being shot down on top of us. On the regular occasions when this happened, it became a tremendous competition between my young friends and me to see who could abduct the most pieces before the arrival of the authorities.

By the time it was all over in 1945, our collection of relics might have rivalled the Imperial War Museum's. Even after the most flammable items had been handed in by anxious parents, we could still muster an almost complete engine of a flying bomb, some large but mostly unidentifiable chunks of a Dornier 110, a tail unit of a Hurricane and over 900 shells of various calibre—all live.

Major sources of enjoyment throughout the school holidays were war games, and we fought many campaigns in the woods and fields surrounding this pleasant part of the country. Having taken sides at the beginning of the summer, clannish loyalty would be guaranteed throughout. It was all taken very seriously, with definite rules strictly adhered to, and if outsiders wished to join in they were vetted and had to agree to hideous initiation before they were allowed to take part.

Our fictional skirmishes were played out not only between imaginary Germans and English but sometimes between Roman legions and Christians. On some occasions where history became caught in a sort of time warp, we had ancient Greeks fighting off the Vikings, and even squadrons of strange creatures from some far-off galaxy doing unmentionable things to the French.

Whatever conflicts we engaged, in, there was one overriding rule. It was all strictly Boy's Own stuff.

To my horror, all this was suddenly about to change, when one weekend in early July the parents delivered a shattering blow. A girl called Madeleine, the daughter of some close friends, whom I'd met before on two occasions, was coming to stay with us for two whole weeks, and I was expected to let her join the games. This, I knew, was going to ruin everything.

As I feared, when the fateful day came, I had to take her into my platoon. The next fortnight would seem like an eternity.

I did hope that she might go shopping a lot with Molly, but she didn't. In fact, Madeleine became more and more enthusiastic towards combativeness, and she was beginning to look a bit too permanent. Worse still, she might even stay on for the rest of the holidays.

It was actually on the second Tuesday when it happened. She and I were crawling through the long grass and had stopped at the top of a ridge to spy on the others below us. It was one of those tranquil windless days. We were lying quite still. Her legs had fallen across mine and, suddenly, they felt warm and strangely satisfying.

This was an entirely new but quite enjoyable sensation. We were both all of nine years old then, but all these years on I can still remember exactly how it felt.

It was the moment of my first sexual awakening—that balmy far-off day when girls ceased to be a pain in the back-side, but instead triggered a totally new feeling, also below the belt. As I lay there intoxicated by something that I didn't fully understand, listening only to the sound of droning insects, our battle and, for that matter, the whole world, drifted further and further away.

My side lost that afternoon, but it didn't bother me a bit, for I'd already surrendered—unconditionally.

4

It was at about this time I started to become a dissident. It all began one morning when I decided to ignore the written instructions and quite deliberately opened the wrong end of a packet of Weetabix. I'd not expected anything too dramatic to happen, but at the very least anticipated that the biscuits might all fall out of the bottom. The result, however, was disappointing, merely preventing future satisfactory closures of the packet.

Nevertheless, it marked a small turning point in my life. From that day on I would make emphatic changes. I vowed that in future I'd intentionally step on the lines between paving stones, having previously believed it unlucky to do so. I would now walk down stairs at a normal speed after having flushed the lavatory, and not try to make it down three flights to the safety of the ground floor before the cistern finished filling up. If I saw a ladder I would, in future, walk under it.

Molly would risk life and limb by stepping off the pavement and into the road to avoid doing so. Crossed knives were also unlucky so, when putting them away having washed up after meals, each knife was carefully segregated into separate compartments in the cutlery drawer to avoid the risk of a cruciform. If anyone else put them away, Molly would rearrange them later, believing that no violence would occur within the family as a result.

I would in future ignore all these superstitions. There then followed my 'wrong way round' period. This demanded that I put my left leg first into my underpants and trousers and also put on my left sock and shoe in that order. Even my shirts and jackets received the same left-limb-first treatment. These particular actions were, followed by stringent inspection before leaving the house in case something vital had been overlooked.

It was around this time that my dog, Punch, got sick. He was my first pet dog, my shadow. He followed me everywhere, even to the loo, and he slept on my bed. He meant the whole world to me.

One day he became ill and was taken off to the vet. Of course, he never came back. I was told at the time that he'd gone to Grandma Bengtsson's to recover and he'd stay there until we next visited.

I couldn't wait for the day when we'd drive down to her. When that day came, I packed all his toys, his food bowl and his water bowl to take with us. On the journey there, Vic suddenly remembered that he had to stop and make a phonecall to someone. Of course, it was Grandma.

Before we arrived, I was told to hug and kiss Grandma on arrival. I thought, 'Bugger Grandma, I just want to hug and kiss Punch.'

'Where is he?' I asked, as soon as we'd parked.

'Oh, we didn't know you were coming today, and he's staying with some friends in Portsmouth.'

That was obviously far enough away.

That evening I couldn't get over the disappointment. On the following day, I had to go on a long walk with Aunt Cordelia. She explained to me while we were out that they should have told me the truth about Punch. As he was such a special dog, Jesus wanted to look after him until I went also to Jesus, and that he'd sent down an angel to take him up there. He wouldn't grow any older, but would stay a pup, because when you went to Jesus you remained the same age.

The second evening at dinner I said, 'Why didn't you tell me the truth about Punch? Cordelia has.'

Everybody stopped eating, and I repeated what Cordelia had told me.

Molly had to go to the bathroom suddenly as she seemed to have something in her eye, but though I missed him dreadfully, the matter wasn't discussed at any length after that night.

Over the years, in spite of my Catholic education, I've had an on and off relationship with religion. At the moment it's about halfway. If by some miracle (after my contribution to global warming) I go up to that place in the sky and Punch isn't there, I'll ignore Jesus, and kick the shit out of Cordelia.

The 1945 summer now drifted away. The swallows had gone, the hols were over. It was now back to the Xaverian College in Brighton, where I enjoyed my remaining scholastic years. They were mostly happy days—possibly less so for the masters. Remaining only a mediocre batsman throughout didn't help, but being a terrifying bowler for use against the visitors and away fixtures did, and I'm sure it was this fact plus the fees and little else that prevented my expulsion.

My parents arranged extra coaching in maths, science and music including piano, organ and clarinet. This was most agreeable as it enabled me to escape French and Latin. I failed to see how 'John has the pen of my aunt' was likely to be of value on later excursions into French-speaking territories. And as far as Latin went '*puella stat*,' or 'the girl stands,' was definitely without value. I now could think of many interesting positions that young ladies could adopt, but standing certainly wasn't one of them.

'*Semper in excreta*' (always in shit), my own motto—equally appropriate now as it was then—didn't rank too highly either, in spite of it being one of my more imaginative compositions.

Regarding compositions, it was the *Nocturne in B Flat* by Chopin that was to play another small role in my education. I'd chosen to play this work as my entry for the Brighton Music Festival, and it was under the guidance of Ms *Jones*, a lady picked by Molly to take on the difficult mantle of music tutor, that it became evident that my left hand was woefully lacking. Even after umpteen attempts at the piece there was little or no improvement.

In order that I concentrate all my efforts into the bass clef, Ms *Jones* held my right hand firmly in her lap in a way that prevented escape, and allowed it no possible intrusion to the keyboard. After a little while she said something along the lines of, 'I think you enjoy putting your hand there, don't you?'

It was at her instigation that it was there and she who was making removal impossible. I wasn't at all sure that I did like it where it was, but withheld comment.

After I'd played the piece several times more, right hand still firmly detained, I was suddenly promised that if I improved my rendering she might, as a reward, allow me to touch that part of her anatomy properly. She was a dumpy little thing with fair hair and soft, pretty hands. She always smelt of Imperial Leather soap, and was very old. But then to a young boy someone in their early thirties appears ancient.

Anyway, the prospects of being allowed to handle her crotch lacked charm and I considered transposing a flat for a natural, as a sort of dissuader, but dismissed this ploy in favour of playing the opus slowly and quite literally playing for time.

She liked it.

Ms *Jones*, I discovered, was soft all over, as ten minutes later on top of a white candlewick bedspread I passed another important milestone. It was a splendid 13th birthday present.

I hadn't imagined that Ms *Jones* would be quite so heavy, but then on that particular afternoon I also hadn't considered the possibility of her sitting on top of me astride my knees while slowly removing my belt, and even more slowly undoing my flies, pausing only to check out pertinent developments in the Y-front department.

After making a few minor adjustments, she gently lowered herself down. Up until then I'd often wondered how, where and when it might happen, and this was it.

My eyes were closed, but as she leaned forward and stroked my hair, I opened them. As she tenderly raised herself up and down, her face displayed the faint smile that appeared usually throughout adagio passages— prior to a high point.

I lay quite still. The feeling was so good it could, as far as I was concerned, last forever.

Then it was all change as she rolled over, pulling me on top, taking care to avoid disengagement. The action didn't last much longer, as by now I'd completely lost control.

We just lay there side by side. It was some moments before she spoke. When she did it was in a whisper.

'It's our secret,' she said.

I didn't answer for a moment or two and before I could, she repeated, 'It's our secret,' adding, 'isn't it?'

I certainly wasn't going to tell anybody, and told her so. I don't know how it had been for her, but for my part it had been quite a performance. Forget the music.

I suppose I can further compound a dreadful pun and say that for me it had been a tonic so far. It certainly had the edge on the lemonade and cup-cakes that up until then had been her usual 'treats'.

The following Saturday lesson—at the piano, that is—lasted barely long enough to complete half a dozen scales, before we had our clothes off and engaged in other finger exercises, Ms *Jones* having first put on a record of the Chopin works—not in any way to enhance the programme but, I suspect, to convince the neighbours that her hands were busy at the keyboard.

Punctuality was never my strong suit, but I was always on time, and sometimes even early at Ms *Jones*'s smart little Edwardian house. Maybe it was simply this phenomenon that caused speculation at home, or perhaps Ms *Jones* had another favourite pupil who'd talked in his sleep. Doubtless my sudden enthusiasm for the pianoforte had been noted, adding to suspicion, because lessons were suddenly curtailed by Molly. Stopped, without so much as a cadenza, variations on a theme, or too many encores.

I don't suppose that many schoolboys can say that they've done it to the *Nocturne in B Flat* or the *Revolutionary Study*. Under similar circumstances today, youngsters might complain that they had been sexually interfered with. But in my day one would keep severely quiet in the hope that the parents would continue to pay for the lessons.

After this interlude, I did on a number of occasions walk very slowly past that little house, in the hope of seeing her. Ms *Jones*, though, had already left the district. This was confirmed when about a month later I witnessed the Brinsmead piano being navigated down the path along with other effects—some more familiar than the others—and heading off in a large light-brown Carter Paterson van in the direction of Bolton or Birmingham, or somewhere else far off.

Oddly enough, it's not any of Frederick Chopin's compositions that remind me of the first time I 'did it'. What does, in fact, are bloody cup-cakes with pink icing on top.

Of course, I'd kissed quite a number of girls prior to this, but none had approached the Velcro-ic quality of Ms *Jones*'s lips.

The music section on my end of term report was tactfully left blank. I always had a feeling that my form master, Brother Campion, had a good idea what had taken place during my extra lyrical tutoring. He once told the whole English class that Bengtsson's essays were like a music mistress's skirt—'short enough to be interesting, but barely long enough to cover the subject.'

The Xaverian did its best, and having survived numerous threats of expulsion, I left quite voluntarily in 1949.

By now I possessed a library of reference books covering most subjects, but it was, however, some of my non-textbooks, together with the dynasty of salt water that I had inherited from my grandfather on Vic's side, that prompted a desire to follow the seafaring and adventurous traditions of the Bengtssons. In fact, the blame could be equally proportioned between Vic, Nelson, Grandfather Kurt and Biggles, as they were largely responsible for my strange outlook on life. Seagoing was more or less tribal to the paternal side of our kin.

It was obvious to all that I didn't have the potential to become a second Einstein and neither the desire nor capability to dethrone Sir Adrian Boult from his conductorship of the BBC Symphony Orchestra. An imminent vacancy for Chancellor also looked unlikely.

But to persuade Molly that piracy or smuggling would be a more suitable vocation was going to prove difficult. A foray of sorts into a respectable discipline might help to prove the point.

That spring, my grandfather on Molly's side duly arranged a position for me at Coutts Bank and I became an office boy. Today this too might have been seriously considered a career in piracy, but in those days banking was still a vaguely moral pursuit. Catching the 7.08 a.m. train from Brighton to Victoria and spending eight frustrating hours in the ledger department, before rushing for the 5.25 p.m. train from Victoria back to Brighton, was a most boring business. The fear of becoming trapped in this treadmill like its superannuated servants, who were now destined to falter their way through its musty transepts until Nirvana, their lives and souls mortgaged to the company years before, terrified me.

After only two days I set about planning my escape. Molly had taken guard for all such eventualities, so all the mysterious illnesses I developed, fictitious crooks and queers in whose company I made this daily pilgrimage, together with lots of other ploys that I came up with, had absolutely no effect on her.

Why Grandfather had opened this particular door for me I was at a loss to know. Both my grandparents were always very fond of me and I of them, so I couldn't imagine what I had done to vex him to this extent. Perhaps all the doors in the city were sadly similar, and he believed that Messrs Coutts were fractionally less dreadful.

Spring turned into summer and it dragged. I watched my friends developing tans whilst I remained a sickly commuter white. Even if I took the odd unofficial day off I had to stay out of the sun in case any change of colour might be detected. At one stage I considered breaking a leg, but it's difficult to be accurately selective or to judge the degree of damage. I didn't wish to risk spending the summer in hospital as that would sacrifice the weekends as well.

On hearing that a neighbour's daughter had caught measles, I spent the whole of one weekend with them hoping for spots to appear all over me, to be followed by quarantine until at least September. Not one mouldy blemish showed up and I continued in the peak of condition.

The lucky break came when one of the women who worked in the same department accidentally damaged one of the accounting machines. *Ann* had been there for a number of years and was worried about losing favour. I had actually cleaned this apparatus earlier in the day and a sudden thought occurred to me. If I were to take the blame for the mishap by saying that I might not have put the parts back in the correct order, she would be exonerated and I would receive a black mark—which might make me a candidate for future dismissal.

My explanation was accepted and the matter almost forgotten, when the stupid woman confessed that she had broken it and that I was simply being chivalrous. I couldn't admit that I had accepted the responsibility in the hope of getting the sack, and now looked humiliatingly gallant.

Ann was in her thirties, a divorcée with amazingly pretty schoolgirly legs, lived in central London and, unbeknown to me at the time, had a gargantuan sexual appetite. This gorgeous little blonde was now under the apprehension that I fancied her. She was bloody right—I did.

Cigarettes, mars bars and various other items all started coming my way. During tea breaks and at lunchtimes she would seek me out and chat endlessly. I didn't mind. In fact, I felt quite flattered.

These activities had not gone unnoticed by our overlords, and heaps of shallow advice was being handed down by Mr Hedges, the chief of the department.

'I should find myself a nice girlfriend if I were you,' and, 'There's plenty of time for that sort of thing when you are older,' were examples.

His over-skinny wife Olive, who looked more like the chattel of that cartoon sailor man, Popeye, also worked in the ledger department and wrongly considered herself to be second in command, was more blunt. In stage whispers she would be heard to mutter to her cronies contributions such as, 'Filthy little beast!' or 'She is old enough to be his mother,' and 'He will wind up in trouble, you'll see!'

Olive didn't like me anyway because I am sure that she knew that I had nicknamed her the 'Filleted Earwig'. Actually, her indelicate comments only helped to fuel the impending affair.

A controversial film called *Pinky* was showing in the West End at this time and after a number of broad hints from *Ann* I agreed to take her to see it. Friday came.

4 p.m.: finish.

A quick 4.30 p.m. change in the loo, followed by a 5.30 p.m. sandwich in Marco's in Windmill Street.

7 p.m.: meet *Ann* outside the Empire in Leicester Square.

11 p.m.: phone home to report failure to catch the last night train to Brighton.

11.30 p.m.: arrive at *Ann*'s flat and, remembering advice previously received from Vic scheduling the deadline for climbing into girls' beds, discover I am an hour and 45 minutes adrift—for it was 11.45 p.m. when I pulled the covers over us.

Since my earliest experimentation with sex I'd realised there was more to it than the straightforward basic horizontal mode. But to be suddenly faced by most of the 64 reputed positions listed in the *Kama Sutra* was, at best, daunting. That the whole programme should be carried out in complete silence had not for one minute been my expectation, but I certainly hadn't anticipated the level or duration of noise. I could only marvel at the soundproof qualities of Victorian architecture, but for which there would undoubtedly have been a rush of rescuing neighbours, as *Ann*'s unbridled squeals might at times have fostered in the less well-informed the belief that mortal wounding was taking place.

This lady was untamed. She was to chastity as Icarus was to aviation, and Herod to babysitting. She not only had an immense capability for carnal control, but also an expectation of sex so vast that it couldn't even be contained outdoors.

In spite of the *Jones* variations on a theme I was still quite naïve. We'd all read some pretty surprising prose at school contained within some dubious continental literature prior to its confiscation, most of which was quite explanatory. But until then I was still under the impression that oral sex was simply sitting down and having a chat about it. Any shortcomings in my sexual erudition were most definitely corrected by the debriefing I received throughout that hot September night. I vaguely remembered Saturday and went home on Sunday.

I was rather expecting Molly to hit the roof when I returned, but she didn't. Numerous covert top-level communiqués had passed between bank and home base and, as a result, she was playing it cool. Some days later she asked quite casually, 'Who is *Ann*?'

'A girl I know. Why?' I replied.

'She is older than you, isn't she?'

'Yes, I believe she is.'

'Sounds like a brazen little hussy to me.'

That was all she said, but at that moment I could see the door opening for my escape from this awful penance. If I were to play my cards right, *Ann* could become my light at the end of a boring tunnel. I might be leaving the bank sooner than in my wildest dreams.

Meanwhile, back at the bank there was more advice and now questions, all of which had taken on a more searching attitude.

Mr Hedges could hardly contain himself. He fenced all round the burning question but didn't actually ask, 'Did you go to bed with her?' I led him on but didn't tell him. Of course, he didn't care what junior staff did after working hours. His interest was probably fanned by jealousy.

Ann was bloody good looking—a stunner in fact—and I could imagine what was going on in old Hedges's mind. That trim little body. And, yes, those legs. Faintly tanned, with a dusting of blonde downy hair that one only noticed when the light was behind them, depending from what angle and, of course, from what distance they were viewed.

I now spent much more time with her, each weekend passing in a haze of whisky and tangled bedclothes. I'd hated London at first. My problem now was that I was growing fond of it. Even the view from the bedroom window had taken on a certain appeal. Mind you, as I lay gazing at the rooftops veneered with pigeon-tormented tiles, contrasting against an endless blue afternoon sky, I could have been anywhere in the world.

But this was London and I was with her, and I felt relaxed. Too relaxed. What if she, my light at the end of the tunnel, might turn out to be a train coming the other way? What if she, who took what seemed like hours to put on make-up for just a short walk in the park; she, who made it almost impossible to take a bath without becoming entangled in lines of drying bras and pants; what indeed if she, my very instrument of escape from this prosaic boredom, might actually start to undermine my resolve to do just that?

Strangely, it was *Ann* herself who settled it for me. One Saturday she decided to visit her mother who lived in East Ham and I went with her. Neither of us thought it wise for me to be seen at her mum's house, so I was to explore the East End for a couple of hours and we would meet up later at the Tube.

As I wandered along Connaught Road I could hear the sounds of the river—busy tugs and other commercial traffic—and I was soon drawn towards the Royal Docks. Upon my arrival at King George V, a friendly policeman let me slip through a gate and I slowly made my way round the dock. In spite of it being the weekend, there was plenty of activity here, including the unloading of three large freighters, and it wasn't long before I became totally engrossed.

As I watched, I realised I would have to become part of it. It wasn't only the sight and sounds that were having this effect, but even the smells of some of the crates of cargo, redolent of strange and exotic places, told me that it was time to leave the bank and go to sea. I would leave by Christmas, I told myself.

At home, this announcement now fortunately met with no visible maternal opposition, and the situation was thoroughly (if only secretly) endorsed by Vic.

I stayed at Coutts for the Christmas party to which I had contributed whilst I had been there, where amongst the curled-up sardine-and-tomato sand-wiches I became more than a little drunk on cheap British sherry.

Through a mist of poor quality festive season cigar smoke I watched them all. Cadaverous old Hedges creeping around looking as though he was only trying to save on funeral expenses, and Olive Oyl who would have been pleased to pay them on his behalf. The manager and his ample-bosomed secretary, who was wearing make-up that looked as though it had been applied with a trowel, were both dressed up to the nines and keeping a respectable distance from each other, just in case of comment. Old Jones from the book-binding department in deep conversation with some of the printers, probably giving very technical details of how he kept his glue pot hot. And the two chaps from accounts whom nobody was quite sure about.

What in God's name could they all find to talk about—having such exciting lives? Although Percy Green, the assistant manager, had once accidentally set fire to his waste-paper basket. It was the talking point for weeks. Now if he'd set fire to the bank, or even himself, I could have understood it. But there you are.

And, of course, there was *Ann*. I would certainly miss her, and I wondered for how long she would miss me.

A shudder ran down my spine. Just suppose that it was all a dream, and I wasn't really leaving after all. That night I made damn sure that I caught the last train to Brighton.

On the face of it, I'd learnt very little about banking, but I had a very good idea what Adam must have got up to, and I don't think it had a lot to do with stealing or biting apples in someone's holy garden. Thank God for the *Ann*'s of this world—because not only did she provide me with my franchise for freedom, but she also set the standard by which I would judge all legs in future.

When men come to like a sea-life, they are not fit to live on land.

- Samuel Johnson

5

After descending the jetty ladder, I walked soft-footed across *Myzpah*'s pristine deck, and directing my voice (rather meekly, I'm afraid) down an open hatchway, I called, 'Below!'

Although Vic had assured me that this was the correct jargon, and even leaving out the 'Ahoy' prefix, I still felt quite embarrassed about using it. Somehow it conjured up visions of pirates with patches over one eye and parrot shit down the backs of their jackets, all hopping about on one leg shouting things like, 'Avast and belay there!'

Nevertheless, it worked, because a head appeared.

'What do you want?' it asked in an educated Scottish accent. With a newly acquired confidence, I replied, 'I'm the new deckhand, Martin Bengtsson.'

'You are, are you? Ever been to sea before?'

'No sir,' I replied.

'Don't sir me! I'm Douglas the engineer.'

I was tempted to say, 'Aye-aye, Douglas,' but said, 'Okay,' instead.

'Come down, laddy, and I'll show you where to stow your gear.'

The companion-way ladder led into the engine-room, which was quite brightly lit. A pump, which obviously belonged to the engine, was sitting on the deck in pieces, which must have accounted for the tapping noise.

'That's your locker and bunk aft of the engine. It's the warmest fucking place in the ship, and you'll be glad of that, because this can be the coldest fucking job in the world. It's also the noisiest fucking place, but that shouldn't worry you too much, because when you do get time to get your fucking head down, you'll be so fucking tired that you won't fucking notice it. And you'd better bloody believe it,' he added—not so much to emphasize the point but, I suspect, to display his highly versatile vocabulary of swear words.

After cramming my belongings into the designated space at the foot of a rather hard-looking anti-narcotic bunk situated some three feet from about 600 horsepower, I felt it was time to take stock.

I'd have been quite wrong if I'd imagined that all trawlers were fitted out like *Myzpah*. The galley, forward of the engine-room, contained not only well stocked food compartments, but also similarly burdened wine racks. There was too, an abundance of spirits, port and sherry. I later discovered that most of this grape juice came about by a swapping arrangement between *Myzpah* and some French trawlers a few miles off the coast. On the port side of the galley sat a black and white Aga breathing warmly beneath a large pan, from which emitted some interesting smells.

Further forward, where one might expect to find the fish-hold, was the saloon, richly embellished in oak, mahogany and brasswork. Two more cabins were ahead of this, and finally right up in the forepeak of the ship, was the loo.

This decorative apparatus by Wedgwood, I was to discover later, had one major problem. Being in that most forward part of the ship it experienced the most violent rise and fall, so even in moderate weather it obliged users to cope with the issue of a semi-weightless crap long before latter-day space travellers had to face such a challenge.

The opulent fitting out of this stately vessel had been carried out during her building to indulge the whims of her original owner, a wealthy eccentric gentleman fisherman.

Having familiarised myself with her Tardis-like layout below, I decided to take another look at the mysterious equipment on deck.

My second conclusion was pretty much the same as the first and I was none the wiser. In this situation the best thing to do was to sit down and have a cigarette.

The day had started fine enough, but now some small nimbus clouds appeared, suggesting that they might be planning something covert with the sun and Neptune was gently stirring the surface of the ocean.

Put another way, by five o'clock it would most likely be pissing down and blowing ten sorts of a bastard.

Some out-of-season visitors had now gathered on the jetty, making me feel that I should be doing something useful. There was also the added danger that one of them might ask something technical. As yet, my knowledge of the industry could be documented on the back of a tuppenny stamp. I was, after all, only the new fourth hand, employed to replace the late Len Peddleton. Len had recently gone to meet that man in the sky who, rumour had it, knew more about fishing than anybody else.

'Is there anything I can be getting on with, Douglas?' I asked, shouting down through the hatch.

There was a clearly audible snort from below.

'Don't be a fucking idiot! Never volunteer!'

I wished I hadn't and vowed not to do so in future. I also avoided looking up at the jetty until I'd heard the visitors leaving.

Shortly after three, Mark the skipper appeared. From his walk, an educated guess might have led one to believe that he was more than slightly drunk. He turned out to be a man of few words. Looking at me, he said, 'You must be the new hand. Let's eat.'

I was to discover that Mark always remained in the pub until the last moment prior to sailing, subscribing to the theory that it was better to spend it all rather than risk being lost at sea with some still in his pocket, or even worse, leave any that his widow might get her hands on.

We went below followed by John, the fourth member of the crew, who had just arrived. So this was late lunch. All laid out like an upmarket restaurant.

The day's menu was the beef stew I'd encountered earlier. Cooked in red wine with onions, garlic, mushrooms and a whole lot of other things, it had been simmering all the morning and was delicious. This was followed by spotted dick pudding with heaps of fresh cream, and rounded off with a selection of cheeses and Bath Olivers, brandy and coffee, the early stages having been gratified by a bottle of your better-than-average claret.

Douglas doubled as cook. I hoped that he was equally competent at engineering. He and his ex-wife had owned and run a restaurant, and from the quality of this day's provender, this didn't surprise me.

Throughout this first meal, I was able to weigh up the others. Douglas was about 45, stockily built—in fact, overweight—and five foot nine. His brown military-length hair was going grey at the sides. The reddish nose in the centre of a florid, unshaven face suggested a long-term fondness for the bottle.

He wore a heavy hand-knitted sweater, damaged and repaired badly at the cuffs and elbows, and totally shapeless brown corduroy trousers that had seemingly not been involved with an iron since the day they came off the tailor's peg—not shabby, but worn without many holidays. His heavy, reddish-brown leather shoes, sporting thick corrugated soles and leather laces, completed his scruffy assemblage. It did, however, bear a hallmark of past quality.

The uninformed would have almost certainly placed him in very different surroundings. With the exclusion of his profanities, of course, he might have been a laird, a resting actor, a lecturer, or even a struck-off doctor—but not a fisherman.

Mark was about 40, slightly taller than Douglas, with dark unkempt hair. He also didn't portray the archetypal fisherman. He looked more like a painter and decorator. The dark-blue overalls spattered with paint, covering a greyish-white shirt and black ordinary shoes was, I discovered, his seagoing and his going ashore gear.

The only exception was a change of footwear at sea, when both he and Douglas wore not rubber wellingtons or sea boots, but Royal Marine leather parade boots purchased from the Army Surplus Store. I was told that they had more grip in heavy weather, so to buy some.

Mark's only notable feature was that his left eye was marginally out of line with its chum, possibly the result of a fight or accident. It had the effect of giving him a persistently fixed stare, like that of a ventriloquist's doll. Tucked inside the neck of his overalls, he wore a small crucifix on a slim chain. Personally I had no objection to this custom, as long as it was worn for the purpose for which it was intended. As it doubled not only as a toothpick, but also as an instrument for earwax removal, I found it quite disgusting.

I assumed that it was this artefact that had given Mark the shoreside nickname of Isaiah, and it took me some time to rumble that he had been so christened by a wit from another trawler, as a result of one of his eyes being higher than the other.

John, who came from a long-established fishing family, actually looked like a fisherman. In his early twenties, he was dark-haired and didn't have a lot to say for himself. A sweater, jeans and sea boot man.

It was quite evident that these fellows were no ordinary fishermen. It was equally apparent that *Myzpah* was no average fishing boat.

Having polished off the meal, I was drifting into that sleep-preceding warm glow, and there was nothing I'd have liked more than to try out my new bunk. Not a chance. Mark rose from the table and in an almost sober voice announced, 'Right, let's go then.'

As previously predicted, it was now blowing hard from the south-west and raining. We swung on the berth and let go.

20 minutes later we headed for the saluting lighthouse, and I logged to memory that this was the prelude to a future in which I was determined to succeed, no matter what the cost. I was young, fit and ambitious—but above all, adventurous. I needed to be.

There was never a harbour bar at Newhaven, because the entrance was continuously dredged to give the cross-channel ferries enough water to pass in and out at almost any state of tide. As we swept from the shelter of that long and friendly breakwater out through the shallows, *Myzpah* stood on end. I thought she'd never stop going up.

We crashed down the other side of the first wave and right through the next. She recovered just long enough to get halfway through the following one, before being smothered again. She shivered, and so did I. It seemed that the whole world had gone mad, but we ploughed on into the teeth of a howling southwester. The wind had more than picked up—it was like a tempest from hell. I hoped that *Myzpah* was about to live up to her name. 'The Lord watch over us whilst we are absent one from another.' Old Testament.

These weren't just very large waves. They were mountainous steep walls of water so close together that *Myzpah* didn't have time to rise, but crashed through them. She shuddered repeatedly as several tons of water thundered down on her decks again and again. I was sure that she couldn't survive this onslaught for much longer, and wondered how long this would go on before Mark turned her round. He couldn't, of course, even if he'd wanted to, as any one of those seas would have turned her over.

After some ten minutes of this torturous bashing, which seemed like an eternity, the breaking seas gave way to huge swells that no longer crested. *Myzpah* bravely slid up and over most of them, diving through only the occasional one.

It was now getting dark and under the light of the compass, suspended in its gimbals, which were working overtime, I hoped that the pure-white pallor of my face wasn't visible. I was experiencing that sort of fear that not only made it possible to smell adrenaline, but almost to identify its colour.

Eventually we reached deeper water and, as the swells became further apart, the motion became less extreme.

I was sure that Mark would now turn around and we'd struggle back into harbour. I was wrong. He'd obviously played this perilous gambit before, keeping one hand on the wheel and the other on the throttle control, shutting down the revs each time *Myzpah* nosedived to avoid any damage to the engine, as her unburdened propeller broke clear of the water.

Steering wasn't too demanding as the mizen-sail kept us head to sea and wind, like the weather-vane on a town hall roof. I've always disliked those darkly Victorian custodians of establishment, but at that moment in time I'd have given my eye-teeth to be looking at one, or better still, touching one.

Hanging on to part of the inside structure of the wheel-house and trying desperately hard not to appear as frightened as I inwardly was, I yelled to Mark above the noise, 'How far do we go out?'

'About 35 miles,' he bellowed.

From this reply it was plain to see that they were all totally raving mad, and that my life expectancy had distinctly shortened.

That night I became suddenly closer to God, and with him started immediate negotiations on a long-term contract which, for my part, sought an option to adjourn my mortality to a more convenient and distant date in return for any number of things, including becoming a better son to Molly and Vic—less selfish, more thoughtful, and generally a better all-rounder. That was, of course, if I ever saw them again.

'Are you enjoying it?' Mark enquired between the crashes of the seas.

'Not particularly,' I replied.

'Vic will want a full report on you during this trip,' he shouted above another thundering wave.

'If this weather doesn't improve, he'll be getting it through a medium!' I yelled back.

His answer wasn't wholly reassuring. In a loud voice like Olivier delivering, 'Once more unto the breach, dear friends,' he roared, 'Women and cowards on land may lie; the sea's a tomb that's proper for the brave.'

He took lively pleasure in reciting some more jolly little unvarnished truths.

'Remember,' he delivered, 'those who go to sea are only ever two inches from death,' meaning the thickness of the timbers. I didn't feel at all like it, but retaliated, in an effort to shut him up.

'Don't worry, I'll be all right. I'm too young to die.'

In the light of the compass, he gave me a withering look, and snapped, 'There's no age limit. It's not like driving, drinking or shagging.'

I've always attached little importance to the average man's opinion, and wondered how many apprentices had been treated to these attestations during their first storm. However, his third proclamation I've always believed in firmly.

'You must treat the sea with a measure of reverence,' he continued, 'because it's the most powerful . . .' He broke off to pull the wheel over another spoke. 'Because it's the most powerful . . .' he repeated, raising his voice above the wind, 'natural element on earth. You must also have a reverence for the fish we take, because they are now the only food left on the planet that man still goes out to hunt.'

Thinking he'd finished, I started to say something. He hadn't finished, and shouted me down.

'So remember always that you have to give something back to the ocean in return. And that, my son, is respect.'

In a friendlier attitude he next suggested that I get my head down for a couple of hours and then I could share the next watch with John. This advice was very welcome, and after a struggle I managed to clamber below. Almost on hands and knees, I squeezed my way past a hot and noisy diesel engine and crawled into my bunk. In spite of the deafening roar and the motion, I didn't need rocking to sleep. I went out like a light.

As a matter of interest, I've never suffered with seasickness—all credit due I'm sure to that original voyage, when my teeth were clenched so tightly together I couldn't be sick. There wasn't room.

Mark shook me at midnight and I joined John in the wheel-house. The wind had dropped and the sea state had moderated. We discussed the merits of sailing in such capricious conditions. There was, of course, a reason for this—money. I already knew that fishing boats' crews were paid on a share basis. The bigger the catch, the bigger the wage packet. What I hadn't realised was 'market timing'.

If *Myzpah* could land her catch before the other vessels, the prices in the market in Brighton would be higher, owing to demand. So if she was on the fishing ground a day, or even two days before the competition, she could return and take advantage of this event. It was clear that John endorsed this habit. Now that the weather had improved, I was already beginning to come round to this way of thinking, and wished I'd not been so panic-stricken earlier, hoping that my fear hadn't been too obvious.

It was still quite rough but, strangely enough, almost enjoyable. What was even more enjoyable was the sudden bright light that appeared below at 4 a.m., followed by the smell of bacon and eggs that wafted up from the galley. Douglas was at it.

We reached the fishing ground at ten, and shot the trawl. We were now running down the wind, and having hoisted the huge russet-coloured mainsail, Douglas dispensed with the engine. This was more like it. Just the creaking of the rigging and the slight groaning noise of the timbers as they moved slightly, one against the other.

Three hours later we hauled the trawl. It produced eight boxes of fish. We shot the gear again. The next haul produced a further six boxes. 26 boxes later we headed for port, in company of the *Boy Eric*, a larger Newhavener who had also adopted our bad-weather sailing technique.

It wasn't always bad weather. Sometimes the sea was as flat as a pancake, but if we were caught out in a blow we'd sit it out and heave-to. Apart from the *Eric*, all the rest of the fleet would run for cover and disappear, like a dole queue caught in a cloudburst.

Myzpah spent much time at sea. It was hard work, but we were well fed and handsomely paid. I soon learned to steer and handle a watch. *Myzpah* didn't have a vast array of equipment to master. Her gear wasn't so much state of the art as state of the Ark.

The compass had a large, aggravating bubble in it, which Vic had once suggested could be removed by topping it up with gin. The bubble stayed. If the remedy had required water, tea or even pee, I'm sure the offending air pocket would have gone, but any form of C_2H_5OH would never have been appropriated for such a frivolous task.

By the early fifties, most trawlers had ship-to-shore radio telephones. *Myzpah* didn't. She did, however, have a wireless receiver, a rather aged Vidor battery job. This was an essential item of her navigation equipment. Screwed down to a shelf in the wheelhouse, it was permanently tuned to the BBC on 1500 metres, this being the frequency on which the weather forecast was transmitted and largely ignored by us all. But owing to its old-fashioned rod aerial, it only functioned when pointing 90 degrees towards London. This was our 'direction finder'.

Most navigators use slightly more conventional methods to obtain navigational fixes (the sun, stars and sextants etcetera). We were different. All our positioning was in relation to Lime Grove.

There was an echo sounder for indicating the depth of water beneath the vessel. It stood embarrassingly in the corner of the wheel-house. It was, of course, broken and always showed a reassuring five fathoms (30 feet). Similarly the wind speed indicator always instilled a measure of confidence, because even in a gale it never registered more than force two on the Beaufort scale.

In spite of these shortcomings, we wound up on Seaford beach on only one occasion in fog. This mishap wasn't caused by a shortage of alcohol in the compass but, I suspect, possibly a surplus of it in the crew.

Of course, I didn't appreciate how much pressure we were putting on this elderly vessel throughout those early months, *Myzpah* put up with a lot of heavy weather. Thanks to the mastery of her builders she came through unscathed, with few near misses. I've little doubt that this was in no way attributable to any serious degree of seamanship managed by us.

Eventually the winter storms gave way to more regular tranquil conditions. This, of course, resulted in lower profits by allowing the smaller boats to work more frequently, thus influencing the market. Mark had a remedy to offset this financial shortfall. It was nick-named 'Meeting Petit Jean'.

This consisted of sailing south by 15 west on prearranged days whilst P.J., a rather small Frenchman who owned a large trawler called *Antoinette*, sailed north by 15 east until we met. A swapping arrangement then took place. He handed over copious quantities of brandy in exchange for money. Not very different from shopping in any present day French hypermarket, except that *Antoinette* wobbled about a bit. From May till September, *Myzpah* was 'supporting' a number of hotels and pubs in Newhaven, Peacehaven, Seaford, Lewes and Brighton.

In June we were given an unexpected six weeks' break from fishing. A film company who were half way through production of a comedy called *Green Grow the Rushes* needed a replacement vessel to finish some shots, as the one they started filming with had sunk. *Myzpah* fitted the bill.

We were paid not to go to sea until the next gale, as the required shots were of a trawler in heavy weather. In the meantime *Myzpah* was painted yellow, and we waited and waited. The Newhaven harbour tug *Foremost* was also engaged to be the camera vessel, and she was put on stand-by. She also waited.

The following five weeks were flat calm and the sea remained like a mirror. Then along came a little force six. We took the actors out for a quick rehearsal. They were all sick. We were now to be paid to double for the cast during the next blow. It came along the next week—force eight. We sailed now as budding actors, followed by the *Foremost*, with camera and film crew.

The cameraman was sick. He was now about as popular as a pork chop in Tel Aviv.

The 'epic' was finally shot with *Myzpah* making passes across the end of the breakwater, upon the end of which was the camera and its less queasy operator.

It was then back to fishing. Towards the end of September the warm south-westerlies started to give way to the cold north-easterlies, and the prospect of a winter's fishing in the Channel lacked appeal. It was that season of the year when, on weekends ashore, the sound of pushed lawn mowers was exchanged for the smell of autumn bonfires leavening discarded summer garb. But why am I being such a romantic? I meant to say it was the onset of winter, and about to get sodding cold.

Deliverance was offered quite by chance, when a German ex-E-Boat limped into Newhaven with engine trouble. She was on passage to Italy, but as soon as she was alongside, her crew vanished. A couple of days later, the agent for the vessel turned up and Douglas was asked to inspect the engines and see if he could rectify the problem.

He did whatever had to be done to the machinery and the agent was suitably impressed—so much so that we as a crew were asked to deliver the vessel to Fiumicino.

Myzpah was due for a major refit, which would take about two months, so Mark, Douglas and I took on the delivery, leaving John to supervise the overhaul. I had some reservations, having become very used to the lifestyle on *Myzpah*, and from a quick look at the galley, the *Pandora* didn't look up to much.

Molly had grown used to the local seafaring number, but she wasn't a happy lady when I announced that I was leaving for Italy to deliver a gunboat for, as Vic put it, 'a dodgy outfit'.

On the morning of our departure, I slipped quietly out of the house to avoid any goodbyes. On the chair that lived by the front door, I found two pairs of new socks and a ten-bob note, with a St Christopher medal and chain on top of them. The glass that I'd taken my last drink from would now be put away safely and not touched until I returned, as it always was.

In the meantime, Mark had engaged another crew member to sail with us. This was Alex. He would double as deckhand and second engineer.

We sailed on the first of October at 6 p.m. As the lights of Newhaven bobbed out of sight below the horizon, an effect I'd seen many times before, I was setting out on my first real adventure, although I didn't know it at the time. The first of many to come, but back then my thoughts didn't go any further than the prospects of a leisurely two-month cruise in the Mediterranean. A small flock of migrating birds settled on our deck and hitched a ride. This was somewhat reassuring—they must have had confidence in Mark's navigation.

6

Sadly, the parents split up when I was 17, and to this day I've never been able to fathom out the reason. At the time there were no other involvements and neither of them wound up with anyone else after the separation. Well, Molly didn't, and Vic's later flings were on a very temporary basis. They had most things in common—music, theatre, and the arts generally were greatly appreciated by them. Even the same right-wing politics. Molly was a damn good cook and Vic was certainly no fool with a knife and fork.

Their sense of humour differed slightly, hers being of the banana-skin variety and his rather more subtle. His one bugbear was the Women's Institute (WI). Molly was a leading light in the choir, at which he constantly levelled some of his wit, but I'm sure that this, together with the frequent musical gatherings at the house by this fine body of ladies, had little or nothing to contribute to the parting.

Actually this female gang bugged me more than they did him. When my voice broke it was hinted that I might be conscripted into this lyrical assembly. The choir did contain three younger and unattached maidens but I had no carnal thoughts in their direction. To score was out of the question and I had them pencilled in as 'dot balls'. Not by a long chalk was there any likelihood of knicker-throwing groupies stalking the WI concerts, so I filed a strong defence and was mercifully acquitted.

Although they were now living apart, Vic was always summoned to mend fuses, tap-washers, and various other failures, and it was on one of these visits that he became trapped in the house during a WI rehearsal. When the contralto was taken slightly unwell, blaming it on the *coq au vin* from the previous night, Vic whispered to Molly that this malaise should have been anticipated after having it off in the back of a Ford Eight.

She missed the point.

Quite a lot of Vic's humour was wasted owing to Molly's naïvetè, the *double entendre* not usually registering—which was rather commendable. If she'd heard the expression 'a good bonk', she would have assumed that it referred to the French equivalent of Barclays, NatWest, or AIB.

Molly could be quite unintentionally funny. I can remember on one occasion when she had received a new hearing aid—one of the latest with advanced technology—after much research having gone into the choice of this expensive piece of equipment. When I asked her how she was getting on with it, she looked at her watch and replied, 'Ten past three.'

After they split up, the Rottingdean house was sold. Vic bought a seafront flat in Hove and Molly moved into a five-bedroom house in sprawling, unsung Peacehaven. I moved in with her.

At last Molly got her head round the fact that I was no longer a child, but a young man, so we divided the house into two separate apartments. I took over the top floor with my own kitchen but, thank heavens, she still did most of my cooking. Always on Sundays, if I wasn't at sea, Molly's roast beef and Yorkshire pud was a vast improvement on anything I could produce, as at this time my gastronomic achievements relied heavily upon a tin opener. Another advantage in having Molly below was that I could always borrow a plate and eating irons whenever my washing-up reached critical mass—a frequent occurrence.

Having escaped from the bank, I intended that *Myzpah* was to be only a stepping-stone to going deep-sea and that I would learn every aspect of the seafaring trade as quickly as possible. Vic had impressed upon me that as Mark had an extra master's ticket I should pick his brains, question everything and commit to memory. Molly, on the other hand, dreaded my long-haul aspirations and dreamt up endless reasons why I should not go.

Numerous business ideas were suggested, but declined. Even a musical career was proposed, and girlfriends were keenly encouraged, a number of them passing—sometimes only briefly—through my quarters. Molly seldom saw them except for the odd fleeting glimpse, turning a blind eye to my 'goings-on' as long as they created a sort of anchor to keep Martin from drifting off for long and faraway absences. For this reason, I don't think she would have cared if any of them had two heads. She did, however, meet one, late one Friday night.

I'd just passed my driving test and sported a very unpatriotic Yankee car—a Ford Fairlane. Its engine was fine, the interior perfect, but the bodywork suffered a little from the tin-worm. In fact, Vic maintained that it displayed more rust than the current state of the *Titanic*. His advice was not to clean it, and if I did so, to do it gently or risk total disintegration. Anyway, I liked it, and was one of the few among the fishing fraternity to possess 'wheels'.

It spent a lot of the time sitting in the drive at home as it needed a petrol tanker following it to quench its insatiable thirst. Although at that time petrol was less than five bob a gallon, it required a lot of five bobs to keep it running, so I used it economically—about twice a week—but never on Friday nights on which had developed a ritual for me to meet up with Vic and go on a pub crawl in Brighton.

This was prior to any Breathalyser, but on Friday nights the Fairlane would stay at home and I would resort to public transport, usually returning home by the last bus out of Brighton's Pool Valley. Travelling by this method would almost always be an eye-opener, as its assortment of patrons ranged from the totally sober returning theatre-goers to the ready-to-fall-down drunks who, most times, got off at the wrong stop. Sometimes there was even the odd fight.

This particular time I was sitting upstairs on the number 12, reflecting upon my evening out, when a female voice called out my name from somewhere behind. I turned round in my seat and there was Kinky. This nickname simply meant slightly crazy in those days and didn't carry the present connotations—although one might have been forgiven for any mistake after what followed.

Kinky blurted out from three rows back, 'I could have done with you half an hour ago.'

A few weeks previously she had managed to fall down a flight of stairs, which resulted in a broken arm, now in a plaster cast and sling. Last week she'd almost completed the double by tripping over a raised paving stone, measuring her length, and spraining her other wrist, now heavily bandaged.

I knew that I was leading with my chin when I asked why. She continued, 'I had a pee and couldn't get my knickers back up, so I had to kick them off.'

After the mixture of laughter and disapprobation had subsided and I'd ignored the suggestion from some loud-mouth that such an act in my case would have been a first, and a hurried seat-swap with me by the red-faced chap who was sitting next to her, our fellow travellers went quiet, ears pricked in the hope of catching any further revelations.

Nothing particularly galvanising was discussed until I mentioned to her that I was on my way home for a late steak and chips, as Molly always cooked for me after evenings out with Vic.

Kinky sighed, pointing out that by the time she reached home in Newhaven her family would have gone to bed and the handicap that had resulted in the lingerie problem also prevented any culinary activities. After dwelling on this for a few moments longer, she announced, 'I think I'll come home with you.'

I had been about to suggest this quietly, but she got in first.

'Lucky sod,' piped up the same loud-mouth seated behind us.

Very justified, because Kinky was a good-looking girl. No, she was a super-slim gorgeous little blonde, with fabulous legs, and a model's figure. Whereas a certain Lady Godiva had allegedly proclaimed when challenged regarding her equestrian activities that she had a 'divine right', Kinky was streets ahead, having a rather lovely left to match.

Her only conspicuous quality lacking was in the vocal department, as there was always a reluctance to favour the soft pedal.

Upon our arrival at Roderick Avenue we headed for the stairs preparing to alight. This being a popular stop, the bus would be stationary for some moments.

'Don't forget your knickers, love!' It was the slob sitting in the back seat at the head of the stairs.

Kinky stopped, and with her good hand she popped open the clasp of the handbag slung round her neck, and with a little difficulty reached in and produced a brief but delicate pair in black and flame red. She paraded them on her index finger, as might a vanquishing knight display a trophy of conflict. On that note we disembarked.

I had mentioned Kinky to Molly, pointing out that she was only a casual girlfriend—a sort of grace-note, who didn't drink and never used bad language. She was looking forward to meeting her.

The first thing that Molly said after introductions and explanations of injuries was, 'You haven't eaten, have you?'

This was the usual enquiry to any of my friends upon arrival, no matter what the hour. 'I'm sure you can manage a steak. Martin will cut it up for you.'

'Well, I am a bit handicapped at the moment. I've had a number of problems this evening.'

At this point I interrupted with the intention of changing the subject. Kinky had a small stain down the front of her top, and she ignored me and continued, 'With both arms like this I managed to tip a large scotch down the front of me in the pub, which was a bloody waste and complete balls-up.'

I followed Molly out to the galley leaving Kinky by the fire. When we were alone, Molly said, 'I do like your non-drinking, non-swearing girlfriend. She certainly is a stunner. I don't know how you do it.'

It was well after 2 a.m. by the time we finished eating and demolishing a bottle and a half of claret. As we headed for my quarters, Molly, with the faintest smile on her face, said, 'I put a hot-water bottle in your bed dear, but I'm sure that you will be warm enough in any case.'

Later in the morning there was a tap on my door and a quiet announcement, 'Your coffee is outside.' I have always taken my coffee black, but as I slid that morning's tray into my room, I noted that it carried not only an extra cup and saucer but also a small jug of milk.

I suppose in my late teens I did fall in and out of love pretty frequently. There just seemed to be a lot of gorgeous girls around at this time. Even the recently introduced young lady who demonstrated the weather forecast on TV became a turn-on. If there had been the slightest chance to come up against her warm front there would have been an instant rise in temperature and high pressure expected to move in from the south with a risk of precipitation.

Vic once told a number of drinkers on the waterfront that I spent most of my money on women and booze, but shamefully squandered the rest.

My first serious girlfriend was Pam. I fell madly in love with her after all of 24 hours. However, the relationship might have foundered on the rocks in its infancy, all because of a hair-dye.

Pam was a hairdresser. She would occasionally phone me and ask me to guess what colour her hair would be that evening. This was fine and amusing, but after she took a course in colouring, she was looking for a model on which to try out her new qualification. Neither of her two brothers, nor her mother, could be bribed to let her loose on their locks, so I managed to draw the short straw.

Pam chose a colour that, as she put it, 'wouldn't show up too much'. So with much trepidation I soon found myself beneath some very un-sexual rubberware. 45 minutes later I was allowed to emerge and view the result. My entire thatch had become a sort of metallic bronze.

I'm not sure which of us panicked the most.

Buy a hat. I never wear one. Perhaps a beret. Not likely—I might be mistaken for a Frenchman. I'd certainly be arrested in a balaclava.

I'd go French. It covered my hair but didn't hide the bronze line that ran round my forehead and strongly resembled a high-tide mark or the Plimsoll line of the Royal Barge.

No amount of scrubbing would shift it. It would simply have to wear off.

Needless to say, throughout its indelible presence, it did little for my cred along the waterfront, where I became variously referred to as Captain Brasso and, by the less courteous, as Golden Bollocks.

L'histoire n'est que le tableau des crimes
(History is nothing more than a tableau of crimes)

- Voltaire

7

Under normal circumstances it should take about 12 days to reach Gibraltar, as *Pandora's* cruising speed was 22 knots and she'd bunkered enough fuel to do it in one trip. Mark, though, had other ideas. He decided on the holiday route down to the Med, through the French canal system. By this method we could eat and drink our way down without fear of getting lost.

In other words, he would marinade himself in alcohol for 500 miles over a period of five weeks, roughly 100 miles per week, at about 20 miles per bottle.

The theory behind this overland excursion was fine but, in reality, not without snags. The Channel crossing went without event, and the passage from Le Havre to Paris was comparatively easy. It's difficult to stray off course when you're between two river-banks.

It was only when *Pandora* left the Seine and entered the first canal that she was confronted with her first problem. The speed limit set on canals was five knots and *Pandora*, bless her, wouldn't steer under eight. So we spent many happy hours shoving and pulling her off the banks. At one bend, she became so firmly stuck it required a farmer and his son plus two donkeys to shift her.

Add to this aggravation the endless number of locks that had to be negotiated, and only between the hours of daylight, because they're the only times their keepers function. The whole operation becomes very tiresome and slow.

One could easily do it more quickly on crutches or with a Zimmer frame.

Two and a half weeks into the voyage of discovery and barely a quarter of the way down to the sea, we were in for another surprise. One of the lock-keepers calmly informed us that we were, as he put it, '30 centimetres too tall' to pass under the bridge at Montargis, which we would reach in another couple of days, and there was no way round it.

We'd become used to judging the clearances that *Pandora* had to squeeze under previous spans by having me stand on the bow with two volumes of the *Mediterranean Pilot* balanced on my head. If the books went under then *Pandora* would.

We arrived at Montargis and, right enough, we were too tall. There was no chance of passing under the bridge that we were now confronted with, even if I got down on my knees. Possibly at that time we all should have considered a genuflection or two. A small miracle was definitely needed.

I wondered what the festive season might be like in Montargis as, in any case, the canal was too narrow even to turn *Pandora* round.

Mark told Alex to flood the bilges. He did this up to the air intakes of the engine. We gained three inches.

'Sandbags,' said Mark. 'About 100 sandbags. That should do the trick.'

Throughout that afternoon, groups of sightseers gathered to see *les anglais avec le problème*. 100 sandbags later, a quick measurement showed that we'd made a difference of two inches. Only another ten to go.

Another 400 sandbags on the foredeck would probably have done it, but by then they would have been stacked so high that they themselves wouldn't go under the arch.

Mark wasn't at all amused when I said that it was a pity it wasn't a truck we were trying to get through, as we could have let the tyres down.

Just then, the mayor turned up. Every village in France, no matter how small, seems to have a mayor. This one, however, proved absolutely vital.

There followed a lot of hand-waving and orders being given, resulting in small groups of onlookers all going off in different directions, returning some 15 minutes later with large numbers of people of all ages. Some started climbing aboard *Pandora*. After a while you could barely see her because she was bedecked with people all over her. They included the staff and management of a small factory, all the drinkers from several pubs, and an assortment of local residents.

The mayor organised the operation, sorting the thinner ones to one side. When most of the space had been taken up he himself, who couldn't by any stretch of the imagination be described as sylph-like, and had obviously enjoyed his carbohydrates and all the things proscribed by current-day belief, climbed aboard to a spirited applause.

Pandora was now lower in the water by more than the required amount, and we gently eased her beneath the brickwork by hand.

The whole exercise had by now created a sort of carnival atmosphere, and it was another two hours before, after all the drinking, hand-shaking and kissing, we could again get under way.

Miraculously, throughout the whole gala, nobody managed to fall overboard.

On to Chalon. A gentle trickle down the Saône to Lyons, making reasonably good time.

The real test came when we left the Saône and entered the Rhone. We were now making extra-good time, as the Rhone was in full flood after the flood waters from Lake Geneva had been released. And we were being washed down towards the sea, now only 100 miles away, at something like 18 knots—totally out of control, of course, and no chance of being able to stop unless we could turn round and fight the current like a pregnant salmon. No other traffic was moving, of course.

We passed under a bridge (thank heavens, a high one) at Vienne, and whizzed past the town without time to give it a second glance. Avignon, with only half a bridge to worry about, and Arles, went past at a similar rate. But when *Pandora* popped out into the Med at Port St Louis, it felt as though she were being discharged like a cork from a bottle of Veuve Clicquot.

At last we reached Marseilles and, after tying up in the old port, we received a visit from the agent whom we'd last seen in Newhaven. He was pleased to see us, and asked us to meet up with another vessel and pick up some spares for the other ships of the fleet. Subsequently we discovered there were nine others. *Frederico Rossi* was the boss man in Italy, and his ships were collectively known as the Fred Fleet.

That evening we were invited for drinks aboard a rather fine-looking yacht moored ahead of us. She was called *Shirocco*, and our host turned out to be none other than the Irish actor, the late Errol Flynn. It was party night, but perhaps every night in his company was party night.

We left with *Pandora* for Fiumicino late the following day, all nursing the mother and father of hangovers.

'With any luck we should be there by late tomorrow afternoon,' Mark murmured, as we completed the measured distance from Cap Couronne to the Isle of Ratonneau.

After a brief rendezvous with a nameless vessel, we stowed the spares and continued.

'We're making about 20 knots, and allowing for any change in the weather, it's about a 24-hour run,' he continued optimistically.

We cleared the southern tip of the Îles d'Hyères just after nine in the evening, which was about right for the distance covered. Cap Corse, the northernmost tip of Corsica, lay 150 miles ahead. It would then have been a direct run to Fiumicino if we hadn't encountered a north-westerly gale.

This put the wind right on our port quarter, making steering hard work. None of us minded gales. We'd seen them all before. But *Pandora* hated them and made it known.

The major problem arrived at a little after four in the morning, which seems always to be the favourite hour for things to go wrong at sea.

Firstly, the engine revs dropped from 850 to 200, reducing our speed to less than five knots. Secondly, the rolling had become so violent that *Pandora* began taking water.

There was little point in changing course, as there was nowhere to run to, and ahead was only about ten miles distant. The flashing light of Cap Corse gave a single flash every five seconds, inviting us to shelter.

8

Mark made another calculation. By this time it would take five hours to reach the shelter of Macinaggio, but if *Pandora* continued to take in water at the present rate, she'd sink in about two.

Of course, we had no radio, life-jackets, life-raft—or indeed any large lumps of wood that we could cling to, as traditionally depicted in paintings of old shipwrecks. In case of any injury or problems, the *Pandora*'s lifesaving equipment did contain a first-aid kit. But on inspection it merely revealed several aspirins and some damp elastoplast that would have required a nail to hold it in position.

Mark murmured that they who go down to the sea for a pastime will go to hell for pleasure. Of course, he was slightly pissed.

Suddenly he sprang into action and ordered that all watertight doors forward of the engine-room be secured. This might give her enough buoyancy to keep her afloat. We'd already done this, of course.

He told Douglas to punch some holes in an oil drum, fill it with old rags, diesel oil and petrol, then struggle out to the foredeck, lash it to the winch and set fire to it.

'Somebody might just see it,' he shouted, his words slurred and almost lost in the howling wind.

It burned quite brightly for about ten minutes, but St Elmo must have been on duty during that brief exposure, because the crew of an aircraft bound for Nice spotted it, and reported our position.

Shortly after 6 a.m. a large ocean-going tug appeared, and after a great deal of effort and a lot of bad language, a cable was secured and we were taken in tow. 11 hours later we were safely beached in the shelter of a small fishing village at Macinaggio.

The tug's pump dealt without flooding and the captain agreed to tow us to Bastia the following day, when he was sure the weather would improve. Next morning it did. The skipper was right.

Upon our arrival at Bastia, customs gave us a little visit. They took a certain interest in the cases of spares, and opened them. They seemed to give up counting after they reached 2,000,000 contraband cigarettes.

The smokes were resealed on board as evidence in Mark's presence. A signature was obtained and we were all carted off to Bastia prison. After three days we received a visit from the acting British Consul and our friend the agent—who'd obviously been distributing copious amounts of French francs in various directions, as all four of us were released forthwith and allowed to move back on board *Pandora*, though under 24-hour surveillance by the *gendarmerie*.

Mark and Douglas had been well aware of the cargo and intended to share the spoils upon our arrival in Fiumicino. They bolted and disappeared like rats up a drainpipe aboard a Panamanian-registered steamer on its way to a North African port, leaving Alex and me to face the music. Funny, both Mark and Douglas always maintained they were middle class. This proved it. They certainly were—in the middle of the criminal class, the bastards.

Our trial date for smuggling was fixed for five weeks hence, when the arrival of an equivalent visiting magistrate would hear the case. Several restaurants, who I thought at the time were just taking pity on us, took it in turns to feed us. But the reason for this was due to a little varnishing by the owners of *Pandora*. Our rescue tug was paid off for the tow and its Italian crew also entertained and fed us. The grub was something else.

The tug was a backup vessel to a team of Italian divers on contract to clear war wrecks from Bastia harbour. The chief diver to the outfit carried the nickname Sticky-Bomb Boy, having received a decoration for bravery after removing unexploded limpet mines from sunken ships in Alexandria harbour after the war. (Mind you, he'd most probably attached them there in the first place.) He did, however, have a novel suggestion. Perhaps if we stuck a limpet mine on the bottom of *Pandora* the following explosion would destroy the evidence against us.

We turned his offer down.

To add to our comforts, a young lady turned up out of the blue and informed us that she was now our cook and maid. We correctly assumed that this pleasant surprise was due to more monetary lubrication. She was Francesca. And as luck would have it, she took a bit of a shine to me. I was taken on many sightseeing trips by autocar—in other words, by bus.

Although her English was somewhat limited and my French likewise, we managed. All these excursions had to be completed by 9 p.m. each evening to meet with the terms of my bail curfew. But in spite of this we visited Ajaccio, Corte, Calvi, the forest of Vizzavona, where at one time the tallest ships' masts in the world were harvested. We paid a reverent look in on the birthplace of that famous little short-arse Bonaparte, and an equally respectful call at one of Fran's aunts who lived at Miomo. I also saw endless fortresses and Roman ruins.

After about a week I noticed that her skirts had become a little shorter. Week two. Although Fran was quite a big girl, she had those legs. I was young and hot-blooded, and hadn't had it for almost two months, and she was Corsican and passionate.

Week three. Blind panic. Fran not only had two nice legs but she also had an equal number of big brothers. I could see that I might become detained in Corsica rather longer than the soon-expected magistrate might decree.

I confided in Alex.

'While you've been off on your little jaunts I've been busy. I've cured the problem with the engine—in fact I started it up yesterday very briefly. We can sod off if you like,' was his answer to my worry.

'Let's go tonight,' I replied.

Not that there was any hint of any future nativity. I simply had a sudden desire for the open sea.

Pandora was facing the wrong way round for a quick departure, but Lady Luck was on our side that afternoon as between us and the quay was a barge loaded with scrap metal. At about 3 p.m. two chaps arrived with a small harbour launch, and explained that they had to take the barge away, and could we put a rope ashore to pull ourselves alongside while they slid the barge out?

We elected to put our bow rope ashore so that when the barge departed the slight breeze blowing from the harbour entrance would push *Pandora* round. She was now facing the right way to abscond after dark. The little sentry wasn't at all suspicious as he actually took our stern rope so that we could pull ourselves in to complete the manoeuvre.

We relaxed until dark.

The fishing boats were leaving, some with their acetylene lanterns already burning brightly. Our guard was absent. Alex fired up the main engine and I cast off, leaving our mooring ropes still attached to the quay. Without lights we headed towards the harbour entrance, behind one of the larger fishing boats, engine just throbbing at 200 revs. I felt that every pair of eyes in Bastia was focused on us and that we would be pursued at any moment. There was another vessel astern of us but it was a smaller fisherman.

Once clear of the entrance it was full ahead. *Pandora* responded like a released bird of prey. Still running with black lights, we surged past the convoy of fishermen ahead of us. Their crews must have been having a quiet chuckle as they, and for that matter everybody in Bastia, knew why we'd been detained. We decided just to head east and we'd decide what course to take once clear of territorial waters.

Shortly after midnight, the lights of Elba Island showed up on our port bow. We were still running as a darkened ship, and so far we'd seen no other vessels and were beginning to breathe more freely. By dead reckoning, it was about 125 miles to Fiumicino, which would take about eight to ten hours.

I told Alex I was going to get my head down and to call me about 3 a.m. when I'd take over. He didn't and it was already daylight when he shook me. He had a worried look on his face and reported that there was another vessel chasing us. I was still half asleep. Otherwise I wouldn't have fallen for it, knowing that there was very little, if anything, that could match *Pandora*'s speed—let alone catch us. But he continued, 'It's gaining on us fast. And, yes, I can see now, there's a bird in its bows. She's got dark hair flowing in the wind and a cutlass between her teeth.'

When he saw my puzzled expression, he fell around the place laughing, but I was none too amused.

Four hours later we slid into Fiumicino to a hero's welcome.

The reception committee were obviously well prepared to meet us, there being a total absence of authority—the customs in particular. Our approach to the jetty had to be made with care, and slowly, as all these H-craft are big ship control, meaning that the engineer has to be below to handle the engines, taking instructions from the bridge. And without deckhands and adequate mooring ropes, going alongside would be a trifle difficult.

As I gently eased *Pandora* against the quay, two chaps jumped aboard, with ropes, and helped tie us up. They were both English-speaking. In fact, one was English, the other Australian. It was obvious that they knew their way around these crafts.

Once we were secure, a tall man with dark hair, clean shaven and dressed in a light-grey suit, climbed on deck. He introduced himself as Claude. It was obvious that he was in charge—and French. He had a firm handshake and a broad smile. I informed him that I was Martin Bengtsson, to which he replied that he knew that. I introduced Alex and said that he'd become my engineer. Claude replied that he already knew that as well.

The other two joined us. Claude made the introductions. The Englishman was called *Dave Black*. The Australian was simply Oz. No surname was offered—which didn't seem significant at the time. But I was to later find out that nobody actually had a surname for Oz, or any idea where he came from. He'd apparently been living in South Africa for the past ten years but showed no great desire to return there, or to his place of birth. In fact, quite the reverse.

Claude announced that somebody wished to meet us and suggested that we leave. Alex said he would need to shut the engine down, but Claude waved this aside, saying that the other two would take care of everything.

Once on the quay he steered us towards one of three cars parked a few feet away. A driver was already sitting in it. Alex and I climbed into the rear seats. Once Claude was settled in the front we moved off.

The drive took about twenty minutes, during which time I pondered how our impending arrival at Fiumicino had been anticipated, but I didn't let it bother me.

We arrived outside a large house—or rather, villa—partly hidden behind a high wall and rows of cypress trees. The Citroën pulled up in front of a high, ornate set of iron gates. Claude climbed out and pressed a button set in one of the stone pillars. Moments later, he pushed the gates open and waited, closing them again after we'd driven through. He got back in the car, and we drove some hundred yards up a tarmac roadway bordered by neat lawns.

The villa was L-shaped and oldish—but it was difficult to tell how old. Its lower windows were protected by iron bars with a fancy design. The heavy baroque front door at the top of six wide steps was already being opened as we pulled up. The three of us went in and Claude showed us both into a square room at the beginning of a panelled hallway. This room looked out onto the driveway. Claude suggested that we help ourselves to drinks, before leaving us and closing the door behind him.

The room had a fine ornate ceiling, a huge marble fireplace, on the mantel of which stood a gorgeous antique clock inlaid with tortoiseshell. A quick glance revealed that it had been designed by one G. Hisler, which at that time didn't mean anything to me. I later discovered that he was a very coveted designer. Above this hung a rather splendid marine oil painting. The name of its artist I couldn't decipher.

Two glass-fronted cabinets containing decorative china stood one on each side of the fireplace. Another wall was covered with a massive, well-filled bookcase—the sort that one expects to swing open and reveal a secret doorway.

It didn't.

In the centre of the room stood a rather fabulous circular table, with elaborate carved legs embracing an inlaid ormolu top. Under one of the other windows, another table, smaller and also circular, was supporting four cut-glass decanters in a walnut-and-brass-mounted box, an oval silver tray of glasses and an array of bottles.

I took a large whisky and Alex did the same.

There was a hint of perfume in the room. Surveying the stage I said, 'I could live like this, Alex.'

'I'd rather spend the money on other things,' he replied.

At that moment in time I couldn't imagine what other things could be possibly better to spend it on if I had it.

In the far corner of the room a terrestrial globe was on a stand. I wandered over and gently rotated it. The inscriptions were in Italian and Latin. It was almost certainly priceless.

'Beautiful, isn't it?' I commented.

'It wouldn't last ten minutes in my house,' he replied.

After a short while Claude returned and announced that 'he' would see us now. I drank my drink and Alex did likewise.

'There's no big hurry,' said Claude.

We followed him to a sitting room at the end of the hallway. A fire was burning in another fine fireplace. The room was sumptuously furnished with two deep black leather sofas and armchairs, all wood-panelled with large paintings and period brass and cut-glass wall lights.

Claude introduced us to a seated man of about sixty years.

'This is our principal, Mr *Rossi*.'

He was a slight man with greyish hair that had been dark, slim-faced with piercing brown eyes, clean shaven, and he gave us both a friendly smile. His white teeth looked like the real thing. He was wearing a dark grey suit and black shoes. Two younger men were standing beside him. These two were slight in build, with jet-black parted hair. One wouldn't have to be a detective to realise that these were his sons.

Rossi remained seated and offered me his left hand, his ring finger carrying a single gold band, heavy.

The handshake produced a firm greeting. Similar exchanges were made between the other two—Marco and Rico. Introductions now completed, Claude turned and addressing us said, 'He is very pleased with you. We are taking food here tonight, and you will be sleeping here.'

Rossi spoke no English so, after a few more words in Italian, Claude ushered us to our rooms on the first floor. He left us, returning a few moments later, having rustled up a clean white shirt and tie for each of us.

The bedrooms were quite plain. Carpeted; table with mirror and large armoire; no pictures. The beds looked comfortable enough, but after sitting on one of them I decided it was much softer than the ones I had normally liked. The adjoining bathrooms were pretty luxurious, with marble basins set in dark wooden surrounds with brass taps. Laid out on crisp napery were fresh still-wrapped tablets of soap in clean china dishes, nail-clippers, hairbrushes and cologne. The bath was enormous with a shower overhead, all fed by polished semi-Victorian brasswork.

Having cleaned up, I shoved my head round Alex's door and enquired, 'Are you sure you couldn't live like this?'

'I'm having second thoughts,' he replied.

It was now about seven—already dark. Looking out from my bedroom window I noticed the driveway was floodlit, and that two more cars had arrived since we'd been there. I could also hear female voices below, which may have hinted promise—or the fact that we were to be exhibits that evening.

After about an hour Claude tapped politely on each of our doors and invited us down for drinks. All very civilised. We returned to the old man's sitting room. The doors of the small drinks cabinet were now open and all four of them seemed to be drinking the same colourless liquid in whisky tumblers.

The old man shook hands with us both again. I was quite used to this habit, as Vic would also do it even if one's absence had only been for a couple of hours.

'What do you drink?' he asked in English. He'd obviously been rehearsing this as they all laughed politely.

'What are you drinking?' I replied with a smile.

Claude took over and explained that it was a Sicilian aperitif. We joined them. For the life of me I can't remember what the drink was called. I'm writing this 53 years after the event, so you have to forgive me. Most things are indelibly vivid in my memory, some of which I wish were not so. But some details have faded.

One thing that does stick out, though, was my embarrassment at wearing the shirt, collar and tie with denim jeans and deck shoes (fortunately reasonably clean).

I asked Claude to excuse us. He said something to the old man, who replied with a broad smile. Claude translated, also smiling.

'He says it won't notice when we're sitting at the table.'

A little later a well-dressed woman of about fifty came in. There were no introductions, but she had to be Mrs *Rossi*. She gave both Alex and me a friendly smile.

Marco helped the old man to his feet and we headed for the dining room. They didn't take their drinks with them, so I didn't either. Alex did. I'd already cautioned him to be careful what he said to me as we had no idea who apart from Claude spoke any English. I now quietly suggested that he didn't dive into the grub before grace was said.

The dining room was equal to the rest of the villa. Another lovely fireplace with a brightly burning fire, in front of which was an adequate carpet of eastern origin. The rest of the floor was in dark polished timber. In the centre, a super-long elegant table, quite capable of seating 20 to 24 people, was perfectly laid out with just ten places. There were no empty chairs—they must have been spirited away to avoid the bad luck superstition.

The perfumed aroma that I'd noticed before was more prevalent and I realised that it was originating from about a dozen lit candles, held in two gilt marble candelabra. At the end of the room, as far as I was concerned, the *pièce de resistance*—a full-size grand piano in gilt. It was truly magnificent. I wondered who played it, and if we were about to be asked to sing for our supper.

While I was reflecting upon how these people certainly knew how to live, I think Alex read my thoughts, because he tapped me on the shoulder and quietly said, 'I think I've changed my mind.'

The starter nosh was already on the table. Mrs *Rossi* was joined by three other women, all very smartly dressed. Two were obviously the wives of the sons, in their early thirties. The slightly older-looking one was a bit on the large side, the other rather skinny. The third woman was in her sixties and possibly the sister or the sister-in-law of *Rossi*. They were all wearing expensive jewellery. Not dripping in it, but just enough, and it was clearly the real thing.

Grace was said. The starter was smoked fish roe with olive and lemon sauce. This was followed by roast pork with garlic, accompanied by a side dish of fried aubergines and anchovies in a sweet sauce. This I remember very well as I quite successfully reproduced these dishes on a number of occasions.

Throughout the meal the four women talked incessantly to each other and occasionally to their husbands. The larger of the two younger ones, who wore a black cocktail dress that she must have shrunken on or used a shoehorn to squeeze into, ate non-stop—which most likely was contributory to her shape. The slim one, wearing a black and red number, barely touched a thing. She looked the sort who would be scared to death to be locked in the same room as a potato. All the women looked pleasant enough and smiled frequently.

I've never been terribly impressed by Italian wines, but those that accompanied that meal were first class—especially the pud one. I asked Claude to say how much we'd enjoyed the meal and to comment on the wine. He did.

A look of pleasure came over both the faces of Mr and Mrs *Rossi*. Claude told us that Mrs *Rossi* herself did all the cooking, rather than employ a cook who might not be up to her standard. He also pointed out that I'd said the right thing regarding the pudding wine, as it was one of *Rossi*'s favourites, coming from a region about twenty miles from his birthplace in Sicily. It was called Marsala and splendid—and I've drunk a lot of it since.

The evening finished off with coffee and brandies—several of them. Nobody played the piano and I retired about eleven and passed out immediately.

Next morning was sunny, warm and cloudless—and this was December. Claude was already on hand and joined us both for coffee and rolls outside in the garden. From an inside pocket of another smart suit he produced two envelopes and handed one to each of us. They were white envelopes. I don't think that at that time the brown ones had become a fashionable swaddling. Now—was it polite to open them then or later?

Proper or not, I opened mine. $1,000 US for the delivery of the *Pandora* and a further $1,000 for her safe removal with cargo from Corsica. We both received the same amount and thanked him.

'Now,' said Claude, 'you can both go away home, finish if you like, or you can return to your home for *Noël* vacation, and after return here and recover another of our vessels that is likewise detained in another place. What do you think?'

After a moment I asked him what sort of ship it was, and where it was.

'It's the same as *Pandora* but much better, and it's in Yugoslavia, and of course there will be a big gratuity, and there's nothing else on the ship,' he said all in one breath. He went on, 'Today is 17. There is a week before *Noël*. Stay here and think about it for the next two days before you go home.'

'I already have,' I told him. 'What about you, Alex? Are you up for it?' I asked.

'Yes, I suppose so.'

'There you are, Claude. We'll do it after Christmas.'

'He will be pleased,' said Claude, rising from the table.

I noticed that whenever Claude referred to *Rossi* he always used 'him' or 'he'—seldom his name and never his Christian name.

After further discussions with Claude we were to learn that *Helgah*, our next job, was indeed another H-craft, and had been arrested off Split in Yugoslavia while alongside a coopering vessel, and escorted into Dubrovnik, where she'd been for the last three months. Any cargo that she'd been carrying had most likely been sold off by the authorities on the black market—as this was a place where bribery was endemic, and you were never lonely with a quid.

I was looking forward to going home for a break. Alex and I flew out at 11 a.m. the following day and I was back in Peacehaven by 4 p.m. I phoned Molly from a telephone box that was almost opposite her house.

'Where are you?' she asked.

'On my way back,' I replied.

'Where then?' she asked excitedly.

'Not far now,' I said.

'Are you in England?'

'Yes.'

'London?'

'Closer,' I said.

'Where then? Come on, tell me,' she pleaded. I took a deep breath, and said, 'If you pull your curtain back by your phone, I'll give you a wave. I'm in the call box opposite.'

The curtain shot back. I waved. By the time I'd hung up and walked across the road and entered the house, the glass that had been put away when I left was now charged with a very, very large whisky.

9

Vic arrived about seven, and there was a celebratory evening. Although he and Molly had been separated for ages, they were still close friends.

After a few drinks I broke it to them both that I intended to return to Italy after Christmas. Molly rather expected this and tried hard to appear only a little disappointed. I quizzed Vic on what had happened to *Myzpah* during my absence, pointing out what a pair of shits Mark and Douglas had turned out to be.

'Well, I know a little bit about them and the boat,' he said.

'Fill me in,' I said.

'They both got sacked by *Myzpah*'s owner, and I know nothing and care even less about where they are now,' he continued. 'And as for *Myzpah*, all sorts of things have been happening to her.'

Molly jumped in.

'Oh, tell him, Vic. Don't keep him in suspense.'

'Well, son, I've bought her. She's now undergoing a complete refit. And when you decide to settle back here, she's all yours.'

I was taken completely by surprise and suddenly wished that I hadn't been so keen to return to Italy. But it would be a hell of an incentive to come back to Newhaven soon. As far as I was concerned, *Myzpah* was the finest thing afloat.

Christmas came and went, and I put on pounds. I called Alex shortly after and made arrangements to fly out. A week later, we left from Gatwick.

Upon our return, we received the same enthusiastic welcome as before. Claude said there was no desperate hurry to do the Dubrovnik rescue, and that we should unwind and completely relax. We now had a complete new year ahead of us.

We were again staying at the villa, where the hospitality was brilliant. There was a big party planned for the coming Saturday. Fortunately, I could dress for the occasion this time, as I'd even packed a dinner suit.

On the night of the party, the front of the villa was covered in cars, some of which had arrived under their own steam, others chauffeur driven.

The guest list was as extravagant as the fare. It included politicians, theatrical folk, including Gigli, Lord and Lady Docker, Gracie Fields, and Mario Lanza—who was not quite up to the operatic level of Gigli and a rather bad-tempered individual.

Then there was Colombe—five foot three's worth of lovely figure, longish dark hair, totally gorgeous. And what's more, she was specially introduced to me by Claude.

'This is Colombe,' he said. 'She's been forward looking to meet a pirate.'

Thank God she spoke English, or I was going to have to polish my Italian very smartly.

We made polite conversation, during which she commented jokingly, 'I understand you steal ships on our behalf.'

'Yes, I do,' I replied. 'I'm taking another one next week.'

'When you get back we must have dinner, and you can tell me how you do it.'

'Yes,' I thought. 'And about nicking boats as well.'

Claude, Alex and myself had a conference on the Monday morning over ham, eggs and coffee. I enjoyed planning discussions over a meal and still do.

Claude explained in detail the situation in Dubrovnik. It had been surveyed twice. The last time was as recently as three weeks ago. *Helgah* had been held there for the last three months, during which time she'd been moved into the old port—a fairly deserted part of the harbour. She was moved there shortly after being taken.

Alex interrupted.

'So you've no idea how long it's been since the main engine was last started?'

'Yes, you're right,' Claude agreed.

'Well,' Alex continued. 'If her air tanks are low in pressure she may not start. If she's exactly the same design as *Pandora*, we need 40 pounds per square inch.

'Did her own crew take her in, or was it the arresting bunch?'

'Her own crew were arrested, after which they took her into Dubrovnik under escort. But why do you ask?'

'Because,' continued Alex, 'their thoughts, I'm sure, would have been to escape if they could, and they'd have made sure the air tanks were full. If you adjust the safety valve, you can get 150 psi safely. And if they were shut down correctly then, they should be okay now.

'In any case, I need two small camping stoves so I can hot up the bottles and increase the pressure. And if the air goes in hot we stand a better chance anyway.'

Claude seemed quite impressed and agreed to supply anything we might need. He went on to explain that there was a small sailing yacht over on the east coast, in a small harbour at Pescara.

'It's worth only little money,' he said. The idea was that we'd sail this to Dubrovnik, where we would put in with engine trouble.

He continued, 'You're on your way to perhaps Corfu, when you break down. Alex can fix that. You manage to get into Dubrovnik on your overboard engine. Once in there you ask for the mechanition to repair your big engine. I, knowing what it's like there, can say it will take some time while you're waiting.

'You leave the little yacht and steal *Helgah* if possible. If it's not possible you return on the little one. *Helgah* had full fuel tanks at the time she was taken but check them carefully as someone might have stolen the diesel.'

'It's not fuel I'm worried about, Claude, it's air.'

'If you can start up and get away, and notice you're small on diesel, go into Brindisi. We have another ship there, called *Cormorant*. Her captain will give you fuel.

'If you are a success,' he continued, 'Mr *Rossi* will be very pleased indeed. He will also be very pleased at your trying to do the job.'

Two days later we left Fiumicino with heaps of supplies, enough food to feed a regiment, and some very good wines.

Claude drove us to Pescara and showed us the 'little yacht'. I don't know about little yacht. She certainly was a little gem. A Folkboat, built in Poland, and in lovely condition.

We said goodbye to Claude, who wished us good luck. His last words were, 'Don't be heroes.'

That night we sailed. A nice steady force five from the north, and we made good time.

After 54 hours we were about twelve miles short of Dubrovnik. The wind had fallen right away, so we decided to run the main engine for a while. It kept stopping. So we really did have a problem.

By then we were amongst a fleet of small fishing boats with bright lights. Claude's overboard engine, which in fact was a Seagull outboard, only moved us at about two knots. As it started to become light, we waved a rope to one of the fishermen. He got the message and took us in tow.

Two and a half hours later we were alongside and, would you believe it, in the old port, less than 100 yards from *Helgah*. We gave the fisherman $20 US for the tow. He seemed delighted, and was about to leave when an official in a brown uniform started remonstrating with him. He kept pointing at the berth and repeating himself.

'I don't think he wants us here,' said Alex, jokingly.

It was fairly obvious he didn't.

'And why does he keep pointing at *Helgah*? Have we got a problem?'

'No,' I replied. 'It's not a problem, it's our lucky break. I'm sure he wants them to move us alongside her and keep this berth clear.'

I was right, and that's where we wound up. We couldn't have done it better if we'd been gently lowered in by helicopter.

Later that day a mechanic appeared. After turning our engine over by hand, he said nothing to us but started talking to himself, shaking his head. Eventually, on the back of a cigarette packet, he wrote out a two-figure number, followed by a lot of zeroes.

I didn't care if it cost a million dollars, but thought it good policy to shake my head this time. Making a hand action as if patting the table meaning, 'Lower the price,' I waited.

He thought for a while and, after making a few more calculations, reduced the second of the first two figures but left the same number of zeroes. He took a small and rather beaten-up diary out of his greasy overalls, and pointed to a date two weeks away. He left.

After he'd departed, Alex said, 'He hasn't got the faintest idea what's wrong with it, but it will give us time to check next door out.'

We went ashore to find somewhere to eat, crossing over *Helgah*'s decks. And the following day we hung our sleeping bags and blankets over our boom and along *Helgah*'s rail. The more watchers became used to our movements on *Helgah*, the better.

It wasn't until the second morning that another brown-suited bloke asked us for our passports. He took them away and pointed to his office, some 350 yards away, and his wristwatch, making signs that we could collect them later. As it looked for all intents and purposes as if we were going to be stuck there until our engine was fixed, we'd leave collecting the passports for a day or two. We could always sod off without them if necessary.

On our second evening there, Alex made an inspection of *Helgah*'s engine-room, which was, strangely enough, unlocked. As he reappeared, he grinned, and his smiling face said it all.

'90 psi,' he murmured.

During day three we went ashore to eat in a rather horrid little greasy spoon five minutes' walk away. As we passed our uniformed man's office, he called out to us to go in, and handed us back our passports. I noted that from his office window neither *Helgah* nor the little boat could be seen where they were tied up.

I keep referring to her as the 'little boat' as she displayed no name. Vic always used to say that if you only owned a small boat and you wished to impress, you put its name on the transom, and before the name you added the words, 'Tender to'. The reason for this was that the larger boats always had small boats to allow them to gain easy entry into ports. It would seem as if we had a luxury liner waiting for us a mile or so from the coastline.

The weather looked good.

'Let's fuck off tonight,' I said.

We set our provisional departure time for about 3 a.m. While we were airing our bedding again, we managed to slip all our personal gear into the unlocked wheelhouse of the *Helgah*. We'd become part of the scenery and nobody took any notice of us.

At 2 a.m. everywhere was deadly quiet.

'I'll go and see if the little guy in his office is asleep,' suggested Alex.

'Why don't we both go and tie the little sod up,' I replied.

'No, let's just take a look.'

Sure enough, he was spark out in his chair with his feet in another one. Alex reached up outside the office and with a pair of pliers snipped the wire that ran along the top.

'If anybody rings now, his phone won't wake him up,' he whispered.

Once back on board, Alex heated up the air tanks by placing the lighted camping stoves under them. The little breeze that there was kept us against the wall after I'd retrieved the mooring ropes.

'Keep your fingers crossed, Mart,' came the hushed words from below.

He lit a lump of diesel-soaked cotton waste and dangled it over the air intake with a long spanner as he fired up the engine. The moment it turned and sucked in the flame it roared into life. Our usual procedure followed. Shut down to a mere tick-over, and chug quietly away.

I hated the idea of leaving Little Boat, so I tied her behind the *Helgah*. We'd see what she'd behave like when we opened up.

The sea was like a mirror and, once clear of the entrance, Alex gave her the gun. Full speed for half an hour, then throttle back to three-quarters. Although she swayed about a bit, our tow behaved herself implicitly. Fortunately her mast was tabernacle mounted, so we stopped, unstepped it and lashed it down. Alex also unshipped the rudder and, as a result of these ten minutes of modifications, we could tow her now quite happily at three-quarter speed.

We ran two tow lines from each of our aft fairleads in a bridal arrangement and hauled her up really tight. It's probably the longest tow ever completed by an E-boat.

There was no need to put in anywhere as we had plenty of fuel, so we headed straight for Fiumicino.

As we steamed up the *canale* to Fiumicino, having passed between the two concrete moles, some fishermen sitting on each side were treated to a vision of Alex skipping around our deck with two pieces of coloured cloth in his hands, which he waved above his head. He was singing a little-known version of *Jesus Wants Me for a Sunbeam*, and looked like a Morris dancer who'd lost his chums and also most of his marbles.

Claude was waiting on the quay, and delighted to see us. With him were *Dave*, Oz and some others. As we came alongside Oz yelled out, 'Stealing them two at a time now, Bengtsson, are we?'

We left the tidying up to the shoreside party and were whisked swiftly away by Claude to the villa.

The old man was more than delighted. He had visitors at the time and filled them in regarding our recent achievements. Claude added the fact that we'd also returned the small sailing boat. Everybody was all smiles, and there followed drinks and an extravagant nosh. And one of the women actually played the piano and sang.

Later Claude asked me if I was into classical music, and I said very much so, having been weaned on it. He then asked me if I'd like to go to La Scala and hear *Traviata*. The family sometimes had an arrangement for a box, and the visit was proposed for the following week.

I replied that for me it would be a fantastic present and I'd very much look forward to it. He continued, saying we should unwind for two or three days and, if we wished to go anywhere, he would arrange a car and driver.

He made to leave, and as he did so he added, 'I'm sure you will enjoy Verdi. And a certain young lady will be pleased that you are joining them.' And with a broad grin, 'I'm sorry that the performance is not *The Flying Dutchman*.'

I was now looking forward to the prospect of the forthcoming event—and the opera.

A couple of days later, I was aboard *Helgah* sorting out some of my own gear, when Claude arrived. He steered me into the wheel-house, out of earshot of the others, and announced that the old man (although he never called him that) was so impressed with our performance, mine in particular, he'd suggested that if I'd like to stay on I could skipper the *Helgah* on a permanent basis and have *Dave* and Oz as crew. He asked me whether I thought Alex might like to stay on as well.

I could feel *Myzpah* and Newhaven drifting away, but with the money I'd be making I could afford to bring Vic and Molly out here and buy them a small house, perhaps in Tuscany.

'He wants a decision right away, does he?' I asked.

'No, but soon is better.'

I said that I personally would love the job, but I did have a responsibility to my parents. I didn't mention they were separated.

'Bring them here,' he replied.

'Claude, you read my mind. I'll stay, and what's more, I'll make damned sure that Alex does the same.'

He grinned.

He walked out on deck where *Dave* and Oz were sitting smoking, and said, 'Martin is taking over *Helgah*, permanently, probably with Alex. Do you two wish to join him? You will make a good bloody team.'

'Yeah, why not?' said Oz. 'I like a captain who's climbing up the social scale. Do we get to go to the hopera as well one day?'

Claude laughed, jabbed him playfully in the ribs, and left. When he'd gone, I said to them, 'I'm sure we'll get on well together, but don't anyone ever accuse me of climbing socially. I don't have to climb—I'm already up there.'

We all laughed.

'Now,' I said, 'I think it's time we went off and downed a bit of team spirit, and I feel like giving my liver a bit of a challenge.'

We headed for the bar.

10

After Colombe and I were introduced by Claude, we began to see rather more of each other. At first she was just a very glamorous young lady I was proud to be seen with. Usually between trips with *Helgah* I was given the week off. In the early days, she and I went to many parties together as well as frequenting the opera. I sometimes had supper at her flat in the Via di Roma before returning to *Helgah*.

One night I didn't return to *Helgah* and I thought there might be serious repercussions.

Quite the contrary.

Although he didn't say so at the time, I discovered later that Claude was Colombe's uncle, and hoped I might one day become a relative. I thought I was sincerely in love. Bear in mind that I wasn't yet 20, I was holding a serious position within the Mafia and was well respected. Money was flying around everywhere; a hell of a lot was going on around me. I was enjoying life to the full, and here I was living with the most gorgeous girl.

I wasn't in any way out of my depth. She was great fun, loved life and all the trimmings, was well educated at a finishing school in Switzerland, drove an upmarket sports car, dressed to perfection and moved like a thoroughbred. We had everything going for us.

I'm not going to discuss our love live, except to say that it was perfect. Partly for that reason, and as a mark of respect, the bedroom is not for publication.

Five-hundred cases of ciggies to load and stow. It should take about two and a half hours with any luck, always provided that the ancient derrick on the *Calanica*—the dreadful rust-bucket that we are tied alongside—doesn't fall to bits in the meantime, or the old chap that's driving it doesn't meet with the same fate. He looks as though he's in about the same condition.

These were my thoughts as I surveyed the blithe scene on that sunny late June afternoon. From my viewpoint on the bridge it became obvious to me that she was actually called *Catanica* but a chunk of the *t* was missing. It was clear that her owners were on a budget, not subscribing to long-term investment and buying their paint in lots of small tins from an oddments shop, as her multi-coloured paint jobs gave her the appearance of a savagely attacked rainbow. If, on the other hand, the intention was at a later date to hide her in a tropical garden, the variegated camouflage would have been more than adequate.

Although this rendezvous was far away from any regular recognised air or shipping routes and well outside anybody's territorial limits, making the likelihood of detection remote, we were still vulnerable to discovery by accidental or conventional methods. If these coopering ships carried radar, and in a perfect world we too were equipped likewise giving us the opportunity to preview any visitors, we could do something about it. *Helgah* could outrun any patrol boat by at least 12 knots.

However without the presence of this higher technology we would have to rely on good old-fashioned lookout—literally, for on this fine sunny day our lookout took the form of an ancient mariner who was definitely on the wrong side of 70. He was now sitting perched on top of *Catanica*'s mast with a pair of binoculars. To avoid the risk of falling off, he could only visually sweep through 180 degrees, and I hoped that nothing would creep up from behind him.

The other captain lent us two other hands to help speed up the operation. This duo were relative youngsters, each appearing not to be a day over 65. Tedious work, but at least they were in the fresh air. Poor old Alex, on the other hand, had to remain in or near the engine-room throughout our stay, as engines had to be kept running on stand-by in case we needed them for a sudden departure.

Claude was still on board *Catanica*, having appeared briefly from below somewhere as we came alongside, after which he waved and disappeared again. He was impeccably turned out—today in a lightweight white suit of the sort usually worn by tea-planters and sweaty reporters portrayed in classic films set in the Far East. As it looked spotless, I assumed that he must have stood up rigidly and not even risked leaning against anything throughout his sojourn on the ship in order to have preserved it in that manner.

Being fair to this elderly vessel, she was once a fine ship but, sadly, now a bygone. It was only the rust that was holding her hull together, her superstructure being likewise perpetuated by the woodworm linking arms.

By sharp contrast, all the vessels belonging to the Fred Fleet were spruce and ship-shape, both in their livery and maintenance. They had to be. This was the sharp end of the business. Yes, this was the business, and I was enjoying every moment of it.

I'd come a long way in 16 months, from an office boy in Messrs Coutts to a skipper in charge of one of the mob's prestigious smuggling ships—and still only 19. I was the youngest of the crew by at least ten years, but on some occasions referred to as 'Dad'.

This as sure as hell was beating the crap out of catching the 7.08 a.m. train out of Brighton to Victoria five days a week.

Molly hadn't the foggiest idea of what I was actually up to, except that I'd become a ship's captain. This fact might have gone part of the way to putting her and Vic on better terms, he being the instigator behind my deviation from what she termed a 'normal' occupation. He knew precisely about my activities, and was delighted.

Loading was just about finished when Claude climbed on board and joined me on the bridge, bringing my reverie to an end. He put his hands on my shoulders and kissed me on both cheeks. I was never too sure about this demonstrative behaviour of the French, but I could remember quite clearly Vic once commenting that he had no objections to this practice. In fact, he thought it quite a good idea that the French should be encouraged to kiss all of us on both cheeks—providing they gave us time to pull up our trousers before planning anything further.

'It is bloody fine to see you again, my friend. Did you have a good trip up?' he said.

I told him that I was also pleased to see him, and that the run up was uneventful.

'Did you enjoy your stay on *Catanica*?' I asked.

'No, I did not. I have been on that thing all night,' he replied. 'The food was not eatable, the coffee was disgusting and the wine nowhere to be seen.'

I warned him the table wouldn't be much improved today either, and I suspected it would most likely be corned beef sandwiches and warm beer. The hatches were now closed and *Dave* and Oz were lashing down.

'When you've finished, you can cast off,' I told them.

Minutes later we were free and Alex gave us three-quarters ahead.

There were some goodbyes from our hosts, in a mixture of bad Italian and equally bad English. God only knows what nationality any of them were.

I was particularly glad to be clear of *Catanica*, because as we had loaded and settled lower in the water, we'd become close to slipping below the level of a ring of lorry tyres that were lashed round her working side to act as a permanent fender arrangement to accommodate visiting 'shoppers'. I didn't wish to arrive back at base with any damage to my new commission.

There was no wind and the sea was a flat calm as I signalled to Alex to give us full cruising speed. In these almost perfect conditions, *Helgah* raised herself onto her step and began to plane, which was what she was designed to do. This was a similar action to that of a flying boat about to lift off, and enabled her to skim across this mirror-like surface.

Our home run should take about 35 hours or slightly less.

It was a pleasure to have Claude with us, for a number of reasons. Not least was that he liked to steer, and he was welcome to my share. And without wishing to seem arrogant, his repartee was somewhat more engaging than the other three. Their small-talk centred mainly on what each of them intended to do to various ladies when later ashore, both before and after getting totally pissed. I'm also sure that Claude liked to feel that he was one of the crew—a well-dressed one.

I say this as he was always immaculately dressed. He was the essence of good manners, dress sense, and gastronomy. Everything about him smacked of quality—his Swallow Doretti sports car, which he and he alone drove; the one-off automatic pistol, handmade by some renowned Austrian gun-maker, which he was never parted from; his expensive Italian raiment; and the galaxy of glamorous young ladies who usually attended him.

This was more than could be said for *Dave*, a strictly fish-and-chip or hamburger man, who usually stuffed himself with this type of fodder from the fast-appearing mobile vending vans that Claude titled 'movable feasts'.

Once a week *Dave* took a shower, whether he thought he needed it or not. He sometimes changed his kit if he got around to it—but the frequency of this routine was subject to alteration, his regular attire having less sparkle than that of a senile trainspotter. With a little more effort, he would have been well placed to become dress adviser to Wurzel Gummidge. I couldn't imagine on what he spent his money. It certainly wasn't on visits to restaurants or outfitters.

There was never any shortage of money. It was always in crisp US dollars, and those spoke much louder than words, as the lira was devaluing so fast at that time it would have soon required a wheelbarrow full of them to buy a loaf of bread. Luckily for us this exchange rate made those lovely greenbacks go even further.

Dave now joined us in the wheel-house.

'Anything I can do, Mart?' he asked.

'No, chum, you get your head down and take over from me at about ten. I'll call you.'

I preferred him to be on the wheel at night because he could be trusted not to stray off course or run into anything solid, like another ship or a stray lump of land.

The evening passed off without event—except that the sandwiches turned out to be sardine. It was a beautiful starlit night and still flat calm when I handed over.

'Keep your eyes open for Syd,' I said, as I left the bridge.

Syd was skipper of the *Cormorant*, and also returning to base—from Brindisi after major repairs due to collision damage. She being slower than *Helgah* by about ten knots meant that we should catch them up, depending, of course, on what time they left.

I turned in and slept for almost eight hours. Claude was already on the bridge by the time I surfaced. Oz was now on the wheel.

'Wonderful day for the crossing,' said Claude as I closed the door behind me.

I agreed that it was. He continued.

'Most people would pay best money to be on a junket like this. A beautiful sunrise, a calm sea with dolphins all around us, and miles away from all worldly problems.'

'Yes,' I said, 'and they could all be chain-smokers as well. Pity about the cuisine though.'

He smiled.

With almost precision timing, *Dave* arrived with a large jug of coffee, mugs, and a stack of buttered toast, all of which he set down on the chart table.

Now it's usually engineers that ruin charts by sticking oily fingerprints all over them and asking, 'Are we about there?'

Dave's coffee made a refreshing change—for although similarly indelible, coffee stains are margin-ally more translucent than used lubricating oil.

'Any sign of Syd then?' he asked. 'We didn't pass him in my watch.'

'Not yet,' replied Oz.

'Shall we risk giving him a shout?' suggested *Dave*.

'You know he won't answer,' I said confidently. 'He hates using the radio.'

'Oh, the stutter, you mean?' *Dave* continued. 'It's all put on, you know.'

'What is?' I asked.

'The bloody stutter, of course,' he continued. 'It's just a quirk. A put-on quirk.'

'No it's not. He does it whenever he's embarrassed or thinks he might be,' I said emphatically. I continued, 'I knew him back in Newhaven when he had his own trawler. If he had to use the radio it came over as "C-C-C-Calling N-N-N-Newhaven Radio", and everyone knew that it was Syd.'

'You're so wrong,' argued *Dave*. 'Your father invented that impediment after Sydney was caught on Bexhill beach with a load of Swiss watches. It gave him time to think up answers to the prosecution questions. In fact, I'm sure that old Vic was implicated in that time-keeping affair, because he put up Syd's bail.'

'Can we change the subject?' said Oz. 'I'm sick of hearing about Syd's f-f-f-fucking stutter!'

Determined not to give up, *Dave* persisted.

'It's all habit. All put on. We all have them. You have,' he continued looking at me. 'You cross your cigarette ends with your thumbnail. I've watched you do it hundreds of times, and I always know when you've been about. I look in the ashtrays.

'You ought to stop it. It's your trademark. A dead bloody give-away.

'And while we're at it, if Claude gets annoyed, he fiddles with his safety catch, which I find very unnerving.'

'Anything else?' I enquired.

'Oh yes,' he replied.

'If Oz gets worried, he farts a lot. And I find this disconcerting as well if we are all in the wheel-house or any other confined space.'

'Shut up *Dave*. Give your mouth a rest. The reason that you don't fart a lot is because your mouth's always open and you don't build up enough pressure. Anyway, smart-arse, what's your little oddity?' I asked.

'Oh, me?' he replied, grinning. 'I always sit down when I have a pee.'

'I'm obviously supposed to ask why,' I said.

'You are, but I'll tell you anyway. My doctor told me not to lift anything heavy!'

Claude joined in the laughter, but I don't think he fully understood the joke.

Claude took over the wheel, and Oz went out onto the foredeck where he stretched himself out. I think he wanted a bit of peace and quiet.

He definitely did have a bit of a dark side, the roots of which I doubt would ever be uncovered. Australian by birth, but never mentioned the place. He'd lived in South Africa for a number of years, but seldom spoke of it. Didn't like violence of any sort and would steer clear of any potential bar punch-ups. Hated carrying a gun, which was part of the uniform in this arena—and rarely even argued. Nevertheless, if push came to shove in most situations, he could be relied upon.

He'd been asleep for about an hour, when he suddenly sat up. He jumped up and hurried back to the bridge. Throwing open the door he yelled, 'There are gunshots ahead!'

Dave and I dived through the door and stood outside listening. We moved further forward, away from the noise of the engines and waited.

We heard nothing.

Leaving the wheel, Claude joined us. He was looking over my shoulder. After a few more moments he said, 'There are two boats ahead. There—in the haze.'

I strained my eyes and could just make out two vessels close together. One was *Cormorant*, and she had company in the shape of what looked like a patrol boat.

'It can't be a stop and search, he's well outside limits, and light in any case,' said Oz.

After he'd spoken, he hurried back to the bridge and steered towards the vessels.

Dave yelled to Alex for more revs and went quickly below, returning moments later with our firepower—a Bren gun. He climbed onto the flying bridge and clamped the gun to our modified mounting bracket.

We were now some 400 yards off and could see that the other vessel was no patrol boat.

There had recently been talk of pirates stealing cargoes, and this was possibly what was going on, they believing *Cormorant* was loaded. As we closed in,

I couldn't see anyone on either vessel, but *Cormorant* had smoke coming from aft of the bridge.

She was well alight below.

'What the fuck's going on?' shouted *Dave*. 'It can't be . . .'

His sentence was never finished. *Cormorant* blew up, a ball of flame and black smoke.

When this had cleared, *Cormorant* had disappeared.

As we had so much way on, we overshot the scene, our turning circle being more than 150 yards. *Dave* was firing at the remaining vessel with missionary zeal. He raked her from end to end and, as she rolled, I can remember the bullet holes leaving a pattern like the constellation of Andromeda.

Presumably realising that this was having little effect, he now concentrated on the superstructure. This was more dramatic—bits of timber flying everywhere. He stopped, however, after another magazine—I presume because there were no human targets visible.

Suddenly, complete silence. We were all stunned, standing completely still, as if waiting for something else to happen.

We nosed our way slowly back through the flotsam and a thin film of fuel oil, the smell of which clogged the air. This was all that remained of *Cormorant*.

The other vessel looked deserted, the whole scene weird and surreal, the assailant now a comatose hulk.

Dave broke the silence.

'I'll bet the bastards are hiding below. Shall I sink her?'

We were all still so shocked that nobody answered him.

'I'll sink her then, shall I?' he shouted down again.

Regaining some composure, Claude replied, 'No, we search it first. Then we sink it.'

He went on, 'And if there is anybody in the water, be sure that they are not from *Cormorant* before you kill them.'

Claude's face was a study. I'd never seen him like this. He moved thoughtfully into the wheel-house and after a brief word to Alex down the engine room hatch, edged *Helgah* towards the raider.

Dave left the flying bridge and joined me on the starboard foredeck, preparing to jump when close enough. We didn't have to, as Claude put us right alongside and we were able to step across the gap. We walked quickly across the raider's deck, guns at the ready.

Dave, who was mad on guns, had an old service revolver in his hand, and a Beretta stuffed in the back pocket of his jeans. He jumped down through the accommodation hatch and reappeared moments later, shaking his head, indicating there was nobody down there. He then headed for the engine-room, while I walked forward towards the wheel-house, holding my Walther PPK—and my breath.

As I reached the end of the coaming, I came face to face with one of the crew. He was slumped against the raised section, his legs out in front of him. At first I thought he was unconscious or even dead, as his legs rolled from side to side with the motion of the ship that was now lying beam-on to the gentle swell. His head didn't move, however, and his eyes were open, and they were staring—straight at me.

His hand now did move, towards a particularly unpleasant-looking large revolver that was wedged between his backside and the coaming.

It's funny just how much can go through your mind in a split second. In that split second I realised that not only had I never shot at anyone, I'd never even fired a gun in anger.

It was Churchill who'd said that if you are about to kill a man, it costs nothing to be polite. In this situation, however, I didn't have time to reflect too deeply upon this. In any case, 'Good afternoon,' wouldn't have been appropriate, and 'Goodbye,' in rather bad taste.

I can only remember screaming, 'Fuck you!'—and pulling the trigger.

I missed him by about a foot. The bullet smashed into the woodwork to the left of his head. This didn't bode well, as I was only about ten feet away from him, and his hand had now grasped the gun at his side.

Helgah, in the meantime, had drifted round to this side of the vessel. I had an audience of two—both armed, and in a perfect position to shoot him without the risk of hitting me. Why didn't they? No, the bastards were leaving it to me to avenge Syd.

I lowered my aim and fired again.

His guernsey jumper gave a little jerk, as though prodded by some unseen finger.

For a moment he looked totally surprised. Then his head dropped forward. As the vessel rolled on the next swell he slid towards me, then sideways out under the lower hand rail and overboard, leaving a wide smear of blood behind him.

I tried to grab his gun but it followed him into oblivion.

The applause from *Helgah* was short-lived as there were two more gunshots from below. I sprang across the deck and yelled down through the other hatch, 'Are you all right, *Dave*?'

At first there was no answer. Moments later, however, he appeared at the bottom of the ladder.

'There were two hiding in the engine-room. I've shot them both.'

'Did you get their guns?' I asked.

'They didn't have any,' he replied.

We searched the rest of the aggressor but found no sign of anybody, so we started to flood her.

I called across to Claude, 'We've opened the sea cocks, and she's taking in some water through the bullet holes. But she'll still take some time to go down. Shall we torch her?'

'Yes, do it now. This bloody drama will have been heard and most likely seen from the coast. We will soon have company.'

I soaked the accommodation and galley with the best part of 30 gallons of diesel and some ten gallons of petrol that had been stowed on deck in jerry-cans, presumably for the inflatable—now totally deflated thanks to *Dave's* expertise with the Bren. Luckily he'd managed to miss the cans.

He took care of the engine-room, smashing the feeder pipes from header and main fuel tanks, and leaving a couple of partly filled cans in the alleyway. He then splashed more petrol up the stairway to the deck, and soaked a large wad of cotton waste, which he dropped at his feet.

I signalled for Claude to pick us up and he raced in, removing a chunk of the raider's rubbing strake as he bumped *Helgah* alongside.

Dave lit the waste with his Zippo and kicked it down through the hatch. We both leaped aboard *Helgah*, and Claude backed her rapidly.

Seconds later there was a muffled thud as the spilled petrol ignited.

Some minutes later, a larger explosion, producing a row of smoke rings from each of her portholes.

We stood well off and watched her burn. She should have gone down quickly once the fire took hold, but it still took the best part of an hour before the weight of her machinery had the desired effect.

Most vessels sink bow first, revealing propellers in the air before slipping below the surface. This nameless one didn't. She went stern first, hesitatingly, like a recently qualified lady driver reversing into her garage.

She left little trace, the only leftovers being splinters of wood and a tell-tale patch of oil.

It's always a sad occasion when a ship founders, but we were all bloody happy to witness this deliverance into the keeping of Davy Jones, hoping that our secrets would remain safe with him.

After circling the area several times more and widening the circle to make sure there were no floaters, we turned for home. The whole incident had lasted less than an hour, and none of us was relishing the thought of the next 12 or so.

All in all, it had been a perfect sod of a day.

The beach party went off without a hitch. Aided by ten extra hands from shoreside, it took less than an hour to unload the cargo at a new location some 45 miles south of Salerno.

There was now only the other party to cope with—one I'd been very much looking forward to—but now I didn't relish the thought at all. This was a special social gathering at the *Rossi* villa scheduled for the following evening, to which Colombe and I were invited as usual. The guest list included, amongst others, Mario Lanza and Errol Flynn. But I was far from being in the party mood and told Claude so.

He wasn't sympathetic at all.

'You will go,' he said—like a command. 'There are some associates from the US coming and they will want to meet you.'

He continued, 'You are invited and if you show any signs of contrition over your actions today, it will be treated as a weakness and have very bad reflections.'

Reluctantly, I agreed to go.

Dave, who had overheard the discussion, cornered me in the absence of the others, and told me I was getting in too deep. He pointed out that the parties, the free piss-ups, the extra financial lubrication and shagging the niece of one of the bosses might well have a downside. He further suggested that these fringe benefits might be followed by wedding bells, lots of buns in the oven, no nights out, and no chance of escape or sudden death.

There was a hint of jealousy in his tone. In any case the bird he was sometimes shacked up with had seen more hotel bedrooms than the Gideon Bible, but then this probably suited him. That lifestyle certainly didn't suit me. In fact Colombe, and my relationship with her, would most likely be the only thing that might hold me together after this episode.

There were a number of usual watchers on the quay as we came alongside and tied up in Fiumicino. One familiar face was that of the ever-persistent freelance reporter, Duncan Webb. He was never far away and today his face showed it all. He must have had a tip-off and at last thought he was about to land a scoop.

He invited us for a drink, knowing that was what we usually did upon our return.

We declined. He became insistent. *Dave* offered to throw him in the dock.

To give Webb his due, he said, 'You'd better do it now, because this is my job and I intend to write a story.'

Dave obliged.

Everybody laughed as we split up and went our separate ways, but I felt sick to the stomach as I walked towards our flat in the Via di Roma. It would be marvellous if one could cauterize that part of the brain that fixes unpleasant memories. But as this is never possible, I'd put down today's entry in the Log of Misdemeanours—as the episode that completed my conscience bypass.

I didn't tell Colombe what had happened, but I knew she would be told or find out for herself.

I wondered what Vic would think, as he would certainly get to know. After all, he and Syd had been close friends. It appeared that *Dave* and Oz also knew Vic, and, of course, it had been him that first introduced Douglas to the *Pandora*'s agent back in Newhaven. In fact, the whole bloody thing now seemed incestuous.

Just as long as Molly never found out.

The following morning, I met the other two for a drink. They weren't much help, both having that 'I told you so' look on their faces. Or perhaps they didn't. Maybe it was me and the way I felt.

After several rounds of drinks I was just beginning to mellow a little, when *Dave* went for the throat.

'I'll bet yesterday's shooting invited lots of kisses on both cheeks,' he said.

I didn't answer.

'You do know what the *Cosa Nostra* kiss means, don't you'? he continued.

'Don't you bloody well start again,' I replied. 'These people are not the Mafia—the sort that live in American films. They are Sicilian businessmen, okay? Since I've been out here I've not seen a single fedora hat, double-breasted black suit, anyone carrying a sub-machine-gun, or any sedan cars with white-walled tyres.'

I could see that he was going to go on, so I got up, left the bar and went for a long walk along the quay—alone. Enough macabre thoughts were already going through my head without him adding to them.

I kept on thinking of that piece of water where I'd shot him. Maybe he was still floating out there. Perhaps he wasn't really dead, and if he wasn't then, he would be by now anyway. He must have been injured before I got to him, most likely from the explosion, and in any case, he was going to kill me. Did this justify my actions? And how long was I going to feel like this?

I still had the Walther in my pocket. I took it out and looked at it. For two pins I could cheerfully have thrown it in the dock. But I didn't.

Instead, I kept looking at the thing. It had actually killed a man. No, it was only partly to blame. I'd pulled the trigger, and I would have to live with this memory for the rest of my life. Allegedly it had once belonged to Benito Mussolini, having been a gift from Rudolf Hess, before falling into the hands of *Rossi*. I don't suppose that any of them had fired it, treating it as part of the dress code, like I did.

The one thing that would haunt me forever was the recollection of the victim's face. I can see it now as clearly as I did then. The brief flicker of surprise that doesn't seem to occur in movies or on TV, but happens only in reality, not yet having crept into the scriptwriter's vocabulary.

Three weeks after the skirmish, Vic sent out a cutting from the *Brighton Evening Argus*, headed 'Lost at Sea'. It gave a short account of the late Sydney Downer being drowned along with his crew, after the yacht he was delivering mysteriously sank off the Italian coast.

Even today, certain things are a horrid reminder. I dislike travelling through Heathrow. The smell of spent aviation fuel that greets you on arrival has the same whiff as shrouded that piece of ocean off Sorrento on that June day. I loathe that popular Italian song that suggests a return to that place. And if I view a map of Italy, I try to avoid letting my eyes stray to the southern half.

But my world seemed to end altogether when, upon returning from a trip, I was told of Colombe's death. She had rolled her sports car on a mountain road north of Rome.

This stamped something enduring in my mind and for years haunted me. After her funeral I immediately quit the organisation. Claude gave me a big bundle of money and a Citroën and said I'd be welcome to return at any time.

I left and went to Paris.

Since those days I've turned down numerous offers of holdays from friends who've retired to Tuscany and the south of Italy, and have only stepped on Italian soil once since then, and that was to change planes at Rome airport. I remained inside the terminal building.

Colombe somehow had a grip over me, and I lived a fantasy of our memories. There was only one woman who broke that spell—Caroline—but I'll introduce her when the time comes.

II

The planned itinerary now was to drink my way to Paris.

After two extravagant days at Le Dauphin in Menton and two more in Arles, followed by a further week somewhere between Chalon and Dijon, I found myself at the more familiar Montargis (of the 'stuck under the bridge' fame). This needed three, or was it four, intemperate nights and liverish days at the Petit Relais, a mere stone's throw from that very arch, before I managed to depart.

My arrival in Paris was somewhat marred by a longer-than-usual glance in the driving mirror, which revealed just how dreadful I really looked. As a result I decided to hotel it for one more night before inflicting myself on my friends, in the hope that I could get it together over the following 24 hours.

After struggling to park in a very-difficult-to-manoeuvre-if-you're-pissed-or-hungover basement garage of a not-so-posh hotel off the rue Saint Michel, I left most of my gear in the car. After registering, I took to my room only one clean shirt—the one I was wearing—and a saved-up pair of pressed trousers. With luck, these would still look reasonably presentable the next day if I managed not to spill anything over them or sleep in them, as had become usual with most of my other kit.

At supper time I chose something healthy with salad, accompanied by only one bottle of wine. No pud or brandy, just coffee. As a consequence, I retired a little later, only half pissed, and did remember to hang up the shirt before collapsing.

The Haywoods' flat in the rue Muller was, I discovered, not far away, in the 18th Arrondissement, just a few blocks from Pigalle. I found it without any difficulty. During our reunion we all managed to keep off the subject of Colombe.

'I hope that you'll stay with us for a long time,' said Nicole, as she showed me into their guest room.

I knew that this remark was totally genuine, and for that I was understandably grateful. Here I would venture to unwind for a couple of weeks before even considering anything even vaguely resembling a future.

Mark was a freelance writer with a meagre retainer from some obscure German magazine and a slightly larger one from Reuters. He and Nicole lived well enough, the formula seemingly working successfully.

'It pays the rent, and we eat most of the time,' he would joke if asked.

It had also gone part of the way to pleasantly furnishing the two-bedroom garden flat that had been their home for the past four years. Although the trappings were basically Provençal, Mark had obviously brought over a number of items from England, proclaiming a measure of good taste.

In company with a very English-looking Windsor chair, a handsomely patinated George IV Davenport, a huge dark oak and well-filled bookcase, stood an elegant long-case clock from the late 17th century, by John Shepley of Stockport. These pieces must have constituted at least three trips in his equally British Bentley. There was, no doubt, extra money tucked away in the Haywood family chest to support this opulence.

I was quite well off too at this stage. Owing to my departure from the *Rossi* fleet, I'd not only been paid up for the last three runs at $1,000 per trip, but I'd also received $5,000 from *Rossi* himself.

It was therefore on my insistence that I took them out to supper for the first three evenings after my arrival. It wasn't all my benevolence, as it suited me better to be surrounded by activity rather than stay in. Anyway, my hosts knew numerous places to eat well and inexpensively, and I was actually spending less on the three of us than I'd have normally done on myself alone.

On the fourth evening we ate at home and a friend of theirs joined us. This turned out to be Arlette. She was a strange sort of bird—about 20, on the skinny side and as pale as death.

It was, however, a fun gathering. Arlette spoke very good English. I managed to remain moderately sober, giving me the second opportunity in under a week to surface the following day without feeling like rat shit. And Nicole's treatment of the *gigot de mouton de Sologne* was more than commendable.

From then on, Arlette was more in evidence. It was obviously contrived. I didn't mind. I suppose, if anything, I played along with it. Colombe was still in the forefront of my mind and Arlette certainly wasn't going to take the edge off my grief. She was, however, at least taking the sting out of my drinking, which was a good thing. If this had been allowed to continue unchecked at its recent volume, it might have contributed to an early and premature reunion with Colombe.

I'd met Mark in my early days of smuggling, as he and a number of other scribblers, including the rather determined Harry Proctor and the celebrated and equally determined and aggravating Duncan Webb, were at that time all snooping around the periphery of the business. Proctor and Mark chose to loiter mainly around Marseilles, believing this to be the centre of the operation. Webb chose to work at the Italian end of the industry, and as a result he was the only British journalist to be on hand to cover the explosive demise of Sydney Downer.

It was during this time that Colombe and I had become friendly with Mark and Nicole. They'd been back in Paris now for some six months and, upon hearing about the Colombe tragedy, insisted that I go and stay with them.

Having been there for about two weeks and not wishing to outstay my welcome, I was going to suggest that I move on. Mark was working very hard, and so too was Nicole, in her father's marketing firm.

I would tell them my intentions over breakfast the following morning.

Almost as though she were to pre-empt my announcement, Nicole asked me if I'd mind staying on to look after their flat and cat, as Mark was about to take a six-week commission in West Africa. If I agreed she could go with him.

In return for looking after the moggy, Arlette would look after me. I didn't altogether like the sound of that, but I couldn't object after the hospitality I'd received. I agreed and a few days later they flew out, leaving me and the fluffy Persian with the flat to ourselves.

Well, almost.

Arlette arrived around 4 p.m. bearing copious quantities of grub, giving the impression that we were about to outlast another siege of the Bastille. She only lived two floors up, but judging by the positive way she was organising things she was intending to spend much more time in the Haywoods' flat. So far I'd managed to keep her at arms' length, but from now on it might become more difficult.

Supper was *carbonnades de boeuf*—steaks in a sort of batter—and bloody good it was too. After the meal I attacked the residue of about three-quarters of a bottle of Armagnac and passed out. I didn't see Arlette throughout the following day and guessed that she was most likely cross.

I would try to make amends that evening and take her to the Au Roi Des Coquillages, which was a favourite restaurant of hers, on the boulevard de Clichy. At the same time I would make every effort to stay off the sauce.

After a slap-up feed rinsed down with barely a bottle of house wine, we wandered home slowly through the bright lights of Montmartre. Winston the moggy was duly let out. I made coffee, during which time Arlette disappeared. I couldn't make up my mind whether I preferred to think that she had gone to her room on the third floor or mine across the hall.

She had the whitest bum I'd ever seen. In fact, with few exceptions her whole porcelanic body was as white as a Goldsleider figurine, and would have been more at home on an onyx plinth than compromised, as now, against my blue-and-white striped sheets.

I wanted to speak, perhaps to reassure myself as much as anything, but as I lay beside her I thought it more appropriate to withhold comment.

The first thing I noticed in the morning was the crack in the east ceiling plaster, and pondered why I'd not seen it before.

It was Saturday. It was also raining. She looked very sexy, and I fancied her like hell. Not much point in getting up, really. So we didn't.

Just before noon, somebody knocked. Arlette slid off the bed and went to the door. She walked beautifully, but then most continental women do. Possibly it's more evident if they're naked.

'*Qui est-ce? Que voulez-vous? Ce soir? C'est bien.*'

She returned.

'We're eating out tonight. We go to Lasserre. It's very expensive.'

'Why?' I asked.

'Willie has sold a picture.'

So far I'd not met Willie.

'Who is Willie?'

'He lives upstairs.'

'Is he a painter?' I asked.

'No,' she replied. 'He's a queer. And when he has no money, he sells one of the paintings or *objets d'art* that his rich and lately dead lover left him.'

'He doesn't work, then?' I suggested.

'No. I don't think he's ever worked.'

'So what will he do when he runs out of things to sell?'

'Oh, he says he will kill himself.'

'Well, that's novel,' I thought aloud.

Arlette continued, 'I do not think he will really kill himself. It is more likely that he will die from alcoholic liver.'

'I've not tried that,' I said.

'Not tried what?' she asked.

'Alcoholic liver,' I replied. 'I've had it with bacon, or lightly grilled in batter, and many other ways, but not with alcohol.'

'What is this with alcohol? I do not understand.'

'It doesn't matter. It's not important,' I assured her, not wishing to be drawn further on the subject of booze.

'Is there anything else I should know about Willie?' I queried.

'Willie treats us all to champagne and good food on these times. And oh yes, he's a count.'

(No, that's not a misprint, although one might be forgiven for believing it to be so.)

'He sounds like one,' I said under my breath. 'How many does he treat on these occasions?' I asked.

'All of us in the five apartments.'

'He must be a bigger count than I thought.'

So everybody sponges off Willie. I wondered what other bizarre activities happened in this *laissez-faire* setup.

Lasserre, on the avenue Franklin D. Roosevelt, was splendid—its menu unsurpassed, and its levy every bit as excessive as one might expect. I for one was pleased not to be picking up the tab.

Willie, who had this pleasure, was for the most part the centre of attraction, but he later became more preoccupied with one of the waiters serving at the next table. This was Marcel, who didn't appear to have a particularly attractive arse, but then I wouldn't know. I've never been that way inclined.

Most of the remaining apartment-dwelling revellers appeared to be near normal, but on reflection this was open to debate. The general consensus, however, was that in spite of enjoying an entertaining evening, I wouldn't be cultivating Willie as a close chum.

As time went on, I think both Arlette and I realised that ours wasn't destined to be a lifelong relationship. It just so happened that at the moment we were good for each other. At least, I hoped this was the case. We had the same sense of humour, enjoyed the same music, our tastes in art were similar, and bed was totally gratifying in every aspect. But always there was this feeling of guilt and restlessness, which niggled uninvitingly.

At the end of August, the Haywoods returned. Without realising it, I'd now been in Paris for over three months.

I thought it would be nice for them to have the flat back for themselves. In any case, Arlette had already told the landlady that I would move in with her when they came home. My attraction to the local nectar had slowed a little—which was just as well, as I now had to tackle a further two flights of stairs.

The landlady would smile and give me a knowing look whenever I passed her. This was fine as long as she didn't smile too widely, because by the wildest stretch of imagination she couldn't be called attractive, and worse, if she opened her mouth the total absence of dental care meant it bore a strong resemblance to a vandalised piano. But to be fair, she was never short of men. There was usually a steady flow of them at her door in the later hours.

One day she stopped us to say that she was going to a retreat for a month to meditate her sins. Arlette thought this to be most honourable until I explained that I'd been a wicked sod all my life but could easily meditate all my sins in about ten minutes. We both agreed that by this reckoning, Madame Villier must have had a very full life.

Love is the answer, but while you're waiting for the answer, sex raises some pretty good questions.

- Woody Allen

12

Vic was never short of money-making ideas and, strangely enough, some of them worked. While I'd been in Paris, he'd continued refurbishing *Myzpah* as a fishing boat, but not to go fishing. He was at the time buying large quantities of prime fish in Brighton market. Sold by Dutch auction, he would step in and buy the lot before the price fell low enough to interest local buyers. He made a few enemies, but became the original Fisherman's Friend. The catch was then raced up to London in a fleet of small vans and sold at exorbitant prices to upmarket establishments, having allegedly been fresh caught the night previously by his own trawler, *Myzpah*.

Myzpah very seldom dipped her nets in the water, but was used exclusively to wine and dine select potential buyers for fashionable London outlets.

She was being run by a female crew under the command (and I use the word 'under' totally without wishing to malign) of a certain *Roger Dowager*. He was employed by Vic on the understanding that the position was temporary until I returned and took over.

I think Mrs *Dowager* was rather pleased to see me come back and take over as I did, because *Myzpah* had become known, quite wrongly I'm sure, as the 'Newhaven Knocking Ship'.

This label was without any justification. She was simply a showboat. Whatever the girls got up to in their spare time was explicitly down to them, and I had no control whatsoever over the strength of their knicker elastic.

The routine usually was to take guests out a few miles and, if the weather was being kind, feed and wine them, and sometimes play a little cards.

Some weekends we would shoot over to Deauville, where they could lose even more money in the casino. The profit on the returning brandy more than compensated for the cost of fuel and food.

We usually catered for eight passengers. Guests' wives were always welcome, but didn't often appear. Meanwhile, Vic was selling a hell of a lot of fish. We were allowed to fish one night a week, as a little bit of a bonus, and he would buy the catch.

He didn't always take up our offer. One morning he came to examine our catch. It wasn't exactly as fresh as it might have been. He declined it. Picking up a Dover sole and banging it on the side of the fish box, he said, 'I've seen rigor mortis under a number of circumstances, but this little bastard is almost fossilised.'

After a few months, competition started up, led by another fishing boat called the *Tintoretto*, although Vic always referred to her as the Skintoretto. There were others that came on the scene as well, so *Myzpah* remained tied up alongside, still bogusly supplying London outlets.

A little later on, pirate radio stations started illegally broadcasting in the North Sea. Vic became friendly with the boss of one of them, who wanted the competition to be jammed off the air.

Myzpah came out of mothballs.

The pirates supplied the electronic equipment. At the time, any potential radio pirate needed to have a crystal control of their broadcasting frequency. These crystals had to be expertly cut, and could be only purchased secretly in Holland. We had to use an alternative, called a Variable Frequency Oscillator (VFO).

Now electrics and radio are almost a total mystery to me. Vic always maintained that if I wired up an electric fire anywhere, it was warmer to sit round the plug than the fire itself. So after I'd installed the very powerful Canadian transmitter, and our VFO, I was ready to go. It now only required tuning. So an expert was called in to complete this stage.

The instructions in the manual were simple enough, but not my cup of tea. There was a circuit of a certain frequency that one wished to jam on, indicated by a neon bulb. The instructions were that one should 'tune to maximum brilliance of the bulb'.

I noticed that Vic had modified the instructions in pencil. It now read, 'In your case, tune to maximum smoke.' I only had to jam for half an hour at a given time and then stop. And feeling like Julius Caesar, I jammed, I stopped, I got paid.

13

I was still very restless, so I took a skipper's position for a four-month contract to operate a holiday pleasure-boat from Brighton pier. She was the motor vessel *Anzio*, an ex-Royal Naval minesweeper. We were licensed to carry 250 passengers. The contract was to run from June to September.

Halfway through the season, we'd carried about 4,000 holidaymakers on three-hour trips on the Channel. One day a very pretty girl came on board. This was Letitia. She reminded me strongly of Colombe. So I married her.

Of course, it was a mistake for both of us. I was trying to live a past dream, and being totally unfair in trying to mould her into Colombe. And although I never mentioned it to her, it became so obvious that one day, after we'd been together for almost two years, Letitia said to me, 'It's no good, you know. I'm not her, and I can't be, no matter how hard I try.'

It made me realise how selfish I was being. So what was the solution? We now had a young son.

It was decided that we'd have a trial separation for six months, so I signed up with the Union-Castle company, and left on a three-month voyage to South Africa on a steamship. I completed the first round trip and signed on for a second one. This time there were two men among the crew who knew South Africa well and were returning to go diamond buying (illegally, of course) from native workers, on one of the biggest mining concessions in South Africa.

I was totally hooked on the idea. We three jumped ship in Cape Town and worked our way up country buying stones, and dodging the Illegal Diamond Buying (IDB) police. My two newfound chums were known to the IDB from their previous visits but knew how to keep one jump ahead of them. I was a complete novice at the game, and it wasn't going to be long before I was going to get caught.

By now I'd put together a small collection of uncut stones. The way to test them to see if they were the real thing or not is to carry a piece of cut and polished topaz. It, being almost the next hardest mineral to diamond, can only be scratched by one if it's genuine.

The stones I had were all genuine enough but, at the time, if anybody was caught in South Africa with an uncut diamond, it was deemed illegal and carried an automatic prison sentence.

I was ahead on points so I decided to ship out the ones I had, and joined a German cargo ship in Luderitz bound for Antwerp, where I had no trouble at all in selling them.

The guy I sold the stones to in Antwerp was a little Jewish diamond dealer called the Pelican. He encouraged me to make several other trips to South Africa, and I got quite brave dodging the police. I carried a guitar with me, the fingerboard of which you could slide out. It was hollow underneath, and I kept the stones hidden in there. Replacing the board covered them up.

I eventually got arrested with the guitar, searched, and released—and given the guitar back again. Fortunately nobody ever asked me to play the bloody thing. I can't play a single note on it. I decided my musical days in South Africa were definitely over, so I went home to Letitia.

Incidentally, I still have my piece of topaz, and it hasn't received any scratches recently.

I first met Gordon Neville Baber in Medina Villas, a quiet street in the fashionable part of Hove.

He was standing in the road, contemplating a flat tyre on a not-so-posh Morris 21 saloon.

'No ruddy jack,' he commented as I drew level with him. After a brief consultation, a suggestion from me, 12 house bricks removed from his front garden and a measure of luck, the situation was resolved.

He gently drove the car up the newly constructed brick ramp. With the remainder of the bricks employed to block up the rear spring, all that was needed to scatter the ramp was a quick touch astern, now leaving the offending wheel suspended.

Flat off, spare on, replace ramp, drive off. Ten minutes.

'I like initiative,' he said. 'What do you do for a living?'

'At the moment, nothing,' I replied.

'Good. You can work with me. I need a working partner.'

It was at that moment I became aware of what was sitting on the rear seat of the car, clearly labelled, 'Gelignite Polar Ammon,' and in smaller letters, 'High Explosive'.

Tearing my eyes away from the car's cargo, I enquired, 'What do you do?'

I should have expected the reply, I suppose. With a perfectly straight face, he said, 'I blow things up.'

'I've always fancied doing that,' I replied. 'Do you have any choice of targets?'

He smiled, introduced himself and explained that he ran a demolition company and a film stunt agency, and that I now had a partnership.

He somehow looked very much the part. Aged about 45, well built, heavily bearded, greying at the sides. He was sporting a military-style battledress shirt, corduroy trousers and desert boots.

I later discovered that Neville had been in the army in his previous career. Since leaving the army, he had built up this demolition agency and stunt company. These operations suited him well and went some way to satisfying his love for blowing things up and taking regular hideous chances with life.

He'd had a good war, taking part in the Rhine Drop, Arnhem, the Normandy landings and Monte Cassino, and had come through it all unscathed. Although 20 years my senior, he was most likely much fitter.

'Come in,' he said. 'Meet the wife and have some coffee.'

We entered the house and went through the hall into the kitchen. A woman of a similar age was standing looking out of the window towards the garden. She turned as we entered.

'This is Joan,' he said. 'What's your name, by the way?'

'Martin,' I replied.

'Joan, meet Martin. He's going to be working with me.'

I realised at once that she was deaf, and lip-reading. She smiled, eyed me up and down, and said with a mock-puzzled look, 'You look so normal, too. Welcome to the circus.'

'Call me Nev, by the way,' he said as he laughed at her response, and ushered me through to the office.

This was a large room overlooking the long rear garden. It contained a filing cabinet, a desk complete with an aged-looking typewriter, and a pile of telephone directories fanned out like a sweeping staircase. A heap of what looked like bills and sundry papers was stacked up on the floor. I was soon to learn that this was precisely what it appeared to be—the heap system.

Each month the bills were shuffled like a pack of playing cards. The first six that wound up on top received payment. The others waited their turn. If anyone had the nerve to complain about outstanding accounts, they were omitted from the following month's shuffle.

Against one wall stood six more cardboard boxes, similar to those in the car.

I wondered what the neighbours thought. They didn't know, of course. Immediately next door lived the actress Alexandra Bastedo, later of *Casino Royale* fame.

In the conversation that followed, I was pleased to discover that the Baber family were about to move to a house in the Old Shoreham Road at Southwick. I myself was living only about 200 yards away in The Drive. Just far enough away to be out of range of any blast. My gleanings also included the fact that I'd just automatically joined the Sussex Skydivers—a parachuting club of which Neville Gordon Baber was the instructor.

Specialised Explosives Services was a more or less normal demolition company, and this I could live with, although it might be a misnomer. Neville assured me that Specialised Unit Facilities was a stunt business, but didn't go in for crashing cars or falling off tall buildings. It worked mainly with animals.

'You know,' he said, 'a few snakes, spiders, and some big cats.'

'No loud bangs?' I suggested.

'Sometimes the odd pyrotechnic,' he replied.

Ignore the fact that these odd ones were to include *The Guns of Navarone, The Longest Day, A Prize of Arms, The Battle of the V.1.*

The parachuting bit was simply a form of relaxation.

I love animals and told him so, adding that I hoped the spiders and snakes would be big and the cats less so.

The Sunday afternoon treats—being taken up to about 4,000 feet and throwing myself out of a totally serviceable aircraft that still had its wings on—somehow lacked appeal. But what the hell.

I'd known Nev for all of 20 minutes, and it dawned upon me that during that time, I'd most likely qualified for endangered species status.

We returned to the kitchen where Joan had the coffee sorted. She joined us. I realised that she was an expert lip-reader.

'Any family, Mart?' Nev enquired.

Before I had time to answer, Joan interrupted.

'He only wants to find out if you've any next of kin,' she said.

We all had a good laugh, after which I told him—married, with three kids. Letitia had since given birth to another boy and a girl.

I warmed to Nev and Joan immediately and looked forward to this new chapter in my life. Two days later I was drilling holes and placing charges in and under the foundations of what was the old Crystal Palace, in preparation for the construction of a new sports track. I was surprised to discover how quickly I'd become used to handling explosives and detonators. I hoped that the coming weekend I would find that pulling the rip-cord was about to be equally entertaining. Taking chances seemed to have become the norm.

My driving started to improve. We generally travelled with 200 pounds of gelignite and detonators on the back seat, so when I took the wheel, I didn't ever crowd the car in front. I allowed slightly longer distances for stopping, and when passing slower vehicles, always bore in mind a sign I'd once read—'Undertakers Love Overtakers'.

Nev usually transported us at high speed round the naïve and peaceful counties of England.

Nothing ever flustered him. He didn't really have nerves of steel. He simply didn't have any nerves.

The fumes from the gelly can inflict the most blinding headache, known as a 'gelly head', so whether it was chucking down or quite fine we needed to drive with the sun roof open. This was to avoid breathing in the fumes.

We both smoked. As the winding handle of the driving-side window was broken off leaving it permanently closed and the ashtray was missing, Nev used to flick the butt-ends of his almost-finished cigarettes out through the roof.

Bearing in mind what was resting on the back seat, always covered up with a few items of clothing to disguise it, you would imagine that smoking might be discouraged. Not the case.

One day when we were driving through the centre of Brighton with Nev at the wheel, I was more than a little concerned suddenly to smell burning. Turning in my seat, I saw—to my horror—the seat happily smouldering.

I shouted out, 'Fire!' and Nev pulled up and parked, quite slowly it seemed to me. He then reached over and dealt with the offending little blaze by beating it out with a shoe that was lying on the floor.

'Bugger,' he said. 'It's burnt a hole in that pullover, and it was almost new.'

The fire was, of course, the result of one of his cigs not going out and being nicely fanned by the draught. Nev wasn't the slightest bit upset by the mini bonfire on top of all the explosives, but very put out by the damage to the sweater.

In future I was to track the trajectory of all departing butt-ends very carefully.

14

I reversed the shooting brake carefully and quietly up the drive, making sure that when it came to rest, its rear doors were as close as possible to the side door of the house. Nev climbed through to the back as I slid out and walked quickly to the rear of the vehicle.

After a few moments came the whispered instruction from within.

'Okay, Mart. Open up.'

I turned the key, twisted the handle and slowly opened the back doors.

Nev hopped out.

'Let's take him straight in, Mart. We don't want any nosey parkers recognising him and calling the police. We'll show him into the office before we tell Joan.'

'Be it on your head,' I muttered.

'Out, and keep quiet,' said Nev.

Our captive obediently stepped out and joined us on the gravel driveway without a murmur. Fortunately, as usual, Joan had forgotten to lock up, so the three of us crept in and moved silently along the rear hall and into the office.

'You stay here with him. I'll tell her we're back.'

'Don't be long!' I said.

As he left the room, Nev turned to our detainee and said in a quiet voice, 'We don't want any trouble out of you, my lad, so behave yourself. You've been pretty good up till now. Just keep it that way.'

He closed the door after him and moments later I heard raised voices. Joan sounded cross, which was only to be expected, as I imagined that, in his usual tactful manner, he'd just told her, 'Mart's in the office. Let's have some coffee, love. And by the way, dear, we've brought a lion back with us.'

Bearing in mind that the three of us had just spent two and a half hours on the road, Simba was quite inactive. He yawned and jumped up onto the desk, dispatching papers and sundry objects onto the floor.

Nev returned without Joan. He was carrying a threadbare eiderdown, a couple of red blankets and a Sainsbury's carrier bag containing Simba's supper— eight pounds of raw steak. I was relieved to see this, as this 260-pound carnivore might have been contemplating the 12-stone snack that was holding the other end of his tether.

I was quite keen to visit the loo at this stage and left. During my absence Simba polished off his repast. By the time I returned, he looked as though he was ready for his pud.

'He will probably need a crap now, Mart. We'll have to take him in the garden before he settles down.'

'Sod that,' I replied. 'Put some newspaper down. I'm going home. I'll see you in the morning at about five.'

'Okay, but don't make it any later. We've got to have him on the set by eight.'

'Don't worry, I'll be around. I hope that you still are!'

I was now in the thick of working for Nev's sister company—Specialised Unit Facilities—and working with a much bigger moggy than I would have liked. The following morning as we drove along the A27 towards Brighton, dawn was competing with some dark-looking clouds coming up from the south.

Simba was happily ensconced in the rear of the Ford Dagenham brake. He seemed to enjoy travelling and settled down quietly. This was fortunate as the only dividing structure between him and us was the dog guard, held in place by rather flimsy rubber suction pads, which in the past had fallen down after receiving the slightest shove from Nev's dog.

On the occasions this happened, Boxer usually joined us in the front and wound up sitting on my lap. I hoped Simba wouldn't contemplate anything similar. If he did, I was already making plans to change places with him. Not to sit on his lap, but to climb through into the back.

'We have got everything, haven't we?' I suggested.

'Yes, I'm sure we have. His bed, his blankets and his grub. And he's still got his collar and lead on. Can you think of anything else we might need?'

'Lots of bandages and elastoplast,' was all I could think of.

Actually, Simba was very well behaved. Coming from a private collection, it was also obvious that he was totally spoilt. He was just like the proverbial ginger tom from next door, only a bloody sight bigger. Nev had pointed out earlier that Simba would eat off your hand—if you didn't take it away quick enough.

We would continue to need lights for about another hour before it would be light enough to turn them off. This was a bit of a problem, as we lost them just after dropping down into Patcham on the outskirts of Brighton. There were, however, signs of early morning life as we reached the Robin Hood garage, so Nev pulled onto the forecourt.

'Can anyone fix lights?' shouted Nev to a chap filling up a car facing in the other direction.

'Sorry mate, not until the mechanics arrive at eight thirty. I'm only the gas jockey.'

'We'll just have to sit it out until it gets a bit lighter and then go like hell,' I said.

Nev climbed out, screwdriver in hand, and opened the bonnet. A fruitless action, I thought, as he knew marginally less about electronics than he did about brain surgery. A screwdriver in the hands of Nev was about as useful as a pair of binoculars to Nelson, or a Sony Walkman to Van Gogh.

Just then, the passenger from the car receiving fuel walked over.

'Fords,' he said contemptuously. 'We know all about them, don't we? The fuses aren't in there mate, they're under the dash.'

He opened our passenger-side door, stuck his head under the dashboard, and started poking about with some loose wires.

Simba, who until now had been covered up with one of his red blankets to keep him insulated, chose this moment to sit up and see what was causing the delay.

'That's fixed,' announced the helpful but big-headed newcomer as he stood up. It was then he caught sight of Simba.

'Fuck me! That's a bloody big dog!' he exploded.

Simba's blanket now slowly slipped off revealing his full mane. At this point our man took a deep breath, muttered something about MGM, and walked unsteadily back to his car.

'What did he say?' asked Nev.

'Something about MGM,' I replied.

'Oh, he must have been a squaddie. That's short for My Goodness Me. I'll tell you one thing, Mart. Nobody will believe him when he says that a funny thing happened to him on his way to work this morning!'

Upon our late arrival at the studios, we found that some of the early shots were faked ones anyway and Simba wasn't needed until later in the morning.

The first take to include Nev, Simba and me was a short one. I get shot in the shoulder and fall down in it.

Simba is then supposed to jump over my prone body and have Nev for lunch.

The problem was that the lion hadn't read the script. He was persuaded to walk all over me, and in doing so managed twice to step on my balls, but when he reached Nev, he simply stood majestically astride him displaying about as much malevolence as his statuesque chums in Trafalgar Square.

'Right then, let's try again,' said the director. 'Only this time, Nev, try shaking his mane.'

We tried.

It didn't work because this negative head-shaking action gave the impression that Simba might well be refusing a part in any future episode of The *White Hunter* series for ITV.

'Cut! Let's go again.'

We tried.

This wasn't an outstanding success either. Simba had just reached his final position, when a door in the back of the jungle opened, and a white overall-clad scenery painter strolled in whistling *A Handful of Songs*.

'Cut!' screamed the director. It was quite obvious he wasn't pleased.

Simba didn't seem impressed either. Perhaps he wasn't a fan of Tommy Steele either.

'Right. We'll try one bloody more time, but this time could we all try a little harder? And Martin, as you and the beast's rear end are out of shot, when he reaches Neville, jump up and lift his back leg and see if you can throw him off balance. Right. Let's see what happens.'

Not a lot did.

When Simba reached his position, I grabbed his back left leg and heaved it up waist high. Simba just stood there with one leg in the air. This was the first time I'd been called upon to help a lion get his leg over, and my efforts were completely wasted. Hitherto I've not been asked to repeat this deed and I doubt the opportunity will ever occur again.

We broke for lunch.

Soon after restarting, Simba's lady owner turned up, and on seeing that other animals were present, she insisted that her 'pet' be given a jab against some bug or other.

Nev and I were now apparently his handlers, so we held him so this could be done.

The duty vet stuck the needle into the king of the jungle's bum, and this immediately seemed to change his whole outlook on motion-picture production. He let out an almighty roar, leaped forward knocking me flying, and snapped at Nev, catching him in the forearm. Not a serious bite, but enough to draw blood from a toothmark on each side.

We worked on for a couple of hours and then wrapped for the day. Simba and his lady went back to a private zoo somewhere, and Nev and I headed for home.

By the time we reached Crawley it was getting dark. In the half light I could see Nev nursing his arm, so it was obviously smarting a bit. My suggestion that we stop and see a Crawley quack met with a flat refusal.

It wasn't until we were on the outskirts of Hove 45 minutes later that my further insistence was heeded, whereupon we diverted to Hove General Hospital. A sensible course of action as—unlike Simba—Nev hadn't had a jab of any sort for years.

It might be worth mentioning at this stage that both he and I were expected back on set early the following day. We hadn't gone to wardrobe to change as we'd be wearing the same gear again.

We must have looked odd, to say the least, waiting in outpatients dressed in khaki battledress rig, sporting Fidel Castro-type hats, and our beards sprayed with silver to appear grey on camera.

The fact that Nev had a suspicious-looking wound partly covered by a blood-soaked sleeve, which in fact looked like a bullet wound, caused us to be referred in turn from nurse to sister to houseman—and finally, to the boss.

'Mr Baber, I can't go giving you an anti-tetanus injection unless you tell me what this injury is and how it was caused,' insisted the boss doctor tersely.

'It's just a scratch,' replied Nev.

'I'll need more than that, Mr Baber, I'm afraid.'

'Oh for Christ's sake tell him Nev,' I pleaded, 'then we can go home.'

'Very well,' bleated Nev, looking nonchalantly up at the ceiling. 'It's a lion bite.'

'And just exactly where were you when it bit you, Mr Baber?'

'Actually I was Twickenham, old boy.'

'I see,' replied the doctor sarcastically. 'There are obviously more lions at large in West London than there are here in Hove.'

I wasn't sure if he actually believed us, but as long as he treated Nev for his injury, I didn't much care one way or the other.

We finished our stint with Simba the next day, and I was more than relieved to say goodbye to the lion king.

It was less than three weeks later when we received a phone call from the RSPCA. They wanted us to capture and remove a King Rhesus monkey from an address in Worthing. The poor thing had gone mad. Its owner couldn't get near it.

On this occasion Nev decided to take Tall Tony with us. He was one of our part-time workforce and, as his name suggested, was six foot six tall. If the monkey was out of reach, he might be an asset. He was always very willing and good-natured, and apart from the fact that he was nearly always late, he was a useful chap to have around.

His command of the English language left a bit to be desired. Unlike some people who drop their H's, he also dropped his F's. His usual excuse for continual unpunctuality was, "ucking car wouldn't start.' He now lived locally, having at one time resided in Bognor Regis, so it was quicker to pick him up than wait for his engine to dry out.

When we arrived at the address, we were shown down the garden to a half hut, half cage arrangement. This was Monty the monkey's billet.

As soon as Monty saw Mr Finch, his jailer, he became quite truculent and swung from corner to corner of his metal home, making a great deal of noise and showing a lot of teeth.

As we waited for Nev to decide how to catch the little creature, Tony moved closer to the cage, removing his shirt as he did so. Unfortunately this stripped-to-the-waist posture always annoyed Nev because it displayed a large tattoo on Tony's chest. This picture of a nondescript face (that was supposed to be Lenin) did to a degree resemble Nev himself, and it bugged him. But, as I pointed out, one couldn't expect much from a Bognor Regis tattoo artist who probably didn't have a lot of call for members of the Russian politburo.

Nev finished his survey and said, in more or less a whisper and without moving his lips, as though trying not to reveal our tactics to this agile primate, 'When I give you the nod, Mart, open the door. I'll dive in and catch the little bugger.'

As Monty swung away towards the far corner, Nev said, 'Now!'

I whipped open the cage door and Nev dived in. As Monty returned fast, Nev gave him a firm short uppercut and, grabbing him, stuffed him into the hotel-size laundry basket we'd taken with us.

When we arrived back at base, Tony pushed several bananas into one of the lifting holes of the basket, and we listened.

Sounds of banana-eating came from within. Nev knelt down and looked into one of the holes and, standing up, said, 'Have a look in there, Mart.'

I placed my eye a safe monkey's finger's length from the hole. There was another eye looking out.

'We'd better let him out,' I said. 'He can't stay in there. He'll probably be quiet now.'

Tony undid the buckle and lifted the lid. Monty just sat there scowling. Having received one thump under the chin, he thought it prudent not provoke another. We left him loose in the office for the night.

In the morning, a visual inspection of the room through the window revealed no trace of the little brown tree-dweller. A filing cabinet in the far corner of the room was the only area that defied surveillance, and that's exactly where he was. As Nev crept into the room, Monty sprang on his back, sinking his teeth into Nev's neck and hanging on.

Sitting in casualty at Hove General, I had the distinct feeling, rightly or wrongly, that we were being ignored. The duty sister kept flitting backwards and forwards past us without so much as a sidelong glance.

Eventually she was joined by an attractive brunette in her early thirties wearing a sparkling white coat, in the top pocket of which was a folded stethoscope. A lady doctor. They headed towards us and stopped in front of Nev. This pretty lady continued reading from a light-brown card that she'd arrived with. When she'd finished she said, 'I see that when you were last here, Mr Baber, we treated you for a lion bite. What seems to be the problem this time?'

Nev said nothing but, lowering his head, he removed a bandage that he'd been holding to his neck.

She looked at the four punctures for at least half a minute without speaking. I could see what was going through her mind:

'My God, he's been attacked by a vampire bat somewhere in darkest Surbiton!'

The awkward silence continued, broken finally by Tony, who came to the rescue in his usual inarticulate manner.

'Well, Miss, 'e 'as been bit in the neck by an 'ucking griller!'

15

It had become the practice for me to stroll down to Nev's house and join him for breakfast. Most of our operations and plannings, and inquests over previous balls-ups were discussed over this meal.

This particular morning's conference focused on two operations. Firstly, some business we had to attend to for Specialised Explosives Services, the removal of some walls of an old air raid shelter. The second business of the morning concerned a totally illegal arms deal for a central African country. Nothing really unusual about either of them.

In the short time I'd known Nev, we'd blown up a number of Ministry of Defence (MOD) installations, I'd learnt to handle most types of commercial explosives, been press-ganged into joining the skydiving club and made three very memorable jumps. Also because Nev thought it might be a useful attribute, I was now taking flying lessons under the guidance of an Irish instructor at Shoreham airport.

It would now appear I was to become a gunrunner, and I thought my life had been quite exciting before I'd met him.

Three weeks previously, Nev and I had been in Cogswell and Harrison, the Piccadilly gun-makers, discussing a perfectly legal deal regarding automatic weapons for a proposed sequel to the film *The Guns of Navarone*. Someone visiting the premises overheard part of our conversation and wrongly assumed we were in the arms movement business.

Two days later we received a letter inviting us to a meeting with a company we'd never heard of. We attended.

One of the directors, Mr *Smith*, offered us a phenomenal sum in diamonds if we'd smuggle 50-odd cases of Madsen sub-machine-guns, 30 armoured cars, and an unspecified number of personnel to Katanga, the breakaway state in the Congo. We told him we'd think about it and explore to see if it could be done or not.

Five days later we phoned him and confirmed that it could.

The next day, he phoned to say that two representatives from this breakaway state would be calling on us to see the gun from Nev's collection and show us a sample of the promised stones. They were due to arrive at 11.30 a.m. today, so we were discussing how to handle it.

Suddenly Nev looked up from his plate, his fork having stopped midway to his mouth, a neatly folded rasher of back bacon dripping with egg yolk appetisingly skewered to its end.

'Oh Gawd,' he said, nodding towards the window. I turned and followed his gaze. On the veranda hand rail, not six feet away, sat a rat, looking in hungrily.

'We'll have to have that little bugger after breakfast, me boy,' he said. 'There'll be no peace again if she spots that one.'

Just as he finished speaking, Joan asked Nev what he was referring to. Because of her deafness, she had developed a remarkable extra sense, possibly out of the need for survival. Not only had she the attribute of perfect lip-reading, but she knew instantly if any danger threatened, or if Nev was being economical with the truth—both of which were frequent occurrences.

So the lie, 'It's just a little mouse,' was met with total disbelief.

'It was a rat, wasn't it?' she said crossly.

'No, dear. Just a little field mouse.'

Joan didn't like rats at all, and when she had reported sightings of them in the vicinity of the Victorian quasi-castle into which they had now moved, Nev had told her, depending on their range, that they were escaped ferrets, weasels, and even a stray otter, in an attempt to subdue her ever-present desire to move once again into a more normal abode.

After swallowing, he continued, barely moving his lips.

'We must shoot that little bastard and any of his chums, bloody pronto.' Joan returned to the kitchen, muttering something about little field mice as she went.

'Now Mart, what about these blokes that are coming this morning? What do we know about them? Are we being set up? Have they got any bloody diamonds and would you know a good one if you saw one?'

'Don't rely too heavily upon my judgement,' I replied. 'The last ones I handled were worth only £600, and not £25,000.'

'We're just going to have to play it by ear, me boy,' he said, swilling the last of his coffee.

He got up from the table and left the room. I helped myself to some more coffee and lit another cigarette.

When he reappeared he was carrying a Steyr rifle, which he handed to me, pointing out that it was loaded. He also announced that he'd left another one in the loo and in each of the bedrooms that overlooked the garden, with a live round on each of the appropriate window-sills.

'If any of us finds ourselves in any of the aforementioned locations with time on our hands, we reckie for the rat and ambush if possible. Right, Mart, let's have some more coffee and go and see if we can bag that little sod.'

Running away from the house for the full length of the garden were two long beds of lupins. Between them was the rifle range. To the left hand side, about 100 yards away, the nearest neighbour had constructed a pigeon loft. It was in this area that the rats most likely lived.

We started to crawl down towards the loft, one of us either side of the flowerbeds, rifles at the ready.

Owing to Joan's deafness, the house was rigged with lights in each room and so arranged that if the telephone were to ring they would flash to the beat of the bell. In the event of Nev's absence, she could pick up the instrument and say, 'I'm sorry, but I'm deaf. My husband will be back at . . .' whatever time we were expected. If the doorbell were to ring, the lights would come on and stay on until the door was opened and closed, thus breaking the circuit. It rang now, when we were about halfway down the garden.

'The door, Nev,' I whispered across the lupins.

'Don't worry. Joan will get it. It's probably the milkman.'

Some moments later Joan came out on the veranda with two visitors, a Mr Atombi and his aide. They'd arrived two hours early.

In quite a loud voice Joan said, 'My husband and his co-conspirator will be with you in a minute. They have a dear little mouse cornered at the bottom of the garden.' She held her thumb and forefinger about an inch and a half apart as she said 'little'.

As Nev and I walked rather sheepishly back to the assembled group, there was a suggestion of 'I'll teach you to lie to me' behind the faintest smile on Joan's face.

'Target practice, old boy,' said Nev, trying hard to force a grin as introductions were made.

'I am Atombi, Mr Baber, and this is a colleague of mine, we shall call him the Colonel.'

'This is my wife, whom you've already met, and my partner, Martin Bengtsson.'

And looking at his watch, Nev said, 'We were expecting you a little later.'

After the handshakes were finished, Nev steered us towards the open drawing room door. Atombi hesitated and glanced at the automatic weapon propped up on a chair at the far end of the veranda.

'Is that it?' he asked.

'Yes, that's what the business is all about,' said Nev, walking over and picking the weapon up. 'While we're all out here, perhaps you'd like to see it working.'

'Why not?' said the Colonel.

I picked up a target from under the chair cushion and started off down the garden where there were two tiers of sandbags standing in front of the wall. On reaching them I clipped the target to the wires in front of them and took cover behind an old oak tree. From here I could report the hits.

Nev called down to me, 'Are you ready? Just single shots!'

'Yes!' I replied.

Bang! A miss.

'Try up a bit!' My tactful way of telling him that the nine millimetre shell could have gone anywhere on the planet.

Bang! The black and white circles still remained uninjured.

Bang! Another miss—followed by yet another.

I waited, and from my vantage point I could hear them talking.

'It's me that's a bit off, not the weapon,' Nev explained.

'Does your wife shoot, Mr Baber?' asked Mr Atombi. This was where Joan was to score again, literally.

'Yes I do,' she said, lip-reading the question.

'Are you ready, Martin?' she called.

'Yes!' I shouted.

'He is,' relayed Nev.

Bang! Bang! Bang! Quick succession. And the target vanished in bits.

'If you've all finished, I'm coming up!' I yelled.

'Yes, she has bloody well finished!' he yelled back.

Just as I reached the quartet, Mr Atombi turned to Nev and asked in a jovial way, 'How do you account for your wife being a better shot than you are Mr Baber?'

Before Nev had time to answer, Joan, after lip-reading once more, said, 'You see I shoot better because I'm deaf. The bang doesn't frighten me.' Nev flushed visibly through his beard, and after a few moments of awkward silence he ushered us into the drawing room.

Before leaving us Joan asked if we would like anything to drink. Atombi, Nev and I settled for coffee but the Colonel asked for a citrus or soft drink. I knew that he'd be difficult as soon as I set eyes on him. He looked a miserable, revolting little man—short, fat stomach and narrow shoulders. The loud cologne that he reeked of didn't even go part of the way to cover up the smell of sweat and body odour. From the hint of colour I imagined that he was of Franco-Arab extract.

Atombi, on the other hand, was completely different, being tall, very black, with refined features. And I noticed that not only did he possess a firm handshake, which also differed from his minder, but his hands were very well manicured. He also showed a measure of humour, whereas the Colonel was definitely not amused by Joan's previously demonstrated sense of fun.

The Colonel was the first to speak.

'This gun, I think you agree, is not very impressive.'

Nev looked straight at him and said, 'You, or rather your lot, chose them. I personally would have gone for something a little more sophisticated. But I suppose they kill for a price. Remember, we are only concerned with their delivery.'

'Oh Mr Baber, I would prefer you to say they protect within our budget,' insisted Atombi. 'You see, our country is badly off for defensive weapons. And it's not exactly overflowing with money. We are a new country with new ideas—not wishing to import other people's ideologies or survive on leftover and bankrupt philosophies. We have to start again, and we have to use our judgement regarding those who we believe we can do business with. *Smith* has told you that we wish to trade in minerals, and this we can certainly do.'

'Yes, I understand the order of the day is diamonds,' I said.

'You can have zinc, copper or even uranium if you like,' muttered the little fat man, slightly sarcastically.

He sat down and shoved his little finger of the right hand up his nostril. Having rotated it and extracted nothing, I noted a flicker of disappointment as it had retrieved nothing. He repeated the operation with his left little finger, up his left nostril. The result appeared to be the same. I made a mental note not to shake hands with him unless I was close to a washbasin.

'There are many trinkets we could buy your service with,' he went on, 'even coal. But you do have some of that in this country, so I imagine people like you would prefer something of quality.'

'You forgot the camel shit,' I said. 'We love camel shit. And by the way, you may be buying our services, but you're not buying us. Remember that we're doing it for the money and you can't do it at all.'

'Just a minute, me boy, simmer down.'

'Okay Nev, but remember it's us doing them a favour and not the other way around.'

The Colonel got to his feet and walked about on the veranda.

'Pity about that. I'd rather hoped you and Paul would get on all right,' said Atombi. 'You see, it's important that you do, because he will be travelling on the ship with you and the cargo.'

'I hope he's a good swimmer,' I said.

Atombi smiled, and from his jacket pocket he withdrew a small silver-coloured box about the size of a snuff-box. Pushing the lid open with his thumb, he gently tilted it, allowing its contents to spill onto the table in front of him.

Bright, shiny crystals, beautifully cut and looking very genuine. He didn't touch them, but let them fall in random order. They were all certainly much larger than the ones I'd previously peddled. I wondered how much this little lot were worth, and from the look on his face, Nev must have been thinking exactly the same thing.

'Mr Bengtsson, why do you not take them for appraisal now? The result, I have no doubt, will please you. You see, there would be little point in trying to trade in poor quality merchandise when we have no need to.'

'Go on, me boy. Test 'em,' said Nev.

I had a feeling that Atombi's jolly little chum would like to accompany me so I called out, 'Shall we go?'

'No, my friend. I remain here.'

I would have loved to have told this revolting little bastard that in no way was he my friend, nor was he ever likely to become so. But I resisted. He could carry on nose-picking while I was gone.

Leaving them, I went to Messrs Saqui and Lawrence, the high-class jewellers in Western Road in Brighton for an 'insurance valuation'.

One of the assistants in the jeweller's stared in amazement at the gems I placed on the glass-topped counter in front of him. After a few moments' silence he said the manager would have to examine them.

He joined a shorter man in a partitioned area at the back of the shop. They conferred for a few moments, the shorter man looking down at the table or desk that was partially obscured. No doubt they were checking the lists itemising stolen property circulated by the police, to see if they might be a subject of a major robbery.

Having presumably satisfied themselves that I was neither a thief nor a fence, they joined me. The shorter man introduced himself as the manager, then looked down at the six stones. At first he said nothing, then picked one up and examined it carefully through an eyeglass. He placed it back with the others and said, 'I'm sorry, sir, but I cannot give you a valuation right away. They would have to be seen by our expert.'

'Oh,' I said, 'I don't need an exact one. I only want to know if in fact they are diamonds, and just the approximate value of one of them.'

He looked stunned. Here was I with a fortune in gems and I didn't even know if they were real or not.

Without speaking, he picked them up in turn and studied them. Then holding one of medium size, he said, 'I suppose, in Hatton Garden, one like this would fetch £3,000, perhaps even more.'

I thanked him as I swept them into the palm of my hand.

'May I ask where they came from?' he said.

'Africa,' I replied, and walked quickly out of the shop.

Our two visitors were on the steps about to leave as I arrived back. Atombi was first to speak.

'Well, are you happy with your research, Martin?' The touch of familiarity led me to believe that things must have progressed favourably during my absence.

'Yes, I'm quite impressed,' I replied, reaching in my pocket and retrieving the grey plastic 35 millimetre film container in which I'd just transported over £10,000 worth of diamonds.

I popped the lid off, tipped them into the palm of my hand, and offered them back to him, thinking how easy it would have been to have swapped one for a phoney one worth about a fiftieth of the value.

'No, you keep them as a measure of our best intentions,' he said. And before I had time to reply, he offered me his hand and continued, 'We'll be in touch again soon. Neville has the details.'

After descending the steps a grey Mercedes, which was parked opposite the house, stopped outside the door. Atombi and the Colonel got in and at the first gap in the traffic the car moved off rapidly.

'We're going to get a phonecall to arrange another meeting,' said Nev as we turned to re-enter the house. 'Until then, we just have to wait.'

'I don't care if we never hear from them again,' I said. 'This little lot's worth more than ten big ones.'

With the usual morning conference over, we loaded the Morris with 100 or so detonators, 200 pounds of gelly, detonating cable and the inappropriately named Beethoven box—as although this gadget may have composed music to Nev's ears, few others would agree. Having connected this piece of equipment to explosive charges by means of a cable (preferably a very long one) and taken the necessary precaution of placing oneself either underneath or behind something of outstanding strength, it required only the slightest pressure to the tit to bring about the most ear-shattering result.

The Home Office requisite for storage for all explosives was, and I believe still is, a strong-room called an A store. We had one of these on a farm in Steyning, but as this was some ten miles away we kept most of the stuff at the new house, The Turrets, in order to save the double journey each time that we needed some. Neither the authorities nor any neighbours had any inkling of this. Most of the time, at a conservative guess, there would be half a ton or more in the house.

Long-suffering Molly in Peacehaven was another unofficial depot for when we were working in the south-east, and poor old Molly would draw the curtains in this particular room on sunny days to keep it cool, closing the door very quietly and gently after leaving.

There were also other items stored at Molly's house—the box of grenades (but that's another story), an anti-tank rifle and various other bits of junk.

Explosives are totally safe and remain in a stable condition if kept dry and at a constant temperature. If they do start to 'sweat', you've got a problem, because it becomes very difficult and dangerous to handle them, especially when you've got your fingers in your ears.

Throughout the preceding weeks a number of contracts had been effected by Specialised Explosives Services resulting in a quota of famous landmarks changing shape.

The removal of some large tree stumps at a remote farm was managed without any noticeable damage. Similarly, the gun emplacements overlooking Bristol offered little resistance and only minor damage to adjacent environs. The ex-air raid warning control bunker at Goldsmith College gave up without too much of a struggle. Here only peripheral carnage ensued.

Throughout all of these operations, miraculously, no loss of life or limb occurred.

The greater the number of blows necessary on each job, the closer we became, physically, to the actual explosion. This was because the detonating cable that ran to the charges would become damaged at the far end each time it was used, and the spoiled section would have to be cut off and dumped. Nev, of course, was too mean to buy new lengths for each job, so we'd make do. Sometimes we were only a matter of 20-odd feet from 200 pounds of gelly when we fired it.

Most of the risk was overcome by the introduction of the Neville Baber Foxhole Mark 2. This was a tiny two-man shelter constructed out of wiggly tin or, as normal people might know it, corrugated iron and straw bales. Nev built these with true military precision—so much so I felt they really needed finishing off with camouflage netting, or perhaps a bunch of daffs on the top in case it turned out to be our graves.

Thursday, 13 August wasn't a bright-looking day. The morning conference over, 200 pounds of gelly and dets, and a Beethoven box all loaded, we sloshed down some more coffee, Nev made a number of phonecalls, including one to the bank that contained a hint of promise, after which we left The Turrets for Poling.

Arrival at about 11.30 a.m. We found the site agent, Mr Lawson, was waiting for us, and had apparently been doing so since 10.30 a.m., the time that Nev had previously agreed. Although it was late August, it was a rotten morning—windy, chilly and damp. And I was nursing a hangover of mammoth proportions.

Most of the gelignite family are similar both in texture and smell and appearance to marzipan. But eating it is not to be recommended—as I'd found out to my cost. Having handled some of the softer plastic varieties throughout the previous day, I'd managed to store some of it under my fingernails. It made a pretty lethal *mélange* when mixed with hot fish and chips eaten out of the paper on the way home.

This morning was the first time I'd seen the job and what it entailed. Nev, of course, had been there three weeks earlier when he surveyed the work prior to quoting with a contract. When I saw the size of the task and the proximity of the village, I felt like knocking on all the doors of this sleepy little place to apologise in advance to its inhabitants for the appalling *blitzkrieg* that was soon to ruin their peace and tranquillity. Because nobody could ever accuse Nev of being judicious with the tools of his trade.

The contract was to blow up and take out the foundations of the towers and ancillary buildings of the now extinct MOD radar station. This work was being done for the Ministry of Agriculture by a firm called Hall & Co. from Worthing, who were the main contractors. Our part was to blow everything and leave Hall & Co. to clear up the site and the mess, and send out the usual letters of apology.

Like all contractors, they wanted the job done as soon as possible and with little fuss. So they put us under pressure from the outset. For the first few days we whittled away at some of the smaller structures, working our way to two solid blockhouses. These, I felt, would go either at the end of the job, or on a day when Nev felt like emulating something on the scale of the Dambusters. And I knew for certain that when the time came for this obliteration, most of West Sussex would hear about it.

We'd atomised most of the lesser lumps when Nev thought it time to do one of the big jobs. With the aid of a flashlight we examined it from inside. They were very much reinforced, and after thorough consideration and debate Nev calculated the precise amount of gelly that would be needed. I'd already guessed that it would require 50 pounds placed right in the middle of it.

'I think 50 pounds would be enough,' he said. 'We'd better put it in the middle.'

It always was about this amount for this type of bunker, and the result was usually the same—a bloody big bang and the edifice would be spread fairly evenly over about three acres.

We were about to leave and get set up when Nev, pointing to one of the slit windows, said, 'That's buggered it.'

'What has?' I asked.

'Look inside, on that shelf.'

Peering in, I could just make out a bunch of sticks. It was a blackbird's nest with four young in it.

'That's going to have to wait until they fledge, me boy.'

'I agree, but what about Hall & Co.?' I asked.

'Fuck Hall & Co. Leave it to me.'

We adjourned for lunch at the Black Rabbit. Since the Atombi visit something at the back of my mind had been bugging me, and it wasn't until we were on the strawberries and cream that I realised what it was.

'Nev,' I said, 'I've been worrying about fucking the Colonel.'

'Don't worry about it, me boy, you probably won't have to.'

'Don't piss about, Nev. Be serious for a minute. I wouldn't trust that little bastard as far as I could kick a grand piano.'

'I don't suppose you'll have to do that either, Mart.'

'I bloody give up with you sometimes.'

'Okay, so what's bugging you?'

I finished my last mouthful of cream, swilling it down with a drop of Guinness.

'Why do you think that little shit wanted you to demonstrate the Madsen when he must have already handled them? After all, they placed the bloody order, didn't they?'

'Simple, Mart. When you were out having the diamonds valued, it was as good as suggested that they dump *Smith* and let us get alternative weapons for them. I didn't rise to the bait, because more enemies we don't need. I hinted that we could get some German MG42s, which are much better than the Danish gun, but over five times the price. It frightened them off. But as the deal with *Smith* obviously hasn't been completed, it gives us another bargaining chip.

'Have a coffee. I'll make a phonecall to Messrs Hall & Co.'

'What did you tell them?' I asked when he returned.

'I told them that we wouldn't be able to blow the blockhouses while the wind was in the south-west, as the noise of the blast will rock Arundel. They agreed.'

We whittled away at the rest of the stuff over the next few days, leaving only the blockhouses to do. Four days later, the wind had dropped, the birds were a little larger, and Messrs Hall & Co. were still waiting.

Nev rang again.

'Rain is forecast, and this will amplify the bang even more. We'd better wait.'

'Whatever you say, Mr Baber. We'll leave it to you.'

An anticyclone settled in over the weekend—no wind, bright sunshine—but the birds remained grounded.

'Can't blow at the weekend—too many people about.'

'All right, Mr Baber. Try again next week.'

We lay low until Wednesday, when I caught the end of the phonecall. It went like this:

'We really would like to finish the job, Mr Lawson, believe me. But the husband of this lady assures me that she's got a bun in the oven and is almost ready to go into labour at any time, and the house is less than a quarter of a mile away. I dare not risk it.'

'What did he say to that?' I asked, after he'd hung up.

'He didn't even seem to know what a bun in the oven was, or had to do with it,' he replied, grinning. 'I could have confused him even further and said that she'd been bitten by a one-eyed trouser-snake, but think of the embarrassment it would have probably caused in the natural history section of the Brighton reference library.'

That night *Smith* called again to say the meeting to finalise the deal was fixed for next Tuesday, and was to be at the Metropole Hotel in Brighton at 3 p.m.

We looked at the Poling blockhouses again on the Saturday. The nest was empty. A gale was blowing from the south-west. It was pissing down with rain, so we blew them both together.

On Tuesday we would organise an arms deal so that two rival factions would kill each other. But this week we had spared the lives of a family of blackbirds—and both agreed that this was much more important.

10.30 a.m. on Tuesday found us kneeling behind an upstairs window looking down at the Brighton clock tower. We were in a room belonging to our client. They owned a disused air raid shelter underneath the clock tower and wanted the dividing wall removed. And we were about to blow it.

This monument occupies an imposing position on the dividing triangle that has separated Brighton's Western and Queen's Roads since early in the twentieth century. Beneath it, fine examples of Victorian lavatories vie for status with the extinct and locked-up air raid shelter that was linked by a tunnel to our client's basement.

The charges were now in place. 25 pounds of Polar Ammon and gelly should be ample to take out the two walls—hopefully the ones that divided the chambers of the shelter, and not the one that separated the gents from the ladies. When we were placing the explosives, though, Nev had commented that either way he'd guarantee a lot more than the usual quota of loo paper would be used up in both the bogs by the end of this morning's work.

There had not been a cat's chance in hell of getting a permit to blow at this location, as local councils don't take kindly to the idea of the accidental demolition of any of the town's revered obelisks. So the whole operation was to be carried out on the quiet.

That's a joke. Some controlled explosions can be fairly quiet affairs, but most of the ones organised by Gordon Neville Baber were usually very loud.

Having already run our detonating cable through the tunnel and the basement up to this vantage point, we were now poised waiting to fire. Ideally, Nev wanted several heavy vehicles to be rumbling past so that the combined engine noise might help to mask the sound of the bang.

As we waited, two policemen sauntered up and stopped right over the spot. Moments later, a bus came into view from the direction of Western Road, then another appeared at the top of North Street. Nev's finger hovered over the button, and for a split second I had a vision of three projectiles heading off towards earth-orbit—in the shape of two coppers and a clock tower.

As the double-deckers passed each other, Nev hit the tit. The ground gave a hint of a shudder, the vehicles rolled on, the two policemen glanced briefly down at their size 11 boots. All four faces of the clock stopped at 19 minutes to 11.

We collected the money and left, as was usual on unofficial jobs. I loved brown envelopes containing money. I still get a kick out of receiving brown ones, even though most of them nowadays contain bills.

That night we did a quickie for the Newhaven Harbour Board, who asked if we could cut up into manageable chunks an old steam yacht that had been lying derelict in part of the harbour called Sleeper's Hole. These sections would then be dragged ashore and burnt. This location was designated to become the new marina.

We used 150 pounds of special waterproof gelly, which we placed throughout the wreck at low tide. The aim was to blow the thing at high water around midnight, without any publicity. We did. The vessel was covered with about 20 feet of water as we fired the charges. The sudden freedom given to 150 feet of still-buoyant deck and cabin—now separated from the ballast, engine and machinery that it had been part of for the last 80-odd years—allowed it to rise like a U-boat about to engage in surface combat.

After a short while, it slipped majestically out of the harbour on the ebbing tide, assisted by a north-westerly breeze. This top half of a crewless vessel, looking now like a latter-day *Marie Celeste*, nobody noticed. The explosion had been barely audible—although the underground shudder caused a coal-truck to be derailed in a nearby siding.

I'd hate to imagine what had happened to the foundations of the Sheffield Inn, some 100 yards away.

Rumour had it that the best bitter remained cloudy for a week.

16

Breakfast over one day, Nev and I retired to the office. The doorbell rang. It stopped, so we knew Joan had answered it. Moments later, in a raised voice, Joan said, 'Please wait there. I'll call my husband.'

The office door burst open and Joan came in, followed by two policemen in uniforms, and another man in plain clothes. Joan didn't help the impending situation by shouting at Nev, 'Now what have you been up to?'

The plain clothes man said to Nev, 'Are you Neville Gordon Baber?' to which he replied, with a grin on his face, 'It depends what he's done.'

The cop wasn't amused and the other two remained po-faced. The cop continued, 'I have some questions to ask you. We can do it now or down at the station.'

'Why don't you sit down?' said Nev in a quiet voice. 'Give us half an hour, will you, Mart?'

I got up and left the room and returned to the kitchen while Joan followed me out.

'It's something to do with those men that were here the other day with the gun, isn't it?' asked Joan in a not-too-quiet voice.

I put my finger to my lips, suggesting she lower it. 15 minutes later I heard them leave, and Nev joined us.

'Well,' said Joan, 'What's happened?'

'Nothing, dear, absolutely nothing. It's just to do with firearms licences.'

Joan ignored him. He and I returned to the office.

'We've been rumbled over the Atombi deal. I told them that I'd dropped it all because it seemed illegal. I've got to make a statement later. You weren't mentioned, so you can still deliver them if you want to take a chance.

'That side of it didn't come up, but only fishing in the dark, it seems that someone in the Ministry somewhere has signed a bogus End User Certificate and he's in serious trouble. But they don't know about the actual guns, mercenaries, or anything about the diamonds. I'll phone *McLoughlin* and *Smith* and warn them.'

McLoughlin was one of *Smith's* suppliers. The guns were coming from his stores.

After the call Nev told me that the cargo was already loaded. Five armoured cars and 100 FN rifles, but no personnel, so we'd dropped the Madsens after all, it seemed.

'It's up to you, me boy. We're only the delivery side of it, but I'd hate to hand the diamonds back.'

'Of course I'll do it,' I replied, 'but we must let my wife believe that I'm on a regular commercial ship going to South Africa. The sooner I leave Poole the better.'

I met *McLoughlin* and was taken to the ship. She was a coaster that weighed a bit over 8,000 tons. I can't remember her name. She was all battened down and flying the blue-and-white flag ready for instant departure.

There was a crew of eight, three of whom were on board, the other five getting pissed in a bar called The Jolly Sailor. *McLoughlin* knew them so we went and dug them out. Mercifully, there was no sign of the nose-picker, so we were going without him.

We sailed.

Day one, after we'd sailed.

'Where the fuck have you come from?'

I addressed the expletive to six total strangers who'd suddenly appeared on deck.

'We were in the hold,' came the answer from a tall member of the sextet.

No personnel, I was told.

'How many more of you are there?' I enquired.

'There are 22 of us, and it's shit down there.'

'Who's in charge?' I asked.

'Well the doctor was until we left, but now he's seasick.'

'I don't care how sick he is. Get your pox-doctor up here.'

Two of the hatch boards had been lifted out and the canvas folded back. The tall bloke squeezed his way below and after some minutes nobody surfaced. I struggled down and the sight greeting me was messy to say the least. Bodies were spread out in various stages of seasickness. The hold isn't the best place to be, even in moderately heavy weather. The stench was awful, and the air thick with the remnants of sick and piss.

The tall one seemed okay and looked rather apologetic.

'That's the doc,' he said, pointing to a figure curled up on a pile of sacks.

I realised it wasn't the slightest use trying to talk to him, so I said immediately, 'Right, you're in charge now. Up,' I added, pointing upwards.

He joined me on deck. I said, 'I don't care what happens down there, but I do not want more than three of you on deck at a time.' I went on, 'If we're spotted by another ship or an aircraft, I don't want to look like a cruise ship. We are, after all, a freighter. You understand?'

'Yes, but I don't think anyone would want to come up.'

'Get them up in the fresh air, three or four at a time. What's happening over the food?'

'Well we can rustle stuff up ourselves. I don't think anybody wants any just now.'

'We've another 19 or 20 bloody days to go, and my cook won't provide food for your lot, and he isn't going to clear up in the galley after anyone's messed it up down there.'

'Don't worry,' he said, 'We can manage down in the hold.'

'Like bloody hell you can. Nobody's cooking or brewing up down there. I suppose there's alcohol stashed down there as well. I want it brought up here. And no smoking down there either. You sort it out, now. Elect someone to organise the grub and three at a time on deck. Anyone wants to piss or shit, they do it over the ship's side and not in the bilge. And nobody goes into my crew's accommodation. If I think of anything else, I'll let you know. And get that bloody doctor up here. Is he a proper medico or just a pox-doctor?'

'I think he's a proper doctor,' he replied. 'But he's not very well at the moment, as you see.'

'Get him up in the fresh air now. If we hit any really heavy weather, I've a feeling he'll become very busy. You better organise yourself a second in command, and while you're down there, collect up all the matches and lighters. If anyone wants to smoke, they do it on deck. This thing is probably a floating bomb. I don't know what's in the cargo, and I certainly didn't know I had a human one as well. By the way, what's your name?'

'I'm Paul.'

'Well, Paul, I've enough to worry about, so you're in charge of that lot. Now get that bloody doctor up here, and make sure there's no cooking, smoking, pissing or any other bodily functions down in the hold. Okay?'

'I'll do my best, but they're a hard lot.'

Right: In step with Molly and Vic in Folkstone 1939. From the age of about four my parents encouraged me to call them by their Christian names.

I was given every opportunity to grow up basically normal. The fact that I didn't must therefore be my own fault.

Left: Photo taken by Great Aunt Elida. Me at about four years of age, before I'd shot anybody.

Left: Vic in Cuba in 1918. He learnt the 'fiddle' while playing jazz in the bars and bordellos in Havana, where he'd resided for a couple of years.

Below: Me as a cute five-year-old.

Above: At the Tropic of Cancer on a long-haul adventure.

Below: Protecting my head from the scorching heat.

Inspecting garnets from an abandoned mine in Costacabana.
I still have a jamjar full of them.

Right: At a ballet school. I thought I'd look silly in a tutu, so I opted to conduct instead.

Left: Ballet school. I'm obsessed by all things classical, including music.

Right: With my shiny new Aston Martin.

My second wife, Caroline. During the filming of *Buddy Goes West* (above) Caroline was my screen wife, and I played the part of a banker. She told the director there was a misprint in the script.

Left: Susan and I take a break on set.

Right: Hanging out with Joe Bugner, the boxer.

Left: Ginger Gemmel, on the right of this picture, was a great man to work with.

Right: Another suspended sentence.

I've made a lot of money—and enemies—over the years by forging some of the great painters, including Cézanne, Morandi, and Buffet.

'They don't look very hard at the moment, so take advantage of it.'

I returned to the bridge. The mate, engineer and deckhand were on the bridge when I returned.

'I suppose you knew about the passengers?'

The mate answered.

'I thought you did as well. It was supposed to be a secret so we didn't mention it. They're not causing any trouble, are they?'

'Not at the moment,' I said. 'I think they're all dying.'

I took the mate to one side and told him to make sure that he was armed at all times, but actually there turned out to be little trouble. Only one fight, little damage, nothing serious that the pox-doctor had to deal with. As we got further south they started sleeping on deck during the dark hours.

Once he'd got over his initial seasickness, the doctor became quite used to it, and he kept everything nicely under control. He also had all the details of where we were going to meet up with another ship.

I didn't even know at the time. The cargo had got to be delivered a short way up the entrance to the river—the Congo River. I thought we were heading for port, where we would unload. I was wrong.

We ploughed on for days, and when we finally got there we were met by a small vessel that guided us in. You really need a pilot to enter the Congo River. I'd never been up there before and I certainly wasn't going to chance grounding that lot. The small boat guided us in and took us alongside a jetty in a totally remote part, where we unloaded the cargo.

My human cargo were picked up in trucks and driven away. The following day I was also picked up and driven to a small airstrip. It was a very bumpy-looking affair, no aircraft on it, and trees at either end. It looked like the sort of place you could land on but I wouldn't be too happy about taking off from it. However, halfway through the morning a DC3 flew in and unloaded another lot of guys who were driven away.

I joined the plane and we went from there to Cape Town. I hotelled it for two days, and was visited by a representative of Atombi's. He said the rest of the diamonds had been delivered to Nev, so I flew to Nairobi. From there I flew on a standard commercial flight back to London. And that was the end of it for the moment.

Some months later NATO contacted Neville and asked him if he would build secret submarine tunnels under Gibraltar. We packed up and, along with Joan, headed for the sunny Spanish coastline. The Babers fell in love with Gibraltar and decided to stay on for a while longer, but after three months, I decided I should go back and see how things stood between Letitia and me.

Sadly it didn't work out. The reason for its failure was completely my fault, so we split up for good. All credit must go to Letitia, who brought our three children up to be well behaved, normal and genuine, without any help from me.

Si possis, recte, si non, quocumque modo rem
(If possible, with honesty, if not, somehow make money)

- Horace

17

In 1963, I found myself bored with nothing exciting to do. I had little money and absolutely no knowledge of the travel industry whatsoever, so I decided to become a tour operator.

After an extremely unsuccessful visit to the bank, I borrowed £50 from Vic and started Student Travel in Peacehaven.

It immediately became the family joke.

If any of them was about to go shopping locally or embark on any long distance journeys to America or Australia, the usual remark was, 'I'll take one of Mart's buses.'

I wasn't put off and started running a coach from Calais to Sitges in Spain for students once a week. It ran full up on each occasion and I made £1,600 during the first season. The sarcasm dwindled a little.

Throughout the following holiday period, I operated two coaches to Spain, two to the south of France and two to Italy, twice a week. The satire stopped and members of my family started queuing up for jobs.

The bank, with which I now had quite a healthy account, suggested that if I needed to expand further they'd be of enormous assistance to me—and gave the impression they were about to throw money at me. This was an unwise move on their part, as this offer reminded me of just how unhelpful they had been initially.

My appointment with the manager was well received. Upon entering his office I was ushered into a very comfortable chair opposite his desk, secretary sitting to one side. I got to the point immediately, and requested that he close my account and transfer all the cash in it to the bank on the opposite side of the road.

He looked startled and asked the reason. I explained that when I needed him he was at home but the lights were out. Now that I no longer required him I saw no reason why his bank should benefit from my account. So I'd like it moved.

He tried to overcome his shock and obvious embarrassment and urged me to take a little time to consider the move. I looked at my watch for a full ten seconds and announced that I had done that, and would he now carry out my instructions forthwith?

I had recently purchased a large ten-bedroom Regency house in the exclusive part of Brighton, that had a shop and office premises beneath it, so I moved the enterprise here from Peacehaven. A young lady called Liz joined me as a partner—in both senses.

She had a good business brain, and in no time Student Travel Ltd. almost had a license to print its own money. We were now running winter skiing holidays, cruises and operating our own discotheques in the UK and Spain.

Of course, extravagance started creeping in, and it appeared at one stage that we were trying to outdo each other. I already had a vintage Alvis Speed 25 Tourer, but I needed another car as a runabout. So I bought the first Ford Capri to be announced in Brighton. That same afternoon, Liz trotted out and bought an Alfa Romeo—and drove it all the way to Milan to get it tuned correctly.

At that time the registration numbers of Brighton cars started with the letters BUF, DUF, CUF, TUF etcetera and a number and a letter of the year. I asked the main agent for a single number. Silly really, but he obliged. Imagine my outrage when it was delivered— the registration being PUF1E. Puffy!

They changed it.

Jewellery and fur coats, which I strongly disapprove of anyway, started appearing regularly. But it could all be well afforded. I genuinely wanted a horse and advertised for one that was perhaps unmanageable and needed a strong hand, to give it not only a good home but possibly a reprieve as well. A bookmaker answered my ad and I went to see it.

This was Mel, the three-quarter thoroughbred steeplechaser. He said it was totally mad and should be put down, but he'd sell it to me providing I gave him a letter exonerating him from any blame, and that I took it away before his daughter returned home from university on the Saturday, because it would kill her.

She knew it was going but he didn't want her to see it again.

I took delivery the next day.

Now it was almost seven miles from his stable to mine at Peacehaven. Four of the bookie's helpers held Mel while I climbed aboard. When they let him go he took off out through a wood, which I hardly saw because I was so low on his neck to avoid branches. Over a stile across a golf course, which was a popular move. But there was no way that I could possibly pull him up.

About a mile from home he did ease up. I boxed him for the night and went back the next morning. After tacking him up I got on totally unassisted, and he was a different animal. I actually had to persuade him to go.

He and I became the greatest friends. I found out later that the previous owners had been stuffing oats into him every day, he'd had no exercise and the daughter was trying to ride him on alternate Sundays when she came home.

I moved Mel to a stables where he had company. The stables was run by a very pretty girl, and it wasn't long before I was riding more frequently. Liz, who had never ridden before, bought a thoroughbred Arab. She paid a hideous price for it and the first time she rode him under instruction she came off and broke her arm. She never rode again.

Although Student Travel was very successful, it wan't very exciting, and sometimes I felt as if I needed another challenge. Nobody had knocked on my door for some time, asking me to smuggle anything.

It did, however, cause some amusement when Liz shook me one night and said that there was a man standing outside the house, and he had a gun pointing at the window. I advised her that she should take more water with it but she insisted that I had a look.

I arose and peered through the narrow gap in the curtains. Sure enough, there was a man with a rifle pointing directly at the house. Believing this to be a spin-off from the Congo affair, I jumped into a pair of underpants, dashed through the house, out of the back door along a passageway to a small street that led directly into our road. This would bring me out about 30 feet from the man.

I looked carefully around the corner. I could see him, and he hadn't moved an inch. Could I reach him before he had time to turn and fire? Go for it!

I sprinted, and caught him in a rugby-like tackle. He went down and dropped the rifle. I scrambled to my feet, grabbed the weapon and, sticking it between our ornamental railings, rowed it like a Cambridge stroke and bent the thing almost double.

At that moment I heard three doors of a car slam opposite and imagined that he had backup. He did— in the shape of four policemen.

I started to explain what this gunman was doing, when they interrupted and said they already knew. They were his escort—and he wasn't an assassin, but the local council pest controller out shooting pigeons. I'd now wrecked the council's expensive rifle.

I had to admit that its only use in future would be for shooting pests if they were hiding around corners. None of them was even slightly amused by this.

They were, however, surprised by my attire. In the darkness of the bedroom I had climbed into the wrong underpants and, upon looking down, now realised that the pair that I was wearing were black and white with a sexy lace trim—and they weren't doing a very good job of holding things in position.

I left the scene without further explanations. The headline in the following day's *Evening Argus* was 'Brighton Travel Agent Gets the Bird'.

Thank heavens that's all they reported, and there was no photograph.

On Wednesdays it had become a sort of a ritual that I went to Mead's auction rooms in Bond Street in Brighton to buy furniture and bits and pieces for the new house. On this particular Wednesday in July 1967, my interest lay in lot no. 179—a small watercolour about to go under the hammer. I didn't know it then, but this small picture was about to play a significant role in my life.

It was quite a simple watercolour, but captured the mood. The scene in the painting portrayed a group of fishing boats off the Sussex coast from about the turn of the previous century. Although in the past I'd been a frequent buyer at Mead's, purchasing large chunks of Georgian and Victorian furniture, on this notable day my only concern was for this small picture by Richard Henry Nibbs.

The artist meant nothing to me. I simply wanted it.

Its appeal, I suppose, lay in my previous boating connections and it being so evocative of that era which has always fascinated me. On the viewing day previously I had spotted it hanging amongst some rather unimpressive prints and, upon my enquiry, the auctioneer had suggested that it would make twenty to thirty quid. When the hammer fell the bidding had gone way past, ending up at £80. I'd been brave enough to stay in up to £50. After all, there was a limit to how much I could fiddle from the Student Travel petty cash.

After it sold, as if adding insult to injury, the porter who had been holding it throughout came and stood it against the wall right where I was sitting. Done in sepia and darker brown in a thin gilt frame, it measured about 20 by 16 inches. Just perfect to hang over my piano, but sadly this wasn't to be.

During the bidding I'd not been able to see who bid against me or who the successful buyer was. Now, for some unknown reason, I decided to upset myself further by staying on to see who collected it. It was barely three feet away from me, and I couldn't take my eyes off it.

As I sat there gloomily, a number of extreme thoughts wandered through my head. One far-fetched notion was that perhaps I could copy it.

At school I'd been good at sketching, although since then my only grip of the pencil had been confined to marking off courses on seagoing charts and writing out betting slips. Anyway, I'd need it in front of me to attempt such a challenge.

While I was day-dreaming, its new owner came along, gathered it up with some other pictures, and left. I recognised him as a regular from previous visits to the sale room. He was the proprietor of a small gallery in Kensington Gardens, not a stone's throw away.

I went home more than slightly dejected, and throughout the evening with a bottle of scotch, I couldn't get the blasted picture out of my mind.

The following morning, I required some ordinary shopping as well as some aspirins so I needed to go into town. I found myself being drawn towards Kensington Gardens. It would only take a few minutes, I told myself. Just out of curiosity. I'd see what kind of mark-up the dealer had placed on it.

Upon entering the gallery, there it was on the wall facing me. I felt the same curious twinge. £150, according to a small price tag on the frame.

It had now become an obsession. Obviously I could well afford it, but art wouldn't have gone down well back at base. I must try and copy it somehow before it disappeared forever.

With the aid of a rapidly purchased sketch-pad and pencil? No chance. Not in a month of Sundays.

Think now quickly. Photograph it. Yes, that's it. I'll photograph it and have Vic copy it for me, or try my hand at it myself.

'You like that little watercolour, don't you?' I heard a voice in my ear. It was the owner of the gallery. I replied very quickly with the first thought that came into my head.

'Not particularly. But I might have a buyer for it.'

'Well, bring him along then. Were you bidding on his behalf at yesterday's sale?'

'Yes,' I replied. 'He now lives in Spain and collects marine paintings. I wonder if I might take a photo of it and send it out to him to see if he's interested?'

'Unless you leave a deposit I'll have to let it go if I get a buyer. But why don't you take it two doors down to the estate agent's and get a photocopy? That'll be quicker than a photograph.'

'Brilliant.' I did—and five minutes later I had a perfect likeness. I felt a bit of a bastard as I returned the original and left.

At a very reasonable price, the art department at Bredon's bookshop in East Street provided paint, brushes and a selection of watercolour papers. I was ready to go.

Because of my Student Travel commitments and my avaricious lady partner who thought of little else but the company and how much more money it could make, to suggest that I might take up painting as a hobby was fraught with peril, as every working hour should be devoted to the business and making even more money. I'd have to pick the right time to do it over a couple of days.

I mentioned these intentions to a military chum of mine who was full of advice.

'Do it,' he said. 'But don't tell anyone. And consider this. When you're up to your arse in alligators, remember that your original intention had been to drain the swamp. No, me boy. Definitely don't tell her, but do it.'

I failed to see any connection between secrecy and South American reptiles, but heeded his advice and remained silent.

Picking the right time, I hid myself in the room at the top of my house, banning anyone from visiting for an indefinite period while I worked on a future business project.

Copious quantities of art paper found its way to the fireplace before, after about four hours, I'd managed to achieve the required result. In the end I was quite satisfied with my Richard Henry Nibbs.

The following day being Saturday, I visited several jumble sales and picked up half a dozen frames— suitable old ones, complete with faded prints and nicely yellowing mounts. By lifting the back of one of them and carefully trimming my handiwork, I completed the swap and was well pleased with the result. I chose a moment when nobody was about, hung the painting over the piano and said nothing.

'Okay. How much did you pay for it?' demanded Liz over Sunday lunch.

'Pay for what?' I answered innocently.

'The picture of the boats.'

'Oh, a couple of quid at the jumble yesterday,' I replied.

There were no further comments until midway through Monday when she mentioned, 'It's probably worth quite a lot.'

'What is?' I asked.

'That picture, of course!' she snapped. 'I phoned the reference library and Richard Henry Nibbs is a listed artist.'

'I bet you did. But apart from the monetary value, do you like it?'

'Yes, it's quite nice,' she agreed.

'Quite nice? It's bloody lovely!' I replied. By now I was sure that it qualified for immortality.

'Why don't you get it valued?' she suggested.

'All right.'

Just for the hell of it, I would. And if I was fortunate enough to sell it to a dealer I could always do another one for myself. Perhaps even better.

My first visit to an antiques dealer in the Lanes, the Brighton Mecca for antiques, was not very rewarding. Most of the shops didn't handle pictures. I was recommended to try a dealer named Mr *White*.

Upon entering his shop, I found that this Mr *White* was a man to whom I took an instant dislike. He examined the picture, and after a few moments said, 'I wonder if this bloke Nibbs is a listed artist.' Picking up a large volume he pretended to search for his name.

'What a pity. He's not listed,' he said, slamming the book shut.

I knew damn well he was, as I'd already looked him up in a similar book at the public reference library only hours previously.

'How much are you looking for?' he mused.

'About a hundred quid,' I replied.

'Oh, too much for me. I'll give you £20,' he said rather begrudgingly.

'Not likely,' I said. 'I'd rather put it in an auction.' I started to walk out of the shop and had my hand on the handle of the door.

'It's quite a pretty little picture. What's the lowest you'll take?' he said.

'£75.'

'£50,' he said.

'£55,' I argued.

'All right. £55, cash,' he muttered. The deal was done.

I was about to leave the shop when a thought occurred to me. I told him it was one of a pair, and would he like to see the other one? He said he'd have a look at it.

That evening, I produced the quickest Richard Henry Nibbs on record, smacked it into a frame and returned to the lanes two days later. Mr *White* examined it and said he would pay £50, the same price.

'No,' I said. '£55. You know that.'

I took the money, but this little man had upset me so much I couldn't resist what I did next. I turned, looked at him straight in the face, and said,

'You'd better let me know how many more you want, it takes me at least three hours to do one.'

He physically jumped up and down.

'I knew it, I knew it!' he yelled. 'You're a clever little sod and bloody artful!' I was glad that he added artful but would have preferred if he had said full of art.

'So what are you going to do about it?' I asked.

'I'm going to call a friend of mine,' he said, picking up the phone.

'Who is he?' I asked. 'The Chief of Police?'

'No, you bloody fool. He's another dealer who sells in the States and he could move a few of these if the price is right. Can you do any other painters?'

'I expect I could.'

It's amazing that three days previously I hated this man. Now I loved him like a returning long-lost brother. That evening, over a few pints, he introduced me to *Jimmy*, the other dealer.

I broadened my canvas and widened my repertoire of painters whose style I could copy. Several dozen works of art sailed happily across the big puddle and found new homes on the walls of American art lovers.

It was a shame, but unfortunately this operation had to be curtailed very suddenly. The Brighton Constabulary discovered a quantity of stolen silver beneath *Jimmy's* floorboards.

I quickly put Paul Cézanne on the back burner, but he and a number of his contemporaries will re-appear later in my life.

Things were not going well between Liz and me. The company was becoming too big and things were getting sloppy. Her avaricious attitude meant that she just couldn't bear to see empty seats on coaches. She wanted bums on all of them.

On one of our trips to Poland, there had been some last-minute cancellations. Now it took four weeks to get a visa to Poland, but the passports of the ones now not travelling had visa stamps in them, so Liz sent 52 students off to an Iron Curtain country and six of them had the wrong passports.

At the German border the officials simply counted heads and stamped their books. Nobody rumbled coming in and thankfully coming back out again. We later had letters from various students asking why their passports had been to Poland and they hadn't.

One Thursday I drove to Dover as I usually did to see off the passengers on the ferry to Calais, where they'd be met by two 52-seater coaches. They would head off to sunny Spain from there. I counted the passengers. Twice. There were 106.

I put the car on the ferry, picked two of the prettiest girls, and drove them all the way to Spain, taking in an overnight at a swish hotel. They were delighted, as the others would be travelling through the night on the coach. I drove back to Calais in time to see off our Sunday departure—only to discover that we were over-booked again. Two more pretty girls went to Spain by car, this time taking three overnights and expenses.

Liz didn't over-book again. Quite the reverse.

Later, on one of our skiing holidays, she managed to under-book the number of ski instructors we would need. There was no chance to rectify the situation as all the instructors were by now engaged with other students, so I had to take a group of ten beginners.

I was up to Olympic standard—but unfortunately in dominos and not skiing, in which I'm very average. However, under my instruction there were no accidents or complaints, and the group thoroughly enjoyed themselves—especially on the numerous occasions when I went arse over tit.

This was possibly the only time in my career when I've insisted that young ladies kept their knees together. Well, most of them anyway.

As far as Liz was concerned, I was generally skating on thin ice with very sharp skates. A major falling-out was on the cards.

I received my third and final public warning after a brush, if that's the right word, with a little blonde student from Brighton Art College. As it happens, she was very talented. Nothing proven.

Several breakfasts with a chalet maid from a rival company—again not proven.

The increased frequency of my visits to Christine at the stables where I was riding regularly didn't have to be proven. I knew I was about to get the bum's rush—and there had been a suggestion somewhere that as I'd become so fond of sex and travel I should take the most appropriate action—fuck off.

Apart from the standard fiddling of the books and the Inland Revenue tax returns, Student Travel was far too legal anyway. I needed something more exciting, so before I received a sailor's farewell from Liz, I left. There was no golden handshake—more or less a tin one. I received £10,000, the car and, of course, a set of paintbrushes.

I really wanted out, adventure being hard-wired to my genes, and there was nothing with Student Travel on the horizon.

This was to be the birth of Long Haul.

18

I hate sandy beaches with a passion. And believe me, I've seen any number of them, from Dingle to Durban. I agree that most of them look fine on postcards, but that's it. Great to look at, but not to sit on. The bloody sand gets in everywhere—and I mean everywhere. Socks, shoes, underpants, knickers and even food. It's more than possible that sandwiches were dubbed as such after a sandy beach picnic. And it sticks very nicely to suntan oil. They're fine to view from a bar or a hotel balcony (with drinks, of course) but not to partake of any activities thereon—sporting or otherwise.

And as far as sex is concerned, forget it. Not having the biggest one in the world, I certainly wouldn't risk any damage to it by erosion from this intrusive, abrasive grit. Give me high tide on Brighton's pebbles any day. Or night.

Having made my position abundantly clear regarding these granular playgrounds, you might be surprised to know that in 1972 I quite voluntarily spent three months crossing the largest one on earth—the Sahara desert. A mere 2,000 miles to Timbuktu with five young women in attendance on the first trip, and three spies on the other one.

My advert had read, 'A trip of a lifetime. Long Haul invites the adventurous for a pilot trans-Sahara crossing to Timbuktu and return.'

As far as I was concerned, it was heavy on the word 'pilot'. What it really meant was, 'Hasn't been attempted before. Could very well go horribly wrong, and the company won't be responsible for any funeral expenses. And above all, nobody gets their money back.'

Up to this time, not many balanced people had ever visited Timbuktu or were queuing up to do so. This was to be quite a unique undertaking. A number of people whom I'd spoken to about it didn't even know it was in Africa. They had it mixed up with Kathmandu.

Needless to say, there wasn't a desperate rush to join me on this trip, but a trickle of enquiries and provisional bookings started coming in. As my new and pretty girlfriend, Christine, was coming with me to share some of the driving and to provide some immoral support, I only needed four paid-up nutters to make it financially viable.

Young ladies seem to be more adventurous, and in three weeks before the proposed off, I'd received firm bookings and money from three girls and one bloke.

He, however, turned out to be a let-down. A phonecall from him informed me that as much as he wanted to go, he couldn't confirm for ten days or so, throughout which time he would just have to sit on the fence.

I cancelled him as a time-waster. He lost his deposit, but this action possibly prevented him from getting a sore arse. Another of the fair sex took his place.

Now, five young women and me. Had it just been to the Costa del Something-or-other, this situation might have spawned a happier dimension. But what the hell anyway.

Ten days later, we left. I avoided any publicity and a big send-off, and we slipped quietly out of the country via Newhaven and Dieppe. Our first overnight was in Paris. The following morning we were due to pick up visas for Mali, along with some Russell's viper serum. None of these items could be obtained in the UK, as Mali wasn't recognised by the Brits.

That first night was, however, also my first bit of luck. Out of all the hotels in Paris I could have picked, the one I chose was right opposite the Mali embassy. Pure chance. But it impressed the girls, and surprised me. The middle-aged woman in the visa department seemed astonished that we wished to visit Timbuktu, and by her reaction I'm sure that we six were her first ever visa applicants.

People who venture into the Sahara like to call themselves *sahariens*, and most who qualify do so just by dipping their toes in it.

One favourite destination is Tamanrasset, lovingly referred to as Tam. It has a road running from the north virtually right to it, with a few odd bits of well-recognised track. It also is on a small airline route, so not too easy to become lost.

The Paris–Dakar rally—the one in which Mark Thatcher managed to lose himself and his co-driver until being rescued after a couple of days—skirts round the edge of the desert and doesn't go anywhere near the middle. And there's a town every 80 miles or so. One would have to have no sense of direction to go missing. Say no more.

These excursions are on well-travelled routes, and are supported by tons of backup. We, on the other hand, were going straight across the middle, twice. There were 500 miles between oases at one stage, and we were just a convoy of one.

There were no restrictions regarding entry to the Sahara, the Afrique Occidental Français now no longer in existence. (In fact, very little of anything French remains in Algeria.) Previously, any Sahara trips had to be in a convoy, carrying an experienced guide, an extra driver for each vehicle, huge water rations and enough spare parts to sink a battleship. One also had to notify ahead by radio and report one's position daily. Now, anybody who's mad enough can simply go. If they don't make it, nobody's even going to know, let alone look for them.

We did have quite a lot of spares, heaps of water and enthusiasm in spades—but what's equally important, a sense of humour.

Our second night was at a small hotel just north of Barcelona. The third was spent in the Almeria desert, where we tried out our equipment. In the morning, Daphne, who'd put her shoes outside the tent that she'd be sharing with Sally, found a scorpion hiding under one of them. This was a lesson to make sure all personal gear was inspected thoroughly in future. In actual fact, we encountered no other scorpions throughout the entire trip. Later I was to discover that there were very few of these little troublesome creatures in North Africa, but thousands of the little bastards in Spain.

We crossed from Almeria to Oran on the night ferry and rolled off the ship at eight in the morning. Oran was more or less the point of no return as, once south of here, individuals wouldn't be able to bail out and make their own way back. I made this point to each of the girls. Nobody backed out or even appeared dubious.

We headed south and made an uneventful traverse of the High Atlas mountain range. After the descent on the south side we got our first view of the desert— a vast, open expanse for as far as the eye could see.

We were about to become *sahariens*.

The next stop, Sidi Bel Abbes, was the one-time headquarters of the over-glamorised, much-filmed and written about French Foreign Legion—who, incidentally, rarely ventured into the desert proper, and whose exploits were so wrongly portrayed largely thanks to Hollywood.

Apart from this, it had nothing much to write home about. We stocked up with a large quantity of oranges, fresh water, and (God knows why) asparagus, which was very plentiful, before pressing on. Colomb-Bechar was next. Not the most exciting place, with again only one claim to fame. It was where the once-attempted Trans-Saharan Railway petered out and was abandoned, it being too difficult to continue further south.

Up to now we'd been following a *piste* across the sand—a sort of track marked out with the occasional dumped oil drum. 130 miles later, the *piste* disappeared, at Beni Abbes, and we entered one of the most desolate regions on earth—the Tanere. Any recognised route having now stopped, we were amongst the dunes and shifting sand.

It now became like driving on a huge upturned dinner plate, but remaining where you are, the horizon never seeming to get any closer. It was impossible to judge distances with the absence of objects. A permanent mirage danced on the horizon, and the temperature was more than 110 degrees fahrenheit. In this environment you realise the enormity (or perhaps the foolhardiness) of such a challenge.

A day out of Beni Abbes, the mirage was broken by what appeared to be tall steel towers. They turned out to be exactly that, the remnants of another unsuccessful venture by the French. These were oil rigs and the ancillary trappings, simply left and abandoned.

The only thing that remained was an air of melancholy. I think we all felt this, although it didn't come up for discussion. The whole scene was like a mad Dali painting.

Adrar was next, with water in abundance. This was a partly walled town where most normal occupations take place. Two markets, a number of shops, including several cafés, even a shoemaker. I'm sure that the Tuaregs invented flip-flops, as most of them seemed to wear leather versions. People varied from the well dressed and obviously wealthy, to beggars.

There was much evidence of feudalism, and Adrar was a sort of microcosm—totally isolated geographically and cut off from outside influences—where society hasn't changed for centuries. Along with the palm groves and camels, the only modern amenity was a Landrover service station, as these are very nearly the only vehicles that we encountered in the Sahara. Some 90 miles further south I wished I'd availed myself as a customer. When we stopped for a rest and a mint tea, Daphne, who'd become our mechanic—checking filters, oil levels etcetera—calmly informed me that there was little or no oil in the gearbox.

There were no signs of leaks, so this shortage was one of the items missed during the major service in Brighton prior to departure—in spite of the fact that the garage was very well aware of the future expedition. As the front floor had been reinforced along with various other modifications, the task of refilling the box from the top was not on. The only way we managed to get oil into it was by tipping the vehicle over to almost 45 degrees, propping it up and, with the aid of our hypodermic syringe, pumping oil through the drain plug at the bottom. Definitely not to be recommended.

This shortcoming preyed on my mind. I wondered what other vital features may have been overlooked—so much so that every little noise caused me apprehension, and I found myself imagining all sorts of things. Other worries and sleepless nights became the norm. Did they check the oil pressure and the differential before we left? Just supposing it won't start up in the morning?

Of course, it was madness to have embarked upon this trip. It wasn't going to prove anything. We'd been to Timbuktu. So what?

For the first time and, might I add, the only time in my life, I was beginning to experience real fear. Owing to problems not of my own making, I didn't any longer feel in control. And I couldn't, of course, let the others know my feelings.

Now, even 35 years later, I sometimes relive the experience. Especially when tucked up warmly in bed, when it's blowing ten sorts of a bastard outside, I question whether I would rather be solo in the middle of Biscay on a small yacht, dismasted with a buggered engine, or in the middle of the desert with engine failure.

Biscay always wins. You can always rig something and move. In the Sahara, you're dead.

It wasn't without a measure of relief that about 30 miles short of Reggane, we caught up with two other vehicles. One was a 2CV with three French medical students, heading for Niger, the other a VW pickup with two Swiss Red Cross chaps, also making for Niger. They were up to their axles in sand and completely stuck.

We towed them out and pressed on. After a couple of miles we towed them out again. And again. Finally all three vehicles made it to Reggane, where we set up for the night.

Our newcomers were all intending to give up and return the next day. The Swiss at least were well equipped, with a radio receiver/transmitter, fold-up picnic tables and chairs, a small fridge and even an ice bucket. They were also, appropriately, as camp as a row of tents. Never mind.

Reggane. A handful of shattered buildings and trucks. A small group of Arabs, all with strange eyes. I warned the girls that if they touched any of the children to wash their hands before touching their own eyes. Whatever the problem was, it might be contagious.

It wasn't. The Swiss had gone off and explored some of the larger buildings and insisted they show me what they discovered. Inside this blockhouse in large letters in French, English, German—but not in Arabic—was a huge sign which said, 'Danger. High-level radiation'. We were smack in the middle of where the French had carried out their nuclear tests. The eye disease was caused by some sort of radiation sickness.

We broke camp immediately and in spite of it now becoming dark, the French and the Swiss headed back north and the girls and I south. It was a dodgy drive but I felt safer when we'd put 25 miles between us and Reggane.

The following day, Christine was driving and I was spread out like a park on the roof-rack trying to catch up with some sleep. A shadow kept passing across my face. The sun was blazing hot. Keeping my eyes shut, I groped around me to see if the shadow was being caused by a loose rope or something similar. I couldn't locate anything adrift. Shielding my eyes from the sunlight, I opened them. The offending obscurity was being caused by three large vultures flying above us. This is the only time in my life I've ever been mistaken for meals on wheels. However, they gave up after a short while.

Quite soon, we were driving over an area known as the Corrugations. They look just like ripples left behind when the tide goes out on any beach. But they aren't. They're as hard as concrete and driving over them is bone-shattering. You have to maintain at least 40 miles per hour or experience the torturing sensation that feels as though the vehicle and the contents are being shaken to pieces. These Corrugations run for 60 miles. We eventually left them behind.

Three days short of Bordj Mokhtar, the border town between Algeria and Mali, we'd stopped and set up for the night, when about a mile away we saw the lights of two vehicles, also heading slowly south. In the morning, we decided to follow their tracks, as they seemed to be on our course anyway.

Just before noon we caught them up, broken down. One was towing the other on a rigid tow-bar. The driver of the front one spoke perfect French. We asked him if we could pass a message on for them when we reached Bordj Mokhtar. He thanked us and explained that there had been three trucks, but that the other one had already gone on for help. The rear vehicle was canvas covered, and there were voices from within, but the passengers appeared to have no wish to show themselves.

Now Daphne, who, let's face it, was quite a nosy young lady, opened the canvas tilt at the back of the truck and enquired, 'Anyone for tea?'

The occupants climbed out reluctantly. They were Chinese army personnel.

There was an air of embarrassment on all sides. Daphne brewed tea and the atmosphere became less tense.

When we were about to move on, the Chinese became very friendly and gave us presents. Little tins of biscuits marked 'nice biscuits'. It was supposed to be 'Nice biscuits' but they explained that they were nice biscuits. And little tins of milk, labelled 'baby milk'.

We thanked them and carried on. I still have my little red tin and use it as a small tool box. But it was what was inside them that was a bit of a joke. Having broken the seal, there was a foil covering, also sealed, with an individual penknife enclosed to deal with it. Beneath this there was a layer of shredded paper to prevent damage to the biscuit. Now the biscuits. As hard as bricks—definitely the dentist's friend—and totally tasteless.

However, we found a good use for them. A couple of nights after receiving them, we were camped. My coffee arrived. I was writing up my log for the day, and had previously given instructions not to place cups containing liquid upon my wobbly table, so the coffee was standing by my feet. After a few moments I leaned over and picked up the cup. It seemed unusually heavy.

It was. Hanging on the side of it were three gerbils, helping themselves.

Where in the middle of the wilderness they'd come from I'd no idea, but I thought as they seemed to enjoy lukewarm coffee they may appreciate some biscuits to go with it. They did. But when bedtime came, they were still engaged in attacking them, and the 'crunch

crunch crunch' noise was going to keep me awake all night. So I gathered them up—biscuits and gerbils—and put them out under the Landrover.

Only minutes later, Christine nudged me and pointed to the bottom of the tent flap. Little noses with bulging cheeks were returning. They'd preferred the tent to dine in—and the 'crunch crunch crunch' went on until 1 a.m. Having not seen man before, or for that matter tasted coffee or biscuits, they were not at all frightened. One actually slept on my pillow for the rest of the night.

In the morning, they simply disappeared.

The tins of milk we gave away when we reached the tiny village of Bamba. It was received like gold bullion. Another half a dozen tins and I think I could have become a local chief.

At about noon on the following day we came upon a large camp constructed of timber buildings. As nothing should have been in this area at all, I quickly suggested that Daphne photograph all that could be seen as we drove past at a distance of about a quarter of a mile. Clearly to be seen was an airstrip marked out with triangular markers, and a light aircraft.

Once clear, I asked her to remove the film and give it to me, reload the camera and shoot a few meaningless pictures of us in the Landrover, and tear up the new film-packaging box or throw it out into the slipstream. She followed my instructions to the letter, and I secreted the film canister under the dash with medical tape, where it remained until back in the UK.

What we had seen turned out to be a training camp for subversives, run by the Red Chinese.

Later on the same day I spotted five Landrovers following us, and closing. There was no point in trying to outrun, because we'd nowhere to run to. I pulled up.

We were greeted by a ramshackle bunch of troops, led by a major of doubtful rank. However, they were very friendly, and shared with us a number of ice-cold lemonades and some pink ice-cream. The major asked that if anyone at the border town of Bordj Mokhtar should enquire whether we'd seen any troops or not, we say no. Nobody asked anyway.

About 30 miles from the river Niger we drove through low green shrubs. Unfortunately they were covered with sharp, hard spikes. These shards embedded themselves into our tyres, but we didn't realise this until we stopped and camped by the river. On reaching the river, I leapt out of the Rover and threw myself in. I knew it contained hippos and crocodiles, but the sheer joy of reaching it outweighed anything else.

We then started to withdraw the spikes in the tyres with penknives and pliers. They withdrew quite easily but during the process Jill pricked her finger, and said so. Maybe it was the sheer relief of having reached semi-civilisation, or the fact that the pressure was slightly less, but I started laughing uncontrollably. I couldn't stop, and pointed out how stupid the English language could be. One could say with impunity, 'to prick one's finger', but it would be very infra dig to utter the quote, 'to finger one's prick'. And, by the same token, I couldn't remember how many kisses I'd snatched, and I intended to keep very secret how many snatches I'd kissed. Everybody was now laughing hysterically.

We rested here by the river for three days before pressing on towards Timbuktu.

19

'I've got you two passengers to go across next week,' said the voice on the phone.

'I can't run with two. I need five, or four minimum.'

'Don't worry,' it continued. 'You'll be paid for six.'

'How come?' I asked.

'That's not your problem,' it continued.

'Yes, it is my problem. Who are these people?'

'We won't go into details over the phone. Come up to town tomorrow and I'll introduce them to you over lunch.'

'Okay, where do we meet? In your office?'

'No, you suggest somewhere.'

'Okay. The Shah in Drummond Street. How does one o'clock grab you?'

'Fine. See you then.'

The call had come from *John Fitzgerald*, at a well-known adventure travel agency in London. He had been managing me for a short while .

He had been discussing my last trip regarding the Chinese training camp with the Foreign Office. Obviously they had put two people up for a look. I made up my mind there and then not to commit myself to anything unless I was totally satisfied with all the arrangements.

The Shah was one of my favourite eating places in London, so I was there before the others. Well, not quite there, but in a bar 50 yards further up Drummond Street. I'd be precise and walk in at exactly 1 p.m.

I did, and almost followed them in.

We were shown to a table and after sitting, *John* introduced us. David Fletcher and Maureen Summers. Neither of them looked particularly like potential *sahariens*. Both white, and I mean very white. I don't think either of them had been in the sunlight in years.

They came straight to the point. David opened the conversation with, 'The Department are interested in the facility that you stumbled upon in Algeria.'

He didn't say which department and I didn't ask. 'We would like to have a look at it,' he continued, 'and we'd like to leave next week.'

'You won't see much more than I did,' I commented.

'Well, we'll see. We might go into the camp on some pretext or another,' he said vaguely.

'It sounds highly risky to me. And there'll have to be more than two of you, otherwise it will be obvious that we're up to something. Less than four passengers wouldn't be a viable proposition for me,' I persisted strongly.

John interrupted, 'I'll get you one more. Then we will be a party of four.'

Before I turned to protest he continued, 'You will be driving a different Landrover, by the way. So you'll appear to be a party of well-off idiots going to Timbuktu. Actually, you're not going to Timbuktu in any case. You're heading for Niamey in Niger.'

'So when do I collect the Landrover? It will need a checking out.'

'Don't worry, it will be checked very thoroughly before you leave. And in any case, it's just been reconditioned fully and is still under guarantee.'

I replied that a guarantee wasn't much good if you're stuck in the middle of the Sahara and it broke down. And who else would he recruit at short notice?

'I'll arrange another female, so stop worrying. And you'll be paid for six anyway.'

'I'll do it if she's pretty,' I said, laughing.

John laughed as he assured me that this criterion would be on the top of the agenda. The other two barely smiled.

'Oh yes, and make sure she's got a sense of humour,' I insisted.

After lunch the other two left, saying they would make contact with *John* later. He and I returned to his office by cab.

Once back there he went over the complete itinerary. I would drive to Algeciras in Spain. The others would fly down there and meet me.

'You hotel all the way, on expenses. Fuel is also on expenses. You might even get to keep the Landrover. And after you meet up with them, they will pay all the expenses.'

'Thank you, Mr Taxpayer.'

He went on, 'Let them handle everything, even the visit to the camp. I hope you can find it again, by the way.'

'I'll find it, don't worry. And who's the other chick you're going to send?'

'Leave that to me. I know an Australian girl who would love to go on such a trip. She can keep her mouth shut, and she's a toughie. Her name is Lena.

'When you arrive in Niamey, you will receive other instructions.'

'Why when I get there?' I asked.

'I've no idea. That's all I've been told. Your visas are okay, aren't they?'

'Of course,' I replied.

'Good. You leave on Tuesday with Lena. She will go with you to Spain. Just give me a check call on Friday afternoon. Oh, and by the way, here's £200 in advance.'

I thanked him and left.

There were no changes to the plans when I phoned him on Friday. I picked Lena up from Brighton Station on the Saturday. Dark hair, well-worn jeans, a rucksack and a broad smile. Her opening remark to me was, 'Hi, Mart. I understand we're going spying!'

I told her that I hadn't a clue what we were doing. She replied, 'That probably applies to all four of us!'

It was an uneventful drive across France and Spain, and we arrived in Morocco on the following Saturday. We drove straight to Oran after which I followed pretty much the same route I'd done previously. The only variation was that I gave Reggane a wider berth. I even found the place where we'd originally encountered the Chinese in the broken-down trucks.

We drove on a short distance and camped, hoping to hit the training camp by mid-morning the following day. It was a bit later on when we got there, and we drove straight in. Our excuse was that Maureen had been physically sick for 36 hours, and that I, having been through that way before, knew there was a water-drawing team or something like that, and there may have been a doctor on hand.

Unfortunately, there was a doctor, a Frenchman. And although Maureen always looked unwell, we knew she didn't have any sort of a temperature.

The doc led her away to a small white hut, and we three stayed by the Landrover. We were obviously under scrutiny and, not wishing to appear worried, I told Lena to flick some sand over me, whereupon I would pretend to be cross and chase her round the vehicle.

I didn't mean a handful, and when she did it, I was genuinely cross. I chased her and she screamed in fun, and when I caught her, I pulled her down, laid her across my knees and smacked her arse.

She was now laughing and so were some of the Chinese onlookers. I muttered, 'That's given them something else to think about.'

She replied, 'It has me too. Whatever you do, don't stop!'

We both rolled back in the sand and just lay there, laughing. Maureen returned with the doc some ten minutes later. Now she did look really ill. David helped her into the Landrover and the doctor said that she'd probably feel better the next day, and why didn't we camp there for the night?

To say no would have seemed rather trite and suspicious, so we set up camp and started to prepare some grub.

One of the Chinese came over and said, in perfect French, that we should eat with them as their guests. I thanked him but, remembering the biscuits, wondered what we'd let ourselves in for.

Maureen complained to David that she would have to go without and keep up the pretence, and could he smuggle something to her later?

We sat at two long tables in a wooden hut. The food turned out to be great. Rice with noodles, and dumplings of a kind, all with white wine.

Everything was fine, and I enjoyed the tuck. The only thing that worried me a little bit was the pud. Pink ice-cream. Too much of a coincidence, perhaps. Whether any of them recognised me from the last trip I don't know. I certainly didn't recognise any of them.

The doc called in the morning and asked how Maureen was feeling.

'I'm much better, thank you,' she insisted.

We rolled on at about 11 a.m. after much handshaking and thank yous. I must say I felt a bit of a shit taking their hospitality when the other two were spying on them. I also didn't realise until we arrived at Tillaberi that actually the three of them were spying. Lena was one of them.

We stopped for the night and were met by another Landrover with two more spies. They all knew each. The upshot was that Lena, David and Maureen were to fly out from Niamey, and Martin was to return solo. I could fly out with them, but it would have meant leaving the Landrover. If I drove it back I could keep it as, after all, it had been registered in my name and I was down as the owner.

I decided, sod 'em all. I'll drive back.

The first problem was at Tesalit where I was questioned regarding the absence of my passengers. I said that the girls had been taken ill and they'd all decided to fly back to the UK. They weren't satisfied and I was told that I'd be asked more questions the next day.

I didn't wait for the next day. After dark I fled, and made it back to Oran in 29 hours—possibly a record that still stands, but then I don't suppose that anyone else has had the encouragement of armed pursuit.

This was my last venture with Long Haul.

Illegitimati non carborundum
(Don't let the bastards grind you down)

- Anon

20

Vic relocated to the Spanish coastline when Grandma Bengtsson died. He was revelling in his retirement in Costacabana and I visited him regularly there. My trips usually lasted about a year or 18 months. On one occasion I'd been lucky enough to become friendly with Max and his family. Max ran and owned a car hire business that was in competition with Hertz and Avis, who both had airport concessions. Max was allowed to use the airport facilities, but not authorised to tout for business. Any client who used his services, which were less costly than the others, must have previously booked a car from him through the Brighton agency.

However, it didn't stop me from plugging his services, and on days when UK, Dutch or Swedish flights came in, I'd drum up business for him. We worked well as a team, for not only did I have a car free from him on a permanent basis, Max had an arrangement with various film companies who shot in the area. He supplied cars to advance location teams, but also to the producers and directors, and through him I received introductions before any local casting took place.

This was to be the start of a very fruitful line of work. In all, through Max, I worked on 16 productions, nine of which were the classic Spaghetti Westerns. The parts were varied, from small speaking bits to fight sequences and, of course, falling off horses.

Now at this point, I'd like to give away one or two trade secrets. If a man was shot by a six-gun while galloping on horseback he would be blown right out of the saddle and the horse would run on. But in Westerns, it's more spectacular for the horse to fall as well. These horses are specially trained to do just that, and the whole action is done at no more than a very gentle hand canter. It's then speeded up on camera. If you stop and think about it, these madly galloping animals that appear on screen would all be potential Derby winners, the way they're depicted.

Of all the horsey films I've been connected with, none of the animals has ever been injured. If any had, I would be the first to expose the situation.

When I fell off after being shot I was very well padded on elbows and knees, and you ride the Western saddle very long—almost in a standing position. So when I was going to do a fall I used to slip my feet out. You don't get paid any more for being towed.

Very minor parts were always better, and as far away from camera as possible. You can only die once on each film. And after you were used in close-up—or *figuración*, as it was called—you were more or less finished with it.

The only injury I ever received was some busted knuckles. Having owned my own horses, I was quite used to falling off, that being a regular occurrence. But on those occasions I wasn't being paid.

I also got to rub shoulders with a number of stars, including Charles Bronson, Lee Van Cleef, James Coburn, Richard Harris, Sean Connery, Brigitte Bardot and, of course, Big Clint.

The greatest and definitely the most amusing one to my way of thinking was the late Richard Harris. Apart from his brilliant performances, where perhaps they might take two for insurance purposes (with other actors I've seen them shoot a scene sometimes as many as ten times) he was always most helpful to others regarding how to put a sequence over. He also had an insatiable sense of humour.

I was on one film with him called *Riata* (which was eventually released as *The Deadly Trackers*). It was scene one, take one. If this first scene goes well, superstition has it that the rest of the production will go likewise.

He had to appear out of a door of a cabin, draw his gun and fire three times in the air to wake up the town. Simple enough.

'Scene one, take one,' said the clapper boy. Samuel Fuller, the filmmaker, yelled, 'Action!'

Richard Harris came out, drew his gun and squeezed the trigger three times.

Bang! Bang! Click. A misfire.

The props received a bollocking, and a new gun was presented.

'Scene one, take two.'

Click. Another misfire, this time on the first one. Props received a bigger bollocking, and another weapon was produced and tested.

'Scene one, take three.'

Richard Harris appeared from the doorway, drew the gun, pointed it directly at the camera and said, 'Bang, bang and fucking bang! Now I'm off for a drink.'

Later on the same production, he had to walk down one of the outside staircases they have on Western houses with a toy doll in his arms along with his stage wife. The doll was supposed to be his newborn. As he walks down the street afterwards, all are supposed to congratulate him. I was to leap off a completely crazy horse, run over and shake his hand.

We rehearsed this scene for hours. There were three cameras on it, and tracking right down the street.

Right. Scene whatever it was, take one. Action.

Richard appeared at the top of the stairs and started walking down. Halfway down he stopped and, after patting the dummy baby underneath, he turned it over, sniffed it, and swiftly handed it to his stage wife.

Total hilarity broke out. Samuel Fuller tore off his cap, threw it on the ground and jumped on it. After the mirth subsided we did take two. This time it went off perfectly.

On one movie, the director was an Italian called Joe Pollini. I turned up with three pretty blondes and asked him if he could use them.

'Are they friends of yours?' he asked.

'No,' I replied. 'I met them in a bar last night.'

'Can you meet any more?' he enquired.

'I expect so.'

'Good. We've used you in a close-up, but you can still work for me. I need new North American fair-skinned faces in camera each day for crowd scenes. I'll give you a letter to show you are now our talent scout.'

Well, it wasn't the worst job in the world. I'd recruit at night, deliver them to the set in the morning, sit on my arse all day in the sun and then take them back to the city at the end of the shooting and receive 5,000 pesetas a day for my trouble.

There were always a number of balls-ups on these productions. After all, the Spaghetti Westerns were supposedly covering a period in the late nineteenth century in the Wild West. But you'd go to the rushes some mornings and you'd find that a Red Indian was wearing a wristwatch, or there were vapour trails in the sky where a jet was coming in to land at Almeria airport.

During one stay in Puerto Banus with my own humble yacht and the then-current girlfriend Jackie, who is also an artist, we developed quite a lucrative operation.

Jackie was very adept at silk-screening t-shirts. These could be bought in bulk from a small Spanish factory for as little as 15 pesetas each. She could paint either the name of the yachts or profiles on them and sell them for three hundred each. She was also producing them, unofficially, of course, with the design and titles of various Spaghetti Western films and knocking these out to the tourists at five hundred.

She was very creative—a real ideas girl—with super legs but also a slightly jealous streak, these attributes coming to light as a result of drinks on board a rather splendid yacht belonging to the Domeque wine family, resulting from one of my many faux pas.

I was talking to an expensive-looking brunette regarding the merits of oils and watercolours. It was one of those pauses at drinks parties when there's a hush and everybody stops speaking, either to get their breath or to consider another boring topic to review. This bird asked me if I were to paint her in the nude, what medium I would use. The party guests remained quiet. I suppose that I'd downed a few by this time so, without giving the matter much thought, suggested I'd like to paint her all over with yoghurt and strawberry ice-cream and then find myself short of a spoon. Jackie overheard the comment and wasn't particularly amused.

It wasn't, however, until the following day that she settled the issue that would publicly lay claim to me. She spent the afternoon printing t-shirts, as usual, and designed one especially for me. I wasn't allowed to view it until the last moment, after I'd donned the thing and was heading for the quay. Holding my chin in close, I was able to see the design—but upside-down, of course. It was plain white with five large black words across it.

It read, 'I only fuck the best.'

Now I might have considered this to be a commendable piece of advertising had she not followed me down the gangway wearing one she'd prepared earlier for herself.

Hers simply stated, 'The best.'

Financially we were doing rather well, but, of course, I tried to go one better. The border between Spain and Gib was at the time closed. This was a disadvantage for most living in Gib, but I saw instant mileage in the situation. I started running a shuttle service between Gib and Puerto Banus, transporting the otherwise-marooned residents 12 at a time for holidays, on a one-week or four-night basis at £20 a head.

It became so popular the frequency became twice weekly—doubling, of course, my passengers, and also the amount of illegal scotch whisky I was carrying to Spain, and Fundadore brandy back to Gib.

The art project just had to go on the back burner, but I could always revive it later.

Jackie and I split up as a result.

21

There were two notorious nightclubs in Brighton. Absolute dens of iniquity. They shared the same building in Queen's Square, one above the other. The one in the top floor was called the Safari Club. The lower one was the Whisky A Go Go. The police didn't title them separately but referred to the building as a whole. They nicknamed it the 'Bucket of Blood'.

I was a member of both of them and can vouch for the scandalous activities. I was in the Whisky one night when the proprietor emptied six shells into his unfaithful wife. Surprisingly, they remained open throughout his trial for murder, but closed shortly after the verdict.

However, before the shooting, I'd struck up an acquaintance with a group of Arabs. Let me at once dispel any myth that all Muslims are abstinent. Two of them were relatives of the lately deposed Sultan of Zanzibar, and somehow my past in the weaponry and mercenary business cropped up. It transpired they were planning a *coup* to retake the Spice Island, needed an organiser, and I fitted the bill.

I was contacted by a group in Dubai and given a shopping list for weaponry and personnel. This would present no problem and I contacted *Smith* from the Congo episode.

I rang *Smith* and arranged to meet him in London. For some reason he suggested Bond Street Tube station. I was surprised it wasn't a hotel or somewhere. But the man had a price on his head. He was always armed, so I was careful.

Bond Street Tube station is fairly deep down and, walking down the stairs, I was faced by a row of phone boxes. He was standing outside the end one. He saw me coming, acknowledged me, and went into the phone box at the end.

Moments later, a man standing in the phone box at the other end of the row picked the phone up, and after a brief conversation, put it down.

Smith reappeared and came to meet me. I said to him, 'Your chum in the end phone box, don't you want to bring him with us?' I'd rumbled that he'd called him and pointed me out.

'Okay,' he said, 'I'll send him away. I thought you might have a backup.'

'I have. She's the girl standing at the top of the stairs,' because one of my girlfriends was accompanying me. She had her hand in her handbag, and in it was a loaded 45.

'Well, you'd better bring her with us.'

We got in a taxi, and discussed the arms deal all the way from London to Portsmouth and back, throughout which time he kept his hand in his overcoat pocket.

My girlfriend said, 'I wish you'd take your hand out of your pocket. You're making me nervous.'

He did. It was heavily bandaged, because earlier in the day, he'd managed to trap it in the door of the lift.

This time I wasn't expected to transport anything, just to mastermind the operation and organise the assault from Mombasa. It transpired that there was a great deal of support among the inhabitants of Zanzibar and it required only 50 or so trained troops to seize the radio station and Government House and hold it for 12 hours until the new regime, or rather the old and now reinstated administration, would be given recognition and a treaty of defence by the United Arab Republic (UAR).

Part of my commission was to convince the UAR that the *coup d'état* was viable, and necessitated my visiting their embassy in South Audley Street on a number of occasions for discussions with the military people.

After a hell of a lot of running about, including visits with *Smith* to the Sultan, now living in exile in Southsea, Hampshire, as well as endless sorties to London and Mombasa, everything was almost ready.

Fifty legionnaires were positioned in five hotels in Mombasa, while six rigid inflatable boats and weaponry were hidden in two business premises also in Mombasa. A larger vessel was also in the port, ready to convey them down to within six miles of the island.

It was then that one of the group, Khalid, who knew the island intimately, as he'd lived there most of his life, invented the need for himself to visit the island in advance to drum up support subversively. He flew in from Dar es Salaam, which was at that time, I thought, rather risky—not only because Tanzania was now the enemy, but it would expose our hand if not all his ex-compatriots could be trusted.

I was heavily out-voted.

That was the last we saw of him. His cover was blown, he was arrested, tortured, he blabbed and then was shot. The attempted *coup* was completely blown, and publicised in the press before it had even started. It was ridiculous to try and proceed with it, so the project was abandoned forthwith—and the Sultan still lives in a semi-detached in Southsea, 50 years on.

Zanzibar is approximately seven degrees south of the Equator. The river Congo is also about seven degrees south of the Equator. If anybody ever asks me to do anything risky seven degrees south of the Equator, anywhere in the world, they can get stuffed.

22

My lasting obsession with all things traditional—classical music, paintings, houses and their trimmings and most of all boats, my own being a 1921 David Hillyard—has on more than one occasion deprived me of some genuine opportunities, and similarly saved me from minor disasters.

As I stood on the shoreline at Plymouth's Millbay dock one early April morning, I realised it was the first of April—All Fools' Day. Perhaps I was there just to make up the numbers. Being confronted by a plastic catamaran, I was already regretting this latest decision. I should have said no.

I hated multi-hulls then and still do, firmly believing that the Tupperware variety in particular were designed solely to splash around estuaries or sit quietly on marinas at weekends. So when asked to deliver this one some 6,000 miles to Cape Town, South Africa, I should have shouted no. But I didn't. For some reason known only to God, I said yes.

It had only been a brief discussion on the telephone three days before when I'd agreed to take on the job, the slimmest caveat being the condition of the vessel. To back out at this point might have smacked of cowardice. In any case, my current girlfriend Susan and her chum Linda were by now not only excited and packed, but well on their way from Somerset to join me. I imagined that if I cancelled, I would certainly incur a lengthy chunk of purdah and celibacy. But I would, if only for their sake, make damn sure that this ugly-looking lump was up to scratch before leaving dry land—where it might have been admirably more suitable as a container for planting up daffs.

I was wondering what had possessed me to take on this number. If it had been an aberration, I hoped that these were not about to increase in frequency—or worse, become chronic. While I was pondering, a stranger joined me on the shore.

'You must be Martin, our navigator,' he said. This was the owner, Johann, a Dutch South African. Skinny, late twenties, mop of dark hair—and, horror of horrors—dressed in completely over-the-top very yachty jeans, deck shoes, and a shirt with an anchor embroidered on the front.

'Yes, I am Martin,' I replied, not too enthusiastically.

After a brief and unconvincing soft handshake, he offered to row, or rather paddle, me out to the craft.

She was about 100 yards off, moored to a buoy by a rope that was totally unravelled at each end. A number of other ropes were badly frayed, showing the stamp of neglect—and this was visible before I climbed on board.

Having now done so, a further brief inspection revealed that at least four days' preparation was needed before any departure could be considered. I told him so.

He shrugged and agreed, spreading his words thinly.

Below, we sat at the one and only table, which was covered with a plastic tablecloth, to discuss arrangements and go over the boat's equipment. The current inventory wouldn't take long to go through. It was a short one—very short. In fact, it was easier to list the items that were absent than those present. No ship-to-shore radio, no life-raft, no life-jackets, lifelines and harnesses, no fire extinguishers or first aid gear, no charts or even an up-to-date copy of *Reed's Almanac*. Then, of course, no engine—except for an outboard which, he was swift to point out, only worked in harbour with everybody standing aft so that the propeller reached the water.

I listed the requirements and Johann agreed to purchase the deficiencies the following day. One thing that did surprise me, however, was that he possessed a sextant. And, after delving under a pile of newspapers, magazines and dirty socks, he unearthed it. It turned out to be a grey plastic one in an equally disappointing plastic box.

His wife, who for some reason or other was keeping well out of the way, called out from the galley which was further below, to see if we wanted coffee. We did.

When it arrived I was expecting her to be odd in some way, or very ugly, but she turned out to be quite normal. This was Aileen. Late twenties, shortish, plumpish, with long, dark hair. It wasn't, however, her appearance that caught my attention. What did was that the coffee had arrived in mugs made of china, and the spoons to stir it with were metal. I was surprised, and when I reflect back on that particular afternoon, I can clearly remember being gladdened by the simplest presence of china mugs and metal spoons—and the knowledge that the whole bloody boat wasn't plastic.

The absence of the ship-to-shore radio might well be a blessing in disguise. Some of the larger catamarans bore names such as *Magnificat*, *Alley Cat* and *Tom Cat*. One that I knew, whose owner had sunk rather more money into her than his bank had agreed to, baptised his 50-footer *Catastrophe*. But I don't think I'd have had the guts to call up and announce on the airwaves that I was *Pussycat*—very likely wrecking the remainder of my cred on the waterfront. It wouldn't have been so bad if she had simply been called *Pussy*—but she wasn't, her feline title emblazoned in large letters across her bum.

The only state-of-the-art electronics visible were in the shape of a ghetto blaster, slotted into a long shelf where it cohabited with about six cubic feet of pop music tapes. It was adequate for hearing the shipping forecast, but very capable of playing an endless offering of noise—loudly.

As we had no control over the weather once on the way, and would have to put up with whatever was on offer, I made a mental note to sacrifice any meteorological predictions and break the bloody thing as soon as possible. I was, of course, pretty well charted up, and had all my own equipment, but what the hell? He should have some for the boat anyway—so he should buy it.

We agreed what food he should buy. I settled for a freezer full of steak, some good-quality tinned food, veg, wine, old brandy and long-life milk. I pointed out that if anchored up with a bird in good holding ground in the lee of Bum Island, fish and chips might be okay. But if on watch, wet and cold, and it's blowing ten sorts of a bastard, you need something substantial. At least I do.

He didn't even smile.

Throughout that afternoon, Johann went through all the merits of *Pussycat*—how well she handled when carrying the main, mizen and working jib; how well she'd behaved on her trip from Sweden to the UK; the fact that she'd been built in Sweden by a yard called Eriksson and Eriksson. He'd also done some sailing with her in the English Channel.

Those were four major downright lies for a start.

Around 4 p.m. my two crew members appeared on the beach and called out. Johann was about to pick them up and suggested, as the cook wouldn't be joining us until next morning that he should get a take-away while he was ashore. He left, met the girls on the beach, and all three of them headed off into town.

It was while he was absent that Aileen came into her own and somewhat spilled the beans. She was Polish, well-educated, and spoke several languages. She said, 'Martin, I must speak with you.'

'Oh dear,' I thought. 'What's coming?'

'You must not take all that Johann says,' she said quietly.

'What do you mean?' I queried.

She said that, as she put it, 'Johann has a romantic mind.'

'Tell me,' I said.

She went on to explain that he had a vivid imagination and hadn't actually done some of the things he said he had.

'He's not a really big liar, but he likes to exaggerate his past.'

She went on to say that he didn't bring the boat from Sweden, he bought it in the Isle of Wight; she thought that although it was built in Sweden, it came to England on a ferry; and could I try the boat out before leaving for South Africa? She seemed worried, and I said I would do some sea trials anyway.

Later, Reg the cook arrived. We all ate on board, to the soundtrack of Doctor Hook.

When Susan arrived, her only comment regarding *Pussycat* was, 'It's a bit smaller than I thought.' But it didn't look as if she wanted to back out—which would have been a help.

Next morning, Johann and Reg went off to purchase the equipment and stores. I checked the rigging and replaced some of the shackles and other bits and pieces. They returned mid-afternoon and I suggested that we have a quick spin round the bay, back in time for tea.

We had a force four to five from the north-east, and I was quite surprised to see how well she did point up to the wind. I kept a watchful eye on Johann, who didn't do a lot. But I was pleasantly pleased to see that Reg was a good hand, and in the conversation learned that he'd had his own 40-footer, and had sailed extensively round the Scottish Isles and the north and west coast of France.

The next couple of days were spent putting things right that were wrong on board. And three days later, after final checks, the weather forecast good, we visited the harbour office and informed them that we were about to leave, and that our next intended call would be at La Coruña in northern Spain.

'You do know the Dutchman was rescued and towed in by the Brixham lifeboat, don't you?' the harbourmaster's assistant casually mentioned. I said that I didn't, but wasn't at all surprised.

We sailed at 4 p.m.—wind still north-easterly, about force three to four. Eddystone Lighthouse abeam at five fifty, steer two zero zero for Ushant.

For the next three days the wind stayed where it was. Biscay became a little lumpy, and most of the others became disinterested in food, so the ones who still wanted it fended for ourselves. I was happier rotating the watchkeeping with Reg, and letting Johann make up the sandwiches.

It wasn't a bad crossing, and we knew we'd have to let him take a watch at some time. It was only just before our arrival in Coruña that Johann he did—and managed an accidental gybe with the topping lift up. This is a cable that's only meant to hold the boom up when the sail isn't doing the job. The result was a row of broken battens in the mainsail, causing us to arrive at La Coruña yacht club looking a little droopy.

The next day we replenished stores and bought suitable strips of timber to replace battens, and some spare ones. This was just as well, as Johann managed to repeat the gybe when we were off Finistère three days later. This time he took out the mizen.

I had to climb out over the water with a hand drill and replace the battens, hanging on to the end of the mizen beam in quite heavy weather—about force six from the north-east.

I wanted to run down the Portuguese coast, close enough that I could spit on it. Before turning in that night I left instructions to do precisely this. In an offshore wind, we would make pretty good time and be in relatively calm water.

I hit the sack about midnight, and for a little light reading material, took to bed with me the paperwork of *Pussycat.* I wished I hadn't. Another of Johann's white lies cropped up. *Pussycat* was built in southern Sweden by Eriksson and Eriksson, but they weren't boatbuilders. They were builders—in fact, they were bricklaying brothers. They'd put it together from a one-off DIY kit in a large garage, and there were photos to back it up throughout the construction.

At 3 a.m. I was awoken by a change of motion and went up into the cockpit to check. Johann said that he'd become worried because the shore lights looked too close, so he'd let her run off a bit.

'You'd better get her back, or we'll be in mid-Atlantic!' I yelled.

'I can't. She won't come back!' he answered, above the wind.

Reg joined us, and said he'd just picked up a gale warning for that area going eight to nine, and suggested we heave-to. I agreed. In the absence of a proper sea anchor we streamed the drogue.

It turned out to be a long heave-to—nine bloody days in very heavy weather. I won't keep on about the size of the waves—everybody who writes sailing stories does so. But they were sodding big.

There was something very satisfactory about the loo on *Pussycat*. It was a unique cure for constipation. It was raised like a throne in order that the outflow was above the water line. To perch on it without falling off and maintain one's balance during any procedure you had to jam your feet against the inside of the hull. In a heavy sea, the hull physically moved in and out, like some large creature breathing. If you didn't want to go when you first went in there, this action always inspired a happy result.

Below was beginning to smell like the incontinent ward of an old folk's home, and vomit was making below decks very slippery.

Day three. I needed to relax. There was nothing else to do so, with Johann's fishing rod in one hand, and a bottle of brandy in the other, I wedged myself in the cockpit and went fishing, after having a fry-up of everything within reach of the pan while similarly wedged in the galley.

Suddenly, halfway through the afternoon, the waves ceased to break and the swell lessened. I looked over my shoulder to find a large freighter some 100 yards away—and we were now under her lee.

A voice boomed out in perfect English, 'How do we get you off?'

She was a Russian and about 18,000 tons. Attracted by the noise like moths to a candle flame the dregs of humanity crawled out of our cockpit. Johann yelled, 'They can take us off! We're safe!'

'They're not taking anybody off,' I bellowed. 'If they get close enough to do that they'll smash this thing to bits.'

'They could take me off,' he replied.

'So, you can walk on water, like Jesus?' I bellowed, shoving him up against the cabin-top.

He pushed me away, screaming, 'I'm Jewish, so don't give me any of your bloody religion!'

I didn't retaliate verbally. He took a swing at me and missed. Blows were now being landed. All that Johann kept screaming throughout the fracas was, 'They can save our lives!'

Now, in the past I've fought in boxing booths, and they're smaller than the traditional ring. But this was bloody ridiculous. We were now belting each other in an area that was about eight feet by eight feet, going up and down wildly, with four other people in the way.

Eventually the Russian moved off, and I suddenly burst out laughing. I couldn't stop. I could just imagine the Russian operator on the radio telling all and sundry that there's a funny-looking yellow-and-black boat 90 miles off Finistère, in a howling gale. One man's trying to fish and the other man keeps hitting him. Now they're boxing. Probably both pissed. And above all, they don't want rescuing.

As they moved off, Johann kept screaming that I'd killed them all, and *Pussycat* might break up. I told him that I knew *Pussycat* was built like a brick shithouse, because Eriksson and Eriksson would have made sure of that, and hopefully she would stay in one piece.

She did.

On the ninth day the wind dropped and we just sat, totally becalmed, and wallowed. Day ten. Wind westerly, force four to five. We could nearly make about seven knots towards Portugal.

Day 12. We made it into Figueira da Foz and came alongside about 4.30 p.m. What a welcome! Dozens of well-wishers, the press and TV. It transpired that we'd been on TV news for days. An RAF Nimrod had made regular passes over us and reported that we were still afloat.

However, the *bonhomie* was suddenly about to evaporate. Johann could speak Portuguese. I don't. I can manage Spanish, but it's not anywhere the same. Johann's surname, after all, was something like Da Silva. And he was shooting one hell of a line to the young lady TV interviewer. She spoke to us in English and wanted our account. She pointed out that our brave captain, Johann, insisted that we'd stayed on board together after we'd all wished to be taken off by the Russian ship.

I suddenly got a pink mist. He'd pushed me over the top.

The look on Sue's face changed. She knew what was about to happen—and it did.

'You're a lying little wanker!' I shouted. 'It was you who was crapping yourself and wanted to be rescued! And you need shagging with the blunt end of a bloody pineapple or something very adjacent!'

I think it lost something in the translation to Portuguese, but I'm sure the young lady got the message from my hand signals which, after all, are pretty much international.

Some very kind English-speaking folk took Susan, Linda and myself home to their house for a hot bath and a meal, and we relaxed for a full 24 hours. Two days later, in a very strained atmosphere, we left Figueira da Foz for Gibraltar.

I secretly agreed with the girls that I wasn't going to take *Pussycat* any further than that.

The wind this time was north-westerly, about four. So I set a course to take us well clear of the coast to avoid any lee shore risk—totally opposite from the previous run. In the night, what does Captain Johann do? He decides that he doesn't like all that open sea, and changes course to stay in nice and close to the land.

The next three days were spent fighting to stay off the rocks and headlands, and struggling to keep my hands off of him. Finally, by the skin of our teeth, we made it into the Gibraltar Strait. Once we tied up in Sheppard's marina I told Johann six words only, 'Airline tickets. Three of them. Tomorrow.'

He protested. 'No. You've broken the contract. So no tickets.'

I told him, in front of an audience, that the ocean is generally a risky place, even without him on it. With him, any area of water becomes totally hazardous, and that I wouldn't now even accompany him across the pond in Regent's Park. 'So, get the tickets.'

The row went on for a little while and, well, I suppose it's probably an old joke. I couldn't resist the retaliation about the walking on water bit. I said, 'When the rabbi got at you with his pair of scissors, old son, he threw the wrong bit away.'

He didn't laugh, but Johann never laughed at anything.

That evening, Sue, Linda and I checked into the Montaric hotel. I think we were all very pleased to get off that boat. Sue and I went out for a meal, but I'm afraid she consumed a little too much alcohol. This wasn't usual and I suppose it could be put down to relief after the trip. I was supporting her with my arm around her waist, and we were not exactly travelling in a straight line.

Suddenly, I was grabbed from behind, and two guys appeared in front of me and took it in turns to punch and kick me. I couldn't see the one behind, but the two in front were Johann and Reg, who seemed to have suddenly changed sides.

I managed to shake off the one that was holding me just as the police arrived. The two coppers had witnessed the latter part of the punch-up and said that I had a clear case for actual bodily harm and should press charges. I declined, and said I'd sort things out my own way.

An ambulance took me to hospital. I had several cracked ribs, but otherwise no serious damage. I reported to the police the following afternoon and told them that I still had some personal effects on the boat and I was on my way to collect them. A young officer said he would drive me down to the boat to ensure there were no more punch-ups.

I climbed aboard and kicked the door open between the cockpit and the saloon. Reg was sitting playing cards with a stranger. I wondered if he'd been the one doing the holding the night before, as I hadn't seen his face. I collected my things and returned to the police car.

The copper asked me who was on board. I told him the cook and a stranger. He said that if I had anything further to do he would wait, adding that he couldn't see into the cabin from where he was sitting.

It was an open invitation.

I went quietly back on board. They were still playing cards, but stopped at my arrival. Reg knew what was coming and stood up. I only hit him once, but hard.

He went back and sat on the edge of the table, which immediately collapsed under his weight. He didn't try to get up. The other guy didn't move—he just remained sitting. His feet were now surrounded by a deck of well-shuffled playing cards, some loose money, and Reg—who now had taken on a permanent wink, his left eye being totally closed.

I turned and left, returned to the police car, and told the cop that I'd sorted out one small problem.

Susan and Linda took the next day's flight back to England. I was a little upset and went on the piss. Early in the evening I was still on it. I wound up in the Spinning Wheel, and was surprised to find Aileen working behind the bar. It hadn't taken Johann long to get her working, and maybe she'd left him. I asked her what time Johann came in to collect her. She said that he didn't—that the owner of the pub sent her back to the yacht by taxi. I thought that was very unlikely, but I stayed there anyway.

Sure enough, it was less than half an hour before he walked in. He almost stopped dead when he saw me, reflecting on what had recently happened to Reg. I told him that he could have it in the bar in front of his friends, or step out into the back alley. Either way, I was going to beat the living shit out of him.

He started to protest. So I hit him.

The Spinning Wheel bar was fitted out with old memorabilia from the UK, with an old-fashioned non-functional telephone mounted on the wall. It was this phone that he hit on his way down. He lay there and didn't move.

'You've killed him!' Aileen screamed. 'Someone get an ambulance!'

As I left the bar I told her that she'd better make up her mind what she wanted—an ambulance or a hearse, because nobody likes time-wasters.

I was arrested at the Montaric hotel the following morning. Sergeant Rodriguez said that he would hold me pending charges. So I was banged up.

23

The Gibraltar Hilton was a dump, so I was both pleased and puzzled to receive a visit from a stranger who announced that he could secure my immediate release. The promise of instant freedom fell pleasantly upon my ears but, if true, an offer such as this would require authoritative sanctions. There'd be no question of bail in my case or any likelihood of the charges against me being dropped. I nevertheless listened with interest as my newly acquired American benefactor further revealed the reason for his presence.

'I need a captain for my yacht,' he said. 'The job calls for a guy who can handle himself, and from what I hear on the waterfront you might fit the bill.'

I said nothing, firmly believing him to be a madman. Apart from historic rumour regarding my nefarious background, he could know only that my present custodial situation was a result of a fight. Two to be precise.

So why did this newcomer need a fighter? As he talked there was no suggestion that I might subsequently be expected to involve myself in any further pugilistic behaviour and, although I very much wanted to, I didn't question this combative requirement at this stage. My chief interest was now how the hell this man could spring me.

'I'll be shooting a documentary film on the North African coast, and I need someone like yourself who has had a . . . ' he paused, 'slightly chequered career.'

I hoped by this observation he was referring to my exploits in the film industry and not my activities in smuggling, gunrunning or, even worse, my experience with explosives. What concerned me equally was how this alleged American film producer, hitherto totally unknown to me, could be in a position to obtain my deliverance.

As we sat on either side of the table in this austere green-painted interview room, something at the back of my mind kept niggling me, but I couldn't put my finger on it. I was sure I hadn't seen him before. Well, almost. He was a tall, slim, military-looking man of about forty-five, with short, dark hair, greying at the temples. While he talked his slate-blue eyes remained focused on me and, although the sort of person with whom one felt uneasy without really knowing why, at this moment I could see him only as a potential spare key to the cell door.

When I pressed him regarding the subject of the film, a further worrying aspect emerged.

'I'd rather not discuss that now,' he said, 'and if we do come to an arrangement I must have your word that you will observe complete secrecy regarding the whole operation . . . ' he quickly corrected himself, 'the whole programme, I mean. Parts of the script are of a sensitive nature.'

'Where are you going to be filming?' I asked.

'On the other side,' he replied, vaguely. I hoped he meant this in the literal sense, referring to the Straits of Gibraltar, and not the figurative location in the sky.

'When are you starting?'

'Soon,' he replied, equally tenuously.

'How soon?'

'Possibly next week.' I stopped digging, as I could see that he wouldn't be drawn beyond this.

'Okay,' I said, changing the subject. 'How can you get me out?'

'I can and that's all that matters. By the way, my name is Henry Muller.'

'Is that supposed to mean something to me?' I wondered. Perhaps the name wasn't significant. 'All right, Mr Muller. What happens next?'

'Just tell me if you're prepared to work for us.'

'For you, you mean.'

'Yes, for me. And then we can both get out of here now.'

'I am working for you, aren't I?'

For the first time during the conversation a brief smile flickered across his face.

'Right. Let's go,' he said.

After less than ten minutes of formalities, I was out, and walking down Main Street. Before reaching Waterport, Muller stood me breakfast in a small café tucked away behind the market. The patron knew Muller slightly—I could tell this by his comments. This, together with the fact that Cathy's was an obscure place to find, made me realise that Muller was no stranger to Gibraltar and was not a recent arrival—a theory further borne out when we reached the *Neptune*.

She was lying in Sheppard's marina in a berth reserved for larger visiting vessels, and from her appearance, she'd been visiting for some time. A surfeit of marine growth at the water line of three cables fanned out from her bow, and the shoreside mooring ropes showed a duration of chafe that suggested the label of permanency.

Neptune was a classic yacht built in Germany in the 1930s and, being such an aged iron ship, she had the costly problem of needing constant surgery. To own her was like owning a hole in the sea into which one continuously poured money. From my first impressions, a lot of dollar-decanting had taken place. This vessel had undergone a complete refit, including a new main engine and some unflattering changes to her superstructure.

It surprised me to see that she was British registered, her homeport being Southampton. Legally, if not owned by a British national, this would not be allowed. Most other non-European owners, particularly Americans, seemed to favour the flag of Panama.

As soon as we were aboard, Muller said, 'Pick yourself a decent cabin. They're mostly empty, but more crew will be joining us later.'

I chose one on the starboard side, just aft of the bridge companion-way and, fortunately, well away from the engine-room. This would ensure quiet but allow speedy access to the main deck if I were needed.

In spite of the updating she'd received she still possessed the trappings of quality and class, and displayed an air of graciousness—a rarity seldom enjoyed by modern vessels. The stateroom and cabins were still panelled in the original solid mahogany.

I finished stowing my gear and joined him on the main deck. The deck-house, which contained the latest state-of-the-art technology, was of the finest oak, so I was horrified to see two of the crewmen just putting the finishing touches to a paint job which included smothering the outside of this superb timberwork with white enamel.

I was surprised to see included in the array of electronic armoury the Single Sideband radio, its aerial mounted on the forepart of the main mast. SSB is used only for transmitting over great distances providing a high degree of secrecy, and is an unusual toy for anything other than ocean-going commercial vessels. I got another little tinge of suspicion.

Finally, my confidence in Muller was totally undermined when shown the rest of the modification. The replacement engine—a supercharged Caterpillar brought over specially from the United States—should have been lowered through the floor underneath the deck-house, removable for this purpose. Instead, it had been craned in through a large previously cut hole in the steel foredeck and then manhandled aft, not without considerable effort, to its position in the engine-room. The hole in the deck had been covered by welding a huge steel plate over it, and the whole cabin below now had a steel lining.

This entire exercise was plainly just an excuse to reinforce the complete bow section of the vessel, although the cover-up was totally wasted because it created more interaction with an already suspicious shoreside workforce. The strength of her was now in excess of any requirement for Lloyd's or a Bureau Veritas survey. Looking at her, I thought she would make an ideal vessel with which to ram another. Later, I found out that I was quite wrong, and the need to fortify had a much more macabre reason.

On my way ashore I passed a group of yardworkers, some of whom had obviously been employed on *Neptune*.

'Is she strong enough for you, Captain?' one of them quipped sarcastically.

'I think so,' I replied noncommittally, but I realised that remarks like this would only help to create further gossip. I would be glad when we sailed.

This was to be sooner than expected. Next morning, Muller said that he wished to do some sea trials. He went ashore for about three hours and returned soon after 11.30 a.m. By noon we got going, and slipped out of the berth.

'A quick run to Europa Point and back, don't you think?' he suggested.

'Why not?' I replied, and went direct to half speed. Ten minutes later, we cleared the Detached Mole and

I gave her full throttle. Although she handled well, I could see that Muller seemed agitated.

'Have you had any previous trials with her?' I asked him.

'Yes, when I took delivery three months ago. But that was on a crap engine.'

'Well, Henry, she's making about 12 knots, which isn't bad.'

'Maybe, but she did ten before.'

'Look, she's not the right shape to go any faster. In any case, an elegant old lady like this would look very silly doing 20 knots.'

He didn't answer.

As soon as we were back alongside he disappeared ashore and was gone for another three hours. I had supper ashore and turned in early. Next morning, Muller cooked breakfast. He and I and the two lads ate together, after which one of them, Lee, cleared up, while the other, Ben, carried out more desecration with white paint.

Gibraltar was then in the grip of a postal strike, so Muller used to prevail on passengers or aircrew leaving on daily London flights to post his mail from Heathrow. Today it was my turn to, as he put it, 'be Wells Fargo'. I called down to him in the saloon as I was about to leave.

'I'm taking my letters. Have you got any to go?'

'No, but take the car. There are some boxes in customs. Sign for them and bring them back. Be careful with them—they're cameras.'

Having got shot of the mail, I made my way to a small warehouse where incoming goods were checked and stored. I asked a chap in plain clothes if I'd found the correct place for any packages for Henry Muller on the yacht *Neptune*. He grunted, and looked in a blue receipt book—the sort that usually costs you money when it appears. He found three entries, and turning the book round said, 'Sign here.'

Happily, there was nothing to pay. He then pointed out that they were heavy and I'd need a hand.

I enlisted some help, and did it in two trips to the marina to prevent overloading the car. When finished the second run about 2.30 p.m., with the cases safely on board, I went ashore for a liquid lunch. I left Muller, at his suggestion, to sort them out. I returned about 5 p.m. after he'd finished.

On day three, Muller paid off the two lads, who obviously weren't expecting to work on the film, and they left. He went ashore, to be gone all day.

I'd just finished having a shower when I heard footsteps and voices on deck. I emerged, swathed in a towel, to be greeted by four girls, Muller, and another man—all Americans. Bobby, Evelyn, Jo, Carol and Arnold were joining us, and they were to be our film extras.

Well, Bobby, Evelyn and Carol, yes. But no way Jo. I've seen some women you could hire out to haunt houses. This one could have done a pretty comprehensive job on a block of flats. She was apparently in charge of the other females. She certainly wasn't about to become in charge of me. The way she spoke indicated she could have done a good impression of Pol Pot having just stubbed an ingrown toenail on the leg of a solid oak table.

And talking of legs, hers were muscular and without any charity. I wouldn't like to get on the wrong side of her—side being the operative word. Heaven forbid on top of. I wondered where they'd caught her, and what bait they'd used.

She didn't, however, look like the gun-toting type, although I could visualise her roaring through the jungle somewhere wielding a machete.

They took ages to settle in as they had so much gear. In fact, I thought they must have chartered their own aircraft to have coped with it all. The girls had four backpacks, three large plastic holdalls, three suitcases and an assortment of small bits of hand luggage between them.

Arnold, on the other hand, possessed one large seedy-looking trunk. It had either seen better days, experienced a lot of demanding travel, or else the designer dents and scratches had been very carefully administered, with much thought given to detail. Nothing Louis Vuitton about this. It was the sort of tin box in which a cut-price murderer might hide a victim. And what's more he had his name on it in two-inch-high letters.

A.G. Pratt wasn't a name I'd personally want to advertise, and neither was the luggage itself anything that I would wish to lay claim to. I wondered what the G stood for. The A, obviously, was for Arnold, and everyone knows what Pratt stands for, but then perhaps it doesn't in America. He was one anyway, to tote halfway round the world a container of such magnitude that it constantly requires someone else to lift the other end.

He threw a glance in my direction—something he must have done many times before in order to get some unsuspecting body to help him with it. I ignored him, and thought, 'Not a cat in hell's chance.'

It was obvious that none of the girls had done any sailing. Within an hour of their arrival the standard of the ship had deteriorated and, from the sound of the shower pumps, our limited supply of cherished fresh water was taking a frightful bashing. Someone was going to have to tell them about keeping the vessel tidy and rationing the water.

I didn't want to do it. Why spoil any potentially beautiful friendships when they'd only just arrived?

That evening we ate ashore. I assumed they'd just flown in, but one of them let it slip over the meal that all of them had been staying at Both Worlds, a hotel on the other side of the Rock. It seemed odd to me that they hadn't been able to see the ship. After all, it was only five miles. Why was Henry Muller keeping them out of sight?

I went ashore the next day, as there was very little for me to do on board. I was on my fifth scotch in the Spinning Wheel, but luckily Johann's wife, Aileen, didn't work there anymore. Three of the extras walked in and joined me and I introduced them to Brian, the owner, who was a Cockney chum of mine.

'You're always surrounded by pretty crumpet,' said Brian, as I introduced them as our extras. 'I wouldn't mind a bit of extra if it all looks like that,' he concluded.

It was only now that I realised how remarkably pretty they all were. And one in particular, Evelyn, seemed to be the loner of the quartet. I'd ask her out if I got the chance before we sailed, if only to find out a bit more about the forthcoming new epic.

I almost wrecked any chance of that, however, late the same evening after dinner. I returned aboard minus cigarettes, only to find that no one else smoked, so there was no chance of scrounging any. I therefore had a certain amount of explaining to do when I announced to those assembled that I would have to go ashore again as I was dying for a fag.

I seemed to save up my clangers for mealtimes. Two days later, when I had managed to persuade Evelyn out for a sightseeing trip to the top of the Rock, we had a slight collision with another car. This caused us to arrive back some 20 minutes late for the appointed feeding time. My explanation for this delay and our dishevelled appearance caused some great amusement to the seated gathering when I announced, 'I'm sorry that we're late, but we've just had a bang in the car.'

These faux pas did at least help to lessen any tension that was noticeably creeping in.

A week later we sailed for Al Mediq in Morocco. It was during the three-and-a-half-hour crossing that I casually mentioned to Muller that I too had been in the film business, and had worked on several war pictures in England and Spaghetti Westerns in Spain. I'd neglected to mention this before, because we hadn't actually talked socially. I could see at once I was dropping bricks, as one could have cut the atmosphere with a knife. Suddenly no one wanted to talk films except me, and I certainly did.

'How long is this saga going to run for when it's finished?' I asked.

'It's going to be a 90-minute documentary,' Muller replied, unconvincingly.

'How long will it take to shoot?'

'Oh, about five or six days. Maybe even a week.'

'As quick as that?' I said, without too much surprise in my voice.

'Yes, I hope so. That's, of course, as long as it all goes well.'

Now, even with my limited knowledge of the silver screen, it's quite obvious that Muller & Co. knew little or nothing about the motion picture business. Because if a really polished production company manages to print three minutes of useable film at the end of each day's take, they've done very well.

'So what have you got in those boxes down there, Henry, a pair of Box bloody Brownies? Because you sure as hell ain't filming!' I said in a phoney mid-Atlantic accent.

Muller gave me a look as if he'd just caught me in bed with his virgin daughter.

'What the hell do you mean?' he snapped.

'I mean you couldn't even shoot the credits in a week, let alone a real film.'

'Of course not. We're doing the rest back in the States,' he replied, trying hard to regain some composure.

'You're a bloody liar, chum. I know you're shooting, but it's not a film—and those boxes have got guns in them. Right?'

'Okay. So we're not actually filming. But what we are doing is not in any way illegal. Quite the reverse, I promise you.'

'Pull the other one, it's got fucking bells on it!' I said.

'What's that supposed to mean?'

'It means you're a lying bastard, Henry, that's what it means!'

I was getting bloody mad. There had been such a lot of mystery surrounding this bunch all the time they'd been in Gib. I was cross with myself too. Why hadn't my warning bells sounded earlier? Then I could have simply pissed off on another boat and left them.

'So it's not illegal?'

'No, Mart, it's truly not. It's not in any way dishonest. In fact, quite the reverse, and you'll be very well paid if you stay. And, by the way, you're more or less obliged to now.'

'Bollocks I am. I can piss off whenever I like. And the lot of you are certainly not going to stop me!'

I pulled the throttle back to idle and put the helm over.

'What did you do that for?'

'I'd rather be back in prison in Gib than stuck in Morocco with you lot!'

'Look, Mart, don't be bloody stupid. I'll level with you. I'll tell you exactly what we're doing. We're pretending to make a film while we look for someone who's gone missing.'

'Missing missing or hiding?' I said sarcastically.

'A bit of both, I guess. Let's go into Mediq and I'll tell you the whole bit.'

'It's somebody well-known, isn't it?' I interrupted.

'No, they're most probably unknown to you.'

'So,' I said, 'it's a missing double-act, is it? They are machine-guns in those crates down there, aren't they? And like you, the film is all bullshit.'

'Yes, they are guns. But they're only supposed to be props for the film.'

'Don't keep on about this non-existent bloody film! And by the way, can I have one of the guns? I feel a bit outnumbered.'

'Yes, Mart, you can have one.'

He turned and threw a small bunch of keys at Arnold, who then went below.

'Make it a big bastard with a lot of bullets!' I yelled after him. Then, lowering my voice to Muller I said, 'And don't keep calling me Mart.'

After a few moments Arnold reappeared. He placed an unopened box of nine millimetre calibre shells on the chart table in front of me. In his left hand he held an automatic pistol. After throwing an enquiring glance at Muller, who just nodded, he handed me the weapon.

I broke open the box and, slipping the magazine out of the butt, methodically loaded it and replaced it in the pistol. I checked the safety and stuck it in the side pocket of my jeans.

We were now only about two miles off the coast so I saw little point in arguing or turning back.

'We'll talk when we get alongside then,' I said.

The next 20 minutes were taken up entering Mediq and tying up to the jetty. I put *Neptune* alongside astern of two other yachts. One was the Gibraltar-registered

Mayflower Camelot, owned by a chum of mine and a regular passage-maker across the Straits. The other was German registered and unknown to me, called *Heidi.*

Throughout the docking, little was said until I broke the silence, speaking generally to all of them.

'I can do one of two things. I can walk over to that yacht in front of us and get a ride back to Gib. The chap who owns her is a good friend of mine and I know he will be going back today. Or I can take this gun out of my pocket and I can shove it up your arse until you tell me what exactly is going on.'

'Please don't do either,' said Muller.

I was about to put my cards on the table anyway. I didn't answer. I just stood holding the gun and waited for him to continue.

'Question,' he said. 'What are your views on blacks?'

'At this moment you're not in any position to ask me questions. And if I had any views, you'd be the last person on God's earth that I'd tell. But I take it you don't like them?'

'Imagine the scenario . . . ' he started.

'Please stop using bloody bits of film jargon!' I said, interrupting. 'You don't even know what they mean!'

He breathed out deeply as though he were about to lose his patience with a difficult child, or admit defeat.

'Okay,' he said, slowly and less intensely. 'A while back three black men hijacked a Delta Airline jet from LA and flew it into the Algerian desert. You may remember, but it doesn't matter anyway. They took a million and a half in ransom, and then fired the plane, a DC9.'

'So what's all that got to do with you or me?'

He ignored my interruption and continued.

'They are now running a Black Panther organisation, which is a terrorist outfit, from a place in the hills just outside Algiers. They've become an embarrassment to us, and their whole operation, which is becoming a menace, will have to be shut down.'

'An embarrassment to "us"? Who's "us"?' I asked. Again he ignored me.

'We're going to look like we're making a movie. The girls will entice them on board and we'll lift them.'

'Lift them, Henry? Dead or alive? And you still haven't told me who "us" is?'

'Okay. "Us" is me, and you, and Arnold, and the girls. Dead or alive depends on these damned terrorists, but I don't personally care one way or the other. Does that answer your question?'

He was now trying to get a firmer grip on the situation.

'And another thing, while we're about it. You're in for $20,000 on top of your wages. Not bad for a few days' work. And don't forget that you'd still be in jail if it hadn't been for my intervention. So tell me, how do your bloody morals feel now?'

'I didn't ever say I had any. I only want to know who I'm working for. Because it's certainly not public-spirited Henry Muller or little Arnold Pratt.'

'It is,' he replied, 'and you'd better believe it. By the way,' he continued, looking past me through the deck-house window, 'your chum is just leaving with his boat, and I would suggest you don't try hitching a ride with the other one—it's one of ours.'

In the evening, Muller cooked supper, mostly out of tins—or rather, cans. Canned cockles (or, as he called them, clams), canned tomatoes, the stock and even the sterilised cream all originating from the same source. The onions were fresh—well, almost. It was the first time I'd eaten New England clam chowder, and I wasn't over-impressed, especially as it was accompanied by a choice of beer, gin or whisky. Not that I'm averse to the latter—in the correct place.

'Don't you people ever drink wine?' I asked.

Evelyn said there was a bottle in the galley and went off to fetch it. She brought it back. It turned out to be red, but French at least. Nevertheless, I opened it and offered it. There were no takers, so I drank it.

Not much discussion took place over the meal except for trivia. The forthcoming main event wasn't mentioned. I had the feeling that all present were trying to humour me. We'd just finished our canned puds. Carol made coffee—not the real thing, of course. Muller then produced two more bottles—one of port, and the other of Grand Marnier.

'Who would like a Grand Mariner, and who would prefer port wine?' he asked.

They all declined except me.

'I'll have port,' I said.

'Are you sure you wouldn't rather have a Grand Mariner? I'm going to,' he insisted.

'No thanks, I can't stand the stuff.'

The others turned in, leaving him and me sitting drinking.

'Question,' he said. 'What were you doing when you were last in Algiers?'

'Who says I've ever been there?' I replied.

'Your passport does.'

'You've not seen my passport.'

'I have actually, Martin.'

'Have you and bloody Arnold been rummaging through my gear?'

'No, I was shown it in Gibraltar. Actually, Mart, Arnold thinks you're all right.'

'It's purely academic what any of you thinks of me, old son. But come to think about it, I've got a soft spot for all of you. It's called the Goodwin Sands.'

He managed a grin, not being quite sure what I meant. He stood up and poured himself another drink, and handed me the port bottle. I poured myself one and then lit a cigarette. I took a mouthful of port, swirled it around my mouth and swallowed. Suddenly, I realised how tired I was, and tried to remember back to my last question. For a moment it had gone. I couldn't remember what it was.

'You didn't answer my question,' said Muller. 'What were you doing there?'

'Doing where?'

'In Algiers, when you were last in Algiers.'

'I don't know, Henry. But I'll tell you one thing. I shouldn't have had half a bottle of scotch before supper. It doesn't mix with this stuff. Here, what are you saying about the police in Gib showing you my bloody passport when I was banged up?'

'Don't let it worry you. It's history now. But please try to remember Algiers. Would you know your way around the place?'

'Don't keep on about fucking Algiers! I'm sick of hearing about Algiers! Now I'm going to have one more drink and then I'm going to bed. And as far as I'm concerned, you can forget all about the police in Gib. I'm going to because I'm getting too pissed to be bothered.'

I got up, swilled the last of my port, and went to bed.

The next morning, I didn't surface until after 9 a.m. The ship sounded ominously quiet and lacked the usual smell of breakfast. Eventually, I found Evelyn lying on the foredeck reading a book.

'Where's everybody?' I asked.

'They've gone off,' she replied.

'I feel bloody rough. What time are they coming back?' I asked.

'In about five or six days, I think.'

'What?' I shouted, and immediately regretted it. Then, lowering my voice, 'So you and I are stuck in this dump for a week?'

She nodded.

'And you stayed on to look after me, did you?'

'Yes, I did actually. Jo wanted Carol to, but I volunteered.'

'Oh that's nice. But you're really only here to make sure I don't sod off.'

'That was the general idea, but I wanted to stay anyway.'

'Tell me, sweetie, how would you stop me?'

'Why are you always so damned difficult?' she asked. 'You're always so quick to pick on people and condemn them!'

'Sorry, but I feel like rat shit this morning.'

'I'm not really surprised after what you tipped down last night,' she replied, giving a little disapproving smile.

'Okay, my love. Please start looking after me and make me a bloody big, black coffee.'

It was already stifling hot, and by 3 p.m. it would have been unbearable. Lying alongside with no breeze, the steel decks would make the cabins below like a furnace. I must try to rig something that would keep the heat off them.

As I stood there thinking about my head and the heat and how to rig an awning, the coffee arrived. With the aid of a boat-hook, two oars and two jib sails I slowly produced a makeshift awning. Then, with a certain measure of bad language and a lot of help from Evelyn, I managed to suspend the thing between the deck-house and the mizen-mast.

As the coffee had failed to work I went below, poured a substantial scotch, drank it and poured another. Carrying the bottle and dragging my bunk mattress behind me, I struggled back on deck, determined to try out the comfort of the new canopy.

'You're not having any more of that,' Evelyn said, taking the bottle out of my hand as I reached it.

'Oh dear. Not only my wardress and keeper but my guardian angel as well.'

'Look, I'll cook us a good lunch later. But first we must go to find a market that's got some fresh things. Then you'll feel much better.'

'Can you promise that?'

'No, but let's go ashore anyway. I just want to get off this thing.'

Then she said something that wasn't in keeping.

'By the way, I'm on your side.'

It took more than five minutes for me to locate my second deck shoe, by which time she was already waiting on the gangway. I joined her and we strolled off gently towards the town centre and hopefully a not-too-distant market.

She bought enough vegetables to last just for one day, insisting that it was better to buy everything fresh. Mercifully, this reduced the burden of the return hike, but it would necessitate a pilgrimage like this on a daily basis, the thought of which I didn't relish.

We returned to the yacht. A discreet search for the fugitive whisky bottle revealed nothing. My mouth still had a flavour similar to the inside of Gandhi's jock box, and I didn't fancy freshly squeezed oranges as a likely panacea. Fortunately, a light afternoon breeze sprang up and I managed to ventilate the lower decks. The morning's labours had proved somewhat futile as, owing to the inconsiderate transit of the sun, the awning was now giving shelter to a six-foot area of dockside.

'We're having lamb with salad. Do you prefer white or red wine?' came a voice from the hatchway.

'I don't believe it. Where did you discover that?'

'It's French, and there's plenty more where that came from,' she giggled.

For the first time in about two months I was beginning to feel relaxed. The good food, the wine, and, of course, the company was helping.

She talked a little about her family but wasn't totally forthcoming. The more I got to know her the more puzzled I became. She came from what I'd call a normal background. So how the hell had she gotten involved in a situation like this?

It was about 4.30 p.m. by the time we'd finished eating. The breeze had dropped away and it was sultry.

'If it's all the same to you, sweetie, I'm going to crash out,' I said. 'I'm bushed. Do you want to use the shower during the next ten minutes?'

'No, you use it first. I'm going to clear these things away and I'll have one later.'

I stood up.

'By the way, that was a smashing lunch. Thanks,' I said as I headed for the hatchway.

It was muggy below so I took my shower as hot as I could stand it, knowing that as I cooled off from the hot water, I might just get an hour's kip before my body reached cabin temperature. I remained under the spray for a good five minutes, and with a towel round me I flopped out in my cabin as quickly as possible, so as not to lose the effect.

I'd just reached the limbo stage, about to drop off, when Evelyn appeared in the open doorway.

'You're not asleep, are you?' she said.

'No. Is anything wrong?'

'We've got to talk. There are things you should know about.'

She was looking more serious than I had previously seen her, and keeping her voice down.

'Okay. Tell me about it,' I said.

She sat on the edge of my bunk, just looking at me, and it must have been a full twenty seconds before she spoke.

'It's true that I'm supposed to be keeping an eye on you while they're away. But I wanted to anyway so that I could warn you. I don't want anything to happen to you and I'm sure that Arnie is setting you up.'

'What makes you think that?' I asked.

'Bloody Arnie is a killer. No, please don't laugh at me. He's dangerous, and he frightens me.'

'Well he doesn't frighten me, sweetie. He's only knee-high to a grasshopper and about as lethal.'

'Oh no, you're quite wrong. I know he was mixed up in the Lee Harvey Oswald business. I can't tell you how I know, but I do know.'

'Don't worry love, little Arnie is nothing.'

'Martin, when he's about, someone always gets dead. He's always around to clear up any mess that's left behind.'

'Oh, you think I might be the mess after the job's gone down, do you?'

'I'm just trying to warn you.'

'Right. I'll remember never to turn my back on him.'

She half-smiled and said, 'Well at least you know. None of the others did. Would you like some more coffee?'

'Yes, I'd love some, angel.'

As she went off I propped myself up on my pillow. There was no chance of sleep now.

'Who the hell are the others?' I wondered.

I played down what she'd just told me, but nevertheless I was going to have to watch my back from now on. It only just occurred to me that since the little shit had joined us in Gib I'd hardly spoken to him. When they came back, I'd set a trap for little Arnold to see just how quick he really was.

Evelyn returned with another large mug of hot black, and stood it on my side table.

'By the way,' she said, 'I know you don't like Jo.'

'It's not that I don't like her. I'm terrified of her!'

'Well', she continued, 'she can be relied upon if you're in a tight spot. She's a professional, and Marine Corps trained. I don't know about Henry, but Arnold is a psycho.

'I really like you a lot and I don't want anything to happen to you. I know that you don't believe me, but I wanted to stay with you more than anything,' she said.

And with that, she stripped off her t-shirt—which, I realised now, was all she'd been wearing—climbed into my bunk and, removing my towel, spent the next hour proving the point.

24

Our bodies were almost stuck together, making any lateral movement virtually impossible. We conceded the more conventional position and she climbed on top of me. I felt like I was about to be smothered, although this vertical activity was far less adhesive. If there were any medals on offer for stamina, Evelyn wasn't about to settle for the silver. She completely lost control, and her supreme moment came almost immediately. Gasping, she fell forward onto my chest. In a whisper she said, 'I'm sorry, but I needed that. It's been a while.'

I also needed something, possibly in the shape of artificial respiration. The heat in the cabin was almost unbearable, so we didn't linger. Evelyn went for a shower. I downed copious quantities of water, which was tepid and unrewarding, while relaxing in the saloon, where two cigarettes later I was still pondering the situation.

It had been a very welcome interlude since the departure of Susan while I was out of circulation in Gib. However, I discharged any thoughts that this radical activity had been deliberately organised from above, and I couldn't imagine that it was included within the current agenda.

I wondered just how devoted to the cause Evelyn really was, if in fact she was at all. I made up my mind I would ask some searching questions. But I would soften her up a little first.

Later, she put together a magnificent supper. We dined in the saloon in spite of the temperature, as there was rather too much to carry up to the slightly cooler wheel-house. Gammon steaks fried in butter and honey, with real potatoes tossed in more butter with freshly ground black pepper, alongside an extravagant salad of nuts, raisins, finely chopped avocadoes and slices of lime complemented by a French dressing. All this without any evidence of a tin or can to be seen anywhere.

Throughout the meal she was very attentive and seemingly unconcerned that I'd polished off a bottle and a half of Chateau LaTour Carnet and several large anonymous brandies from Henry's decanter. With any luck my whisky bottle would reappear at some stage.

I felt like bed again, but this time, alone. It was still baking hot below so I elected to sleep in the wheel-house with just a thin cotton sheet over me as a defence against mosquitoes and midge attacks. You would have thought with the amount of alcohol I had in my bloodstream they would have left me alone. They didn't. I wished them all a hangover.

Evelyn also settled for the wheel-house. Giving her the benefit of the doubt, I decided it was for the same reason as myself and not simply to keep a watchful eye on me and avoid allowing me too much liberty.

The morning was a little cooler, but it wouldn't last. At my request she prepared a huge standard fried breakfast. During its production I had time to give Henry's unlocked cabin the once over. A quick shufty revealed a number of press cuttings from the *Los Angeles Times* relating to Leroy Eldridge Cleaver. The articles stated that he was a Black Panther leader and an advocate of violence to win power for the American black population. I also found some banking details of transfers of quite large sums of money from the Chase Manhattan Bank to Galliani's in Gib, including one from a date two months previously, and some headed notepaper for a film company based in London. It had a phone number but no names on it.

My forage produced little else except the absence of the Arriflex camera that normally lived, boxed, beside the door.

'They must be filming somewhere,' I said, as we sat down to eat.

'What makes you think that?' she asked casually.

'He's taken the cine-camera with him. It's not in his cabin.'

Her mood changed.

'For Christ's sake, don't ever let anyone know that you've been snooping,' she replied—quietly, but very emphatically.

'Don't worry, I won't. Give me a little credit, please. It would reflect badly on you, and I certainly wouldn't risk doing that.'

'Yes, it sure would,' she confirmed.

I changed the subject, but with every intention of returning to it later.

When we'd finished eating, I strolled out on deck for a cigarette, as Evelyn hated the smell of them. I suggested that we leave right away and complete the day's shopping sortie before it stoked it up again.

No other vessels seemed to have arrived or departed during the night. *Heidi*, the other yacht alleged to be part of the operation, hadn't moved and still showed no visible signs of life. Some small fishing boats were being unloaded and boxes of fish were being loaded into little three-wheeler vans on the quayside. The scene appeared quite normal and totally tranquil.

We took a leisurely stroll into the same market as the day before. Amongst the usual things Evelyn bought a large bag of lemons. I queried the need for these, thinking of the extra burden, and was told that the intention was to produce some healthy lemonade.

'Just like my mother used to make,' she added, smiling.

The walk back was without incident.

Once back on board I set about rehanging our sunshield. Sarcastically, Evelyn suggested that I might rig it this time on the starboard side where it might work properly.

'You stick to your mum's lemonade. I'll fix the bloody awning,' I retaliated.

Twenty minutes later, just after I'd finished the task, the promised lemonade arrived, with a glass jug and glasses all laid out on a tray. Evelyn was now sporting a loose-fitting t-shirt. As she bent down to set the tray on the raised saloon skylight, I could see that that was all she was wearing.

'Don't you ever wear any knickers?' I asked.

'Only if I'm wearing jeans,' she replied.

'What's so special about Jean's knickers?' I whispered.

'Don't be an arse. You know what I mean.'

'What surprises me,' I continued, 'is that when your bum is hidden in trousers, you wear knickers and cover it up. But when it's in full view you don't.'

'I wear them under trousers, as you call them, because the seam in the middle is a bit rough and uncomfortable. In any case, they're unhealthy—just a modesty gimmick invented by the Quakers.'

'Well, sweetie, your lack of them is very unhealthy for me. Whenever you bend down, my blood pressure goes up.'

Laughingly, she asked, 'Is it up now? Because I can cure that.'

'It may be, but forget it. Come and sit down here under my very fine shelter, and tell me honestly all you know about this film company.'

'After your snooping this morning, you probably know more than I do. Henry's very strict about the need-to-know level.'

The fact that she'd used the words 'need to know', which is an expression commonly used in military and security circles, gave me the impression that she probably knew rather more than she intended to reveal to me. However, I pressed on.

'Tell me, who are you really working for, and who's financing it? Because it must be costing a bomb.'

'Martin, I truly don't know. And what's more, I don't want to.'

I didn't believe her, and guessed it was the CIA I was involved with, but I decided not to labour the point.

'Well, my love, just tell me how a girl like you became involved in this film company.'

'I answered an advertisement in a magazine offering adventure and travel. As I'd just split up with my husband, I jumped at the idea. Now that's all I'm going to say, so please don't question me any more.'

'One final question, then I'll shut up, I promise. Do you like what you're doing? And if not, why don't you quit?'

'I don't know,' she replied. 'Now please leave it.'

I could see that I was on a loser so I did shut up.

'Just promise me one thing,' I persisted. 'If you want out at any time, just tell me.'

She didn't reply.

It started to get hot again. The sky was cloudless and there wasn't a breath of wind.

'Look,' I said, 'if they're not coming back for another three days, why don't we take the boat out a little way and anchor off? It'll be cooler. There'll be a day breeze, and we can swim in clean water. We can be seen from the road and Henry or Pratt can call out to us when they arrive back to come in.'

'He'd go raving mad. You know how he likes to arrange things to absolute precision,' she said.

'From what I've seen up till now, my love, Henry couldn't arrange lunch,' I gibed, and continued, 'All right, an alternative. You've quite obviously met the crowd on the *Heidi* and, as much as I dislike gin palaces, it most likely has air-conditioning. So let's go over to them.'

'Two reasons why not,' she replied. 'First, we're supposed to be unconnected in any way, and second, they're also ashore somewhere and there's nobody on board.'

'Okay, you win. I'd love a whisky, please. Where is it?'

'You couldn't have searched for it very hard. It's been in your cabin all the time. No, don't get up, I'll get it for you. You'd better avert your eyes though, in case you catch another glimpse of my fanny.'

At about 5 p.m. I decided to take a shower, and asked Evelyn if she wanted it first. 'No, you go ahead,' she said. 'I'll take one later.'

I'd only been under it for a minute when Evelyn joined me. The atmosphere was steamy, the hot water running down our faces and embracing bodies. I kissed her.

The whining noise from the shower pump drowned out any other sounds, but the yacht gave a slight wobble.

'Christ! They're back!' she exclaimed.

She took off down the alleyway to her cabin, leaving a trail of wet footprints as she went. I stayed under the shower for a few more minutes, then, wrapping a towel round me, ascended to the wheel-house and tried to look suitably surprised to see them.

Henry was the first to speak.

'You look pretty fit. Our Evelyn must have been taking care of you.'

I didn't answer. He continued, 'Where is she, by the way?'

'Probably in her cabin,' I replied.

'Well,' he went on, 'When you're all together we must have a conference. There's been a complete change of plan, a totally new development.'

'Well,' I said, 'it won't affect me very much. I don't know what the plan was in the first place.'

Evelyn now appeared in a t-shirt and jeans. She got in first.

'Oh, it's good to see you're back. This thing's like a sweat-box. Are we leaving soon?'

'Arnie and I are leaving tomorrow,' said Henry. 'We've been recalled.'

25

He went on.

'The girls are returning via Gib on the *Heidi*. Evelyn, if she wants to, can stay with you.'

'What, here?' I exclaimed.

'No, of course not. This vessel has to be got rid of.'

'How?' I demanded.

'If you let me finish, I'll tell you. I'm sure that you and she can take it somewhere and dispose of it. After all, you're supposed to be the expert.'

'You don't want me to blow it up, do you?'

'We'll discuss it in a minute.'

Meanwhile, he turned to the others. 'You get your belongings together. Make sure you take everything. I want no personal effects left anywhere in this vessel.'

They all trotted off below. I smiled, as I could imagine Arnie struggling with his handy-sized tin box.

'Right, Martin. You and I are going ashore for . . . ' He hesitated and looked at his watch, 'about an hour.'

We headed for a small Spanish bar. He knew where it was and had obviously used it before. As we walked in, there were three others at the bar, which was L-shaped.

'You sit there,' he said, pointing to a small table with four chairs in the corner facing the door, and asked me what I'd like to drink.

'I'll have a beer,' I replied.

A few moments later he joined me at the table with two beers and sat on the chair that gave him a clear vision of the door.

'Who's meeting us,' I asked.

'Somebody you haven't seen,' he replied, and continued, 'Regarding the boat, you're supposed to sink it somewhere.'

I interrupted. 'I'm not going to do that.'

'If you'll just shut up for a minute, I'll explain,' he said with a little irritation creeping in.

I kept quiet. He continued.

'The company that we're working for have now decided to abort the whole operation, and they want us to leave no traces behind. They want the vessel sunk, but—and this is up to you—all the papers and documentation for it are on board. If you can find somewhere to dispose of it, it's up to you.'

'You mean sell it?' I asked.

'It means whatever you think it means. I suggest that if you can dispose of it, and there is any money forthcoming as a result, you send half of it to me and keep the rest.'

He paused to await my reaction.

'And that's supposed to be my wages, is it?'

'No, it's a bonus. When the man we are waiting for arrives, I'll pay you some money. I'll also pay Evelyn some when we get back on the ship, so that she can fly back after you've moved the boat from here.'

'I don't care where you go—Spain, France. But do not go back to Gibraltar. Once you leave here and arrive somewhere else you let Evelyn go. I do not want her to know your intentions regarding the boat. Is that clear?'

'As clear as mud,' I replied. 'We're waiting for the banker, aren't we?'

'Something like that,' he replied, looking at his watch for about the umpteenth time.

Moments later, two men walked in. They were not acknowledged by the three already in there, and it was obvious they were strangers to the barman.

Henry went up to the bar and got another two beers. As he sat them down on the table, he said, very quietly, 'Drink a little of that, and then ask the barman where the lavatory is. I already know it's outside. You go out there and head straight for the boat. I'll join you. Don't ask questions, just do it.'

I did as he instructed and swiftly headed back. He arrived a few moments after me.

'What the hell was all that about?' I asked.

I'd better explain that at that period I had a very long beard and hair to match. Otherwise his remark won't seem to be relevant. He replied, 'If we hadn't left when we did, I can see the headline on tomorrow's *Herald Tribune*. It would have said, "Respectable American Businessman and Decaying Hippie Found Stabbed".'

I've no idea who leaked that quote, but for some time afterwards I became known in the yachty circles in the Med as 'the Decaying Hippie'.

While we'd been ashore, the others had packed all their gear and stowed it on the *Heidi*. Henry told them to join it. Evelyn stayed with me.

There were some brief goodbyes, and they were gone.

Henry handed me a bundle of money and said, 'I'm sure you'll be happy with that.'

At the same time he opened a drawer below the top of the chart table, revealing a brown envelope. He tapped it with his forefinger, knowingly, while looking at me, and then closed it. Obviously the ship's papers. He handed an envelope to Evelyn, and told her to be in touch as soon as she was home.

'Right, Martin, start her up. I'll cast off for you. You'd better leave now.'

'Don't worry, we're going,' I replied.

The *Heidi* was already swinging from her berth as Henry joined her. She slid out past us and was gone.

We were already facing the right way to depart, which was rather fortunate, because our speed of 12 knots made us a sitting target.

Just as we were getting clear of the entrance the shots rang out.

'Down!' I shouted to Evelyn.

There was no need to. She already was. I joined her flat on the deck.

One of the windows on the starboard side of the wheel-house copped it. As yet, I didn't know where the others had scored.

We were almost clear and running in the right direction, so we stayed where we were for a few minutes longer. When it was safe to stand up, I put her on a north-easterly course and gave the wheel to Evelyn, and went outside to inspect the damage. In the dark I couldn't see any.

'That was a very unfriendly send-off,' I commented. 'Do you feel all right?'

'I'm fine,' she replied. 'I'm just grateful to be out of that rotten place. Do you think they'll come after us?'

'I shouldn't think so for one minute.'

All the same I kept a strict lookout throughout the night and drank endless cups of coffee.

At first light, I did a damage check. Nothing to the hull, just very obvious bullet holes in the upper timberwork. Seven of them.

'Where are we going?' she asked.

'Alicante,' I said. 'I've a chum there who has a boatyard, and he can do what he likes with her. She'd make a very good houseboat, and with an almost-new engine, that's got to be worth a few bob.'

Bertie Mitchell wasn't even surprised when we slid into his yard. He knew that where I was concerned, boats, bullets and balls-ups were par for the course.

Evelyn stayed with me in Alicante for a week before leaving for the US. I've always liked Alicante and used the place as often as I could. And Bertie was a good friend—a Cornishman who sailed out there with his wife and kids years before and stayed on and set up his own boatyard business. There wasn't much Bertie didn't know about boats.

Slightly up the hill and out of the town there was a restaurant that all the yachties used, but I'm damned if I can remember its name. It really was a scruffy place but the food was excellent.

Evelyn and I ate there each night before she went back. The place amused her. I don't think she'd seen anything like it before. The owner was a great fat man, always laughing. I've seen him physically kick the waiter in the bum in front of all the customers because he wasn't serving quickly enough. You never received a bill. He used to write how much you'd spent and the addition on the corner of a not-so-very-posh paper tablecloth, tear it off, and hand it to you.

I was truly sorry to see Evelyn go. We promised to keep in touch but we never did.

Bertie patched up the holes in *Neptune*, and I advertised for an amateur crew to sail her back to the UK. I simply stuck a handwritten notice on a tree opposite the American Express office, and took the first five that came along.

When we reached Le Havre in Northern France, we hit one of the worst winter gales. Most of the crew left. Just one girl stayed on, and she became my Polish girlfriend. This was Ewa.

The weather continued to blow hard so I put the vessel in the *Bassin du Commerce*. She was now locked in where the water level remains constant and there's no need to alter the mooring ropes, so she could be left.

Ewa and I went to spend Christmas and the New Year with Molly, after which we went to Wales, where a film director chum of mine was going through a divorce and needed someone to run his farm for two or three months.

During this time I discovered that all the weaponry from the previous enterprise that had been left on board had since been discovered by the French police. There was now a warrant out for my arrest, so I had to be extra careful when coming in and out of England. It didn't stop me travelling though.

Ewa and I stayed on the farm for the three months and when she decided to return to Paris, I thought it would be a good time for me to visit some old chums in Costacabana.

This time, my Spanish holiday would have to be a little longer—at least seven years, that being the prescribed legal interval to be absent from the UK jurisdiction under the Statute of Limitations. I'd now have to stay abroad until the big computer in the sky became amnesic.

This situation shouldn't be too difficult to handle—quite the reverse. After all, I knew Almeria pretty well and had many good friends there. Up till now though, my sorties had been relatively transient, only requiring me to travel light. But the packing this time would demand rather more than three pairs of underpants, three shirts, two pairs of jeans and a bundle of non-odd socks. After all, this was to be a working holiday, and the need to dress for some occasions was on the cards.

A Brighton company had been good enough (or was it mad enough?) to employ me to flog villas in Almeria to naïve Brits, and to manage holiday villas. I did, as far as they were concerned, have the necessary qualifications, having in the past sold holidays. They were unaware of my trade in guns, however. Selling houses wouldn't be a difficult problem. My command of the language was a trifle limited, but I'd soon pick it up as I had Italian previously—and I was sure that after two or three weeks I'd get beyond 'I'll have another beer, please.'

After much deliberation, I'd taken with me all that I could squeeze into and pile on top of the Ford Transit van. The Costacabana show house was to become my residence and office. Part of my cargo was a rather large glass-topped desk, a black leather armchair trimmed with chrome fittings—quite vulgar and not at all my taste, though very executive—a huge filing cabinet and an aged duplicating machine.

Having finished packing and stacking the van, it was now solid wall to wall. When I caught the ferry from Newhaven to Dieppe, nobody took the slightest interest in the seriously overloaded vehicle. And, even more pleasingly, immigration almost ignored me. I was on my way.

26

My proposed visit to Costacabana now would have to be my longest stay yet. I hoped there'd be a revival in Western films, and any other work that I could do, apart from flogging houses.

I avoided Paris and went south by Le Mans, Tours, Limoges, Toulouse, where I hotelled it for the night, then down to the coast at Narbonne. I didn't hurry— there was no need to, and I was hauling a heavy load for a Transit.

It became a little heavier just outside Figueiras, where I pulled up for food at a bar. While I was polishing off a *bocadillo*, I was approached by a young lady. She was French. She asked me if I was going south, and if I was, could I give her a lift? Naturally I couldn't refuse, and with a rucksack on the floor in the front of the passenger seat she climbed in and folded herself up. This was Marie-Claire.

I told her I was heading for Costacabana and with any luck we'd make it that evening. She looked about 20. Slim, longish dark hair. Not a ravishing beauty, but a lovely face that occasionally displayed an infectious smile.

By the time we reached Castellon, she looked as though she could do with a stretch, or something else, so we stopped for coffee and a break. We repeated the performance at Alicante. Time was getting on. It was obvious we weren't going to make Costacabana until after midnight or even later, and I was getting tired.

Just south of Murcia, she suggested we find somewhere to camp.

'No,' I said, 'we find a hotel. I don't camp. Besides, I'm hungry.'

We wound up at a small place called Aguilas, only about 90 miles short of Costacabana. No bloody hotels, and only two bars, where we had a rather unambitious paella each.

The beach was sandy, of course, so I removed just enough from the back of the van so I could almost flop out straight on the floor. Marie-Claire slept in a sleeping bag, without a tent, a few yards away.

I went out like a light, but woke in the morning with cramp and feeling like a question mark. I was quite surprised to see Marie-Claire sitting, drying off, in the black-and-chrome swivel job—and naked. She'd taken an early dip.

I reloaded while she now put on a light floral dress. She looked rather fabulous—very impressionist, and somehow fragile. I had a burning desire to kiss her, but resisted.

We were met by Vic as we pulled up at Costacabana. After introductions, looking at her, he asked me quietly, 'Where did you get this one from?'

I explained.

'Oh yes?' he said, totally disbelieving me.

It took over two hours to get everything into the villa and check the water supply and electrics. An inspection of the fridge revealed milk, butter, honey, bread and beer. Naturally this was down to Vic, who knew all about the essentials of living.

Marie-Claire asked me if she could stay for a few days. I told her I'd love her to.

Two months went by, after which Marie-Claire returned to Paris. There hadn't been any serious romantic involvement. In any case, Sue had now come on the scene.

I'd met Susan in Costacabana in the Bar Sussex. This was a bar run by an ex-pat from Newhaven, and it was where most people congregated around midday for the regular mail deliveries. I invited her for a drink and later suggested supper somewhere. We agreed to meet back in the bar at 7.30 p.m. I was there with Vic by 6.30 p.m. when she walked in.

'Ah,' I said, 'This is my date.'

'You're early,' I said, when she reached the bar counter.

'I'm not. I'm Joanne,' she replied.

'Don't piss about. You were Susan at lunchtime,' I said.

'She'll be in shortly. She's my twin.'

They were absolutely identical, and both gorgeous. They were in Costacabana trying to get a villa purchased by their mother finished off as a letting project. Sue and I got it together.

Joanne was married with two youngsters—John (18 months) and a new baby.

One hot evening, I was enjoying a cold beer in a bar in Almeria city called El Barril. The bar was run by a very well-respected English cameraman called Ginger Gemmell who had shot many major films, including *Treasure Island* and *Superman*. It had now become the main meeting place for the Almeria film crowd. As usual, it was quite busy and buzzing with anticipation of another Spaghetti Western coming in.

Another cameraman, called Alan, approached me with a problem. He had a British-registered Mercedes that had been in Spain over six months and was now illegal and about to be snatched. He asked me if I'd drive it back to his parents in Farmborough, UK. He would pay all my expenses and my return air fare and a bonus.

It just so happened that the twins also wanted to return to Somerset, so if I took a chance regarding entering the UK we could all travel together in the Merc. After a bit of debate, I decided I'd do it.

We left and I did the driving, but when we arrived at the coast I chose the Calais–Dover route. It was always busier on that route, and with more people about there was less likelihood of them rumbling me as I went in. Upon our arrival at Dover, we drove through immigration, whereupon the officer stuck his head in through the window and in a loud voice said, 'Passports!'

Joanne, who was sitting in the front of the car with the baby on her lap, put her fingers up to her mouth and replied, 'Shhh! I've just got her off to sleep.'

The officer, obviously a family man and a bit soft-hearted, said, 'I'm so sorry. Carry on. Join that short queue over there and you'll get clear sooner.'

We were in without any problem. I couldn't ring Molly in case her phone was on tinkerbell—in other words, being tapped. So Sue rang her as soon as we were clear of the docks. She said, 'I'm Susan, a friend of Martin's, and I've got a present for you. Can you meet me in Brighton?'

Molly said she would. When we pulled up at the appointed meeting place, I said, 'There she is.' Sue leaned out of the car and called, 'Molly!'

I was wearing a hat pulled right down over my face. She came over to the car, and Sue said, 'Get in, Molly. Your present is driving.'

Molly gasped.

We all sped off to Somerset, where I wasn't known. Molly stayed for a weekend and left for Peacehaven. I remained there for three more days, then decided to return to Spain.

Getting out of England might be a problem. I'd avoid Newhaven like the plague. I delivered the Merc, caught the train to Brighton, and intended to inflict myself on Liz and have her drive me to Southampton the following day.

You wouldn't believe my luck, or rather, near bad luck. It was dark and raining. I was walking through a quiet street in Brighton when a Panda police car pulled up alongside me and a voice called out my name.

It was a copper who'd once been a good family friend. Forget 'good' and 'friend'.

'We've got one out for you,' he announced, turning on his portable radio.

I know my surname is difficult to handle, but he'd known me for ten years. Nevertheless, he managed to spell it incorrectly. The computer always needed the first four letters in a name and date of birth, which he also got wrong.

The reply on his little radio came back.

'Nothing known.'

'Are you sure?' he queried.

'Nothing known,' was repeated.

'There's something wrong here. I know we've got one out for you,' he said, climbing back into the Panda and driving off.

I was only about five minutes' walk away from Liz's house, but I wouldn't go there now. I took a cab out to Hove, booked into a small hotel and phoned Liz.

'For Christ's sake, don't come round here!' she said. 'It's crawling with police!'

He'd obviously now got my name spelt correctly.

The following morning I took a train to Shoreham Harbour where I found a German freighter about to sail, having discharged a cargo of timber. I asked the skipper if he needed any crew.

'I need a chief officer,' he replied.

I told him, 'You've just got one.'

We sailed half an hour later for Antwerp, arriving two days later. I got off, took a train to Paris, but before taking the next one to Barcelona I sent three postcards—one to Molly, one to Susan, and a cheeky 'wish you were here'-type one to the Brighton police.

Upon my return to Costacabana, I discovered there had been a development. The Costacabana Sporting Club had now finally been completed. A grand title, but it was only a 60-metre swimming pool, two tennis courts and a bar, surrounded by a very high wall.

Nevertheless, the cost of memberships and the annual subscriptions were sky-high. This was by design to dissuade the local Spanish from joining. After all, the Costacabana Brits wanted it to be exclusively for themselves—and couldn't have the local Spanish natives joining. The old colonial attitude dies hard anywhere, but particularly in that area, amongst the ex-pats now retired from military and government service, living on fat pensions that go much further in Spain.

The big night was just a week away. Just three days before the grand opening, the pool was already filled with water, and the bar stocked with booze. The shock. Without a lifeguard present at the club on duty throughout the opening hours, a license to use the pool was being withheld. Now myself and another reprobate who, like the natives, were not being considered for membership as it was to be kept for the upper crust only, were possibly the only suitable candidates fit enough to fill the posts. The management were forced to lower their pride and offer us the jobs.

Peter Noon and I were now the lifeguards. The opening times were from 10 a.m. until midnight. He and I would share the hours.

It turned out to be a brilliant career move. It was early May. The weather was pleasant, there were plenty of free drinks on offer and, above all, we were being paid.

Things dramatically improved when June arrived along with the tourists and visitors. Anybody renting a villa through the agency in the UK was entitled to temporary membership. Droves of unattached girls started flying in looking for romantic holidays. The visitors were usually in Costacabana for 14-day stays, so there was a fresh crop every fortnight.

Peter and I started putting in tons of overtime, unpaid, of course. In fact, we were on duty all the time, and would have gladly done the job for free, surrounded by bevies of bikini-clad belles.

Vic said I was beginning to look worn out, and he thought I may be overdoing it. I assured him that life was wonderful and I was fine.

'Well, if you do have any problems, let me know.'

'What sort of problems?' I asked.

'You know what I mean,' he replied.

'I'm afraid I don't,' I insisted.

He continued, with a slightly embarrassed look on his face.

'Well, the job must be very demanding, and from what I've seen . . .' He paused. 'You look as though you're shagging yourself to death!'

'Fair comment,' I replied, 'And I don't, as you so delicately put it, have any problems.'

'Well if you do,' he insisted, 'Doctor Carno has some pills.'

'Vic, I don't need any pills, thank you very much.'

'All right, don't overheat. I'm just giving you some friendly advice.'

'I do not need advice, or pills, okay?'

'Well just remember, Carno has pills, and they really work. In fact, if you don't swallow them quickly, you get a stiff neck.'

We both had a good laugh, as he'd acted and worked very hard to get this little joke across. He was, by the way, over 80 at the time. I don't think he needed any medication either. He had an Australian girl with a young baby living with him. Rumours abounded that I had a half-brother, but Vic just laughed when I repeated the rumours to him and assured me that I was still an only child. The young lady was merely sharing his house.

Early the following April, I decided to go and pick up the *Neptune* from Le Havre and bring her across to Gosport where I'd made arrangements to sell her through Camper & Nicholson.

I had one foot on the ferry gangway and one still on the quay when a stranger asked me if I was Martin Bengtsson. I was then arrested and charged with gun-running. As my last address was Govilon in South Wales, I was carted off to Cardiff prison.

I paid my own bail of £20,000 and led a quiet life until my trial came up six months later. During this time I was offered my freedom by some government organisation, if I agreed to work for them. My legal team had suggested that I plead guilty and take a year or 18 months, because if I pleaded not guilty I was going to be found guilty anyway and I'd risk six or seven years. They didn't know I'd done a deal, of course.

I pleaded not guilty, was found guilty, and to the surprise of my barrister and everyone else, received only a suspended sentence.

When the verdict was announced in court, Molly and Vic were in the public gallery and Vic was heard to murmur in a stage whisper, 'Christ, they're going to hang him!'

27

Having wangled my release, I rather expected to be called upon to do something in return fairly soon. But I heard nothing.

I took a job as a tug master in Brighton marina and life settled into an easy pace. One day I went into a health food shop to buy a sandwich. A stunning blonde was sitting behind the counter. I couldn't help myself.

'What's a girl like you doing in a nice place like this?' I quipped.

I was rewarded with a wry smile. That wasn't enough, so I continued.

'I'm going yachting around the Med for a while. Fancy coming with me?'

'Yeah, why not?' she smiled. Her name was Caroline and she was the most stunning girl I had seen. She was a good 20 years younger than I was, but although I was in my forties, I was fit and very active.

She quit her job the very next day and we spent the next few years bringing boats between the UK and Spain.

The only strange occurrence was on one occasion when we were about to board the ferry to Bilbao at Plymouth.

We were politely asked by immigration to step out of our car and accompany two officers to an interview. Questions regarding our proposed destination and our intended duration of absence were asked by one of them, while the other worked quite frantically at a computer terminal.

After ten minutes or so we were allowed to leave. Our car, in the meantime, had been holding up a queue that was waiting to board. Throughout the two-nights-and-one-day crossing to Bilbao, we received a number of quizzical looks from fellow passengers.

A writer-journalist whom I'd met some years before happened to be in the car immediately behind us. He met me at the bar later and said that it was very unusual to take such an interest in departing people. Had I got a bit of a history that he might be interested in?

I didn't go into any details and the matter was forgotten.

Some time afterwards, upon our return to England when I was back working on the Brighton marina project, an approach was made. This was about three years after I'd received the suspended sentence, so they obviously weren't in a hurry.

I was met on the quay when I came in one evening with the tug by a man in plain clothes, who introduced himself as *Peter McAndrews*. I assumed this wasn't his real name. He asked me how long I intended to stay in England. I told him I really had no idea, but probably at least until the marina contract was completed.

He pointed out that I still owed my freedom to them in London, whoever 'them' was. He said that he'd be in touch.

You may remember that a TV celebrity called John Cleese invented a sketch called the Ministry of Funny Walks. Well, as a result of this visit by Mr *McAndrews*, I now invented a ministry. I called it the Ministry of Nasty Habits. MONH. Because whatever they did appeared to be slightly dodgy somehow.

When my contract with the marina finished, I had a complete change of employment. Through a highly respectable security company I took on the lucrative pursuit of bodyguarding.

My first assignment was to hold the hand of a wealthy individual. Not literally, thank God (I will explain why in a moment). This chap had his Bentley stolen, which was later found by the Brighton police, burnt out, at a well-known beauty spot a few miles away called Devil's Dyke, and he was now receiving threatening phonecalls.

His residence, a large Regency house in a fashionable seafront area of Brighton, was occupied by himself and three other men—all as queer as nine-bob notes.

I had drawn the short straw and had to do the night shift. At about 11 p.m. one of them made up a bed for me just inside the firmly secured front door. It was comfortable enough, but it was actually covered with a gold lamé counterpane. When he'd finished, he said,

'I hope you'll be all right, and I do think you're brave, sleeping just inside the door.'

My reply made him go into hoots of laughter.

'Having met you and some of your chums, I'd feel safer the other side of the door.'

This operation lasted a month, throughout which time there was no sign of any more threats, and as yet no more contact from the MONH.

The second job was to be protector to a couple, married with three children. Again, this had originated from threatening phonecalls. Strangely, these calls came through whenever hubby was out. I became a little suspicious of him, and vaguely steered the conversation around to the absence of calls when he was at home.

A few evenings later, we were all sitting by the fire making light conversation. I noticed that he looked at his wristwatch on several occasions. Bang on 11 p.m. the phone rang. I jumped up to answer it, as I was supposed to intercept all calls before passing them on.

'No, no,' he said. 'I'll get it.'

I let him.

The brief conversation that followed went like this.

'Who are you . . . ? Why don't you leave us alone . . . ? Go away, go away!'

He slammed the phone down.

His replies were so quick and came with so little time between them that whoever was on the other end could scarcely have had time to say anything, let alone make threats. I didn't challenge him, but I lied to him and said that the calls since I had been on the job, including that one, were being monitored by the Brighton police.

His face paled.

There were no more calls, and after another ten days my services were terminated.

Still no sign of the Ministry.

My third contract was much more exciting. It was to be a personal bodyguard to a Saudi prince and his family. He was Prince Bandar bin Sultan, the Saudi ambassador to the US, and my contract was to run throughout his two-month predicted stay in London.

The reason I was given for his prolonged visit was that he was suffering from a back problem, and would be receiving treatment in a celebrated clinic in Harley Street. I found him very affable and easy to get along with.

This time I preferred to do the night shift, the hours being slightly unsociable, but I was rewarded by enjoying the social activities that went on.

I finished one morning, having just polished off £60 worth of breakfast, consisting of half a tin of caviar on toast, the cost of a tin at this time being £120 from Fortnum's. Once the tin had been opened, or anything else for that matter in the food or drinks line, it was never retained in the freezers or the fridges. It had to be dumped. Everything had to be ultra-fresh for the family and guests. So I received quite a lot of perks from the Spanish butler. My beluga brekkies were not unusual.

I'd left the house and was now walking towards Victoria train station where I would take the fast non-stop back to Brighton. I'd only gone about 500 yards when a red Volvo saloon pulled in beside me. The rear window was lowered and a voice said, 'Get in. We want to talk to you.' It was *McAndrews.*

'I've a train to catch,' I protested.

'You'll catch it. Don't worry,' he replied.

I got in. After a short, polite dialogue, he continued.

'The job that you are doing is of interest to us, and we need you to do something quite simple.'

'And that is what?' I asked.

'You'll be given some small pieces of equipment which you will place in certain areas of the house and the clinic in Harley Street.'

'They're bugs, are they?' I said.

'That's what some people call them.'

'Am I supposed to ask what it's for?' I suggested.

'No,' he replied. 'Just do it.'

'When do I get these bugs?' I asked.

'When you arrive this evening at Victoria, you will go into the bar of the Grosvenor hotel. Someone will introduce himself to you and show you how to place them and switch them on. It's quite simple. You'll see.'

They dropped me outside the station.

It preyed on my mind all day. Should I consult my boss in the company, or would that be quite the wrong thing to do? After all, our company was entirely a commercial enterprise. They had nothing to do with official authorities anywhere, as far as I knew. I could only imagine that under certain circumstances, such as when minding a diplomatic person or clients, the company was obliged to submit names of their operatives engaged on such a contract to MI5 or

Special Branch for high-level clearance. And then my name had fallen out of the computer. To them, it was pennies from heaven.

I'd play it by ear for the moment. Perhaps tonight's connection would be more forthcoming.

It wasn't. I don't think my contact knew why either. Only how.

He gave me three items. They all looked the same. Very small black plastic boxes, slightly smaller than the size of two sugar cubes put together. Each had a small flexible tail protruding from one end. They looked like little black mice. The tail was about an inch and a half long.

At the other end there was a small piece that lifted up and underneath, a space to accommodate a hearing aid-type battery. He gave me six batteries, and told me not to put them in until just before using them, as they ran down very quickly.

I was to place one in the Prince's private apartment as close to the table as possible. Another was to go in the handset of the phone. By unscrewing the round earpiece and tipping the small speaker out, there would be room enough to slip the bug in, put the speaker back, and screw it up again. These were my instructions.

'And, oh yes,' he said, 'do it on Tuesday evening.'

It was now Friday.

On Saturday I didn't go straight home, but met up by arrangement with a journalist chum of mine. I won't mention his name again, but it's already somewhere close to the beginning of the book. He was the most respected investigative journalist in Fleet

Street, working for a national Sunday paper. He knew more about this sort of equipment than most.

Briefly, I showed him one of the bugs and asked him how it worked, how good they were and a number of other questions.

'They're a bit crude,' he said. 'They only work over a distance of about 300 yards, and only then if the conditions are favourable. That battery will last only about four days maximum, because they're live all the time. It must be something very specific our friends want to listen to over the next 80 hours or so.'

I told him I had three more replacement batteries, to which he replied, 'That still only gives them a week. You can get these sorts of things now that can fit into a gift pen or a pocket calculator, that only uses the battery when it's turned on at a board meeting or something like that. Much more sophisticated,' he continued. 'Anyway, let me know how you get on there. Maybe there's something we should all know about.

'By the way, what they've asked you to do is a criminal offence—so be careful what you get into. And wipe your fingerprints off them.

'If this was an official job, the phone would be on tinkerbell.'

The house where all this was taking place was in Eaton Square. There were two telephone lines into the house—one for the Prince, the other for the staff. I put one bug in the staff phone, so that all that could have been transmitted were orders for food, conversations in Spanish from the butler and calls made by non-English-speaking members of the galley staff.

The other two bugs remained in our flat in Brighton, batteryless. The Brits wanted to know who Bandar was talking to. They were bound to be disappointed. The only slightly exciting visit was when, a week later, the Prince received several visits from a US general—a General Smith. (Yes, his name genuinely was just Smith.) He was also due to have his back fixed at the clinic of Doctor Ind.

I took no further part in this action, but did note that a van sign-written as a carpet contractor's was parked about 200 yards along Eaton Square for the whole week. And I'm sure that this was the listening-in department.

28

I travelled to and from Costacabana over about eight years. Another little incident from there was when Letitia and my youngest son, Nicholas, came down to have a holiday with me.

'What's got four big feet and isn't at home?' came the voice from below ground.

'Probably a wolf,' I replied.

'Pull me up,' repeated the now slightly more emphatic demand from Nick, whom I'd just lowered down the air vent of an abandoned garnet mine.

'Can you see anything sparkling?' I asked, ignoring his request.

'No, I've got my eyes closed. Now pull me up!'

When he reached the surface, he produced from his pocket a small piece of grey rock. In it were five small reddish-coloured stones. Garnets—or as they're known in Spain, *granates*. Nick and I were in the old mining complex that hadn't been worked for decades.

On a number of occasions I'd heard stories about the old garnet mine at Nijar, and today we'd found it. Better equipped with flashlights two days later, we uncovered a seam of garnets. There were dozens of them.

The problem was how we could polish or cut them. Somewhere back in England, at Molly's house, I had a professional stone-tumbler. This machine was a rotating little drum. After about a week of revolving in it, it would have produced perfect cabochons. But the chances of Molly finding it or getting it out to me were remote. You also needed three types of grinding powder—rough, medium and finally fine.

'What about the valve-grinding paste, and we tumble them in the hub-caps of the car?' Nick suggested.

We tried it. It would have taken forever. In any case, it was embarrassing being told stopping in traffic or at garages for petrol that our wheel-nuts had come loose, as the clattering noise was clearly audible. It would have to become another back-burner job.

I knew there were stone-collecting shops selling specimens of all types of minerals from all over the world in Amsterdam. We'd definitely sell the garnets there.

We sent samples to a friend of mine in Holland. The reply came back that they would sell very well, but the collectors wanted the stones in small pieces of the original rock or, as they termed it, 'in the matrix'. This is where Messrs Black & Decker came into their own.

We drilled holes in small lumps of grey rock from the mine and stuck the stones in with the ever-faithful Araldite. Before it set hard we sprinkled the drilling dust around the stones. The fit was perfect. We ran a production line. All that was needed then was five minutes with a wire brush.

At the time I was driving a Mini Cooper. All the way to Amsterdam it was almost dragging its arse on the road with the weight of rock that we had in the back. We sold all the specimens. I still have a jamjar full of loose bloody garnets.

Caroline and I were together for 12 years before we decided to get married. After our wedding we sailed a yacht to Gibraltar, where we lived on it for a while, and then moved it up to Spain and lived on it there for a while. But we were now back in Costacabana in a villa.

Caroline wished to see the garnet mine. And while I'm on the subject of jewels, I must recount some little gems about Max, who was still living in Costacbana. I mentioned to him that we were planning to visit the mine the coming Sunday. He said he'd like to come as well, so we arranged to go on the trip.

At 9.30 a.m. he pulled up outside ready to go. Now when Max did things, he did them thoroughly, with aplomb. I caught sight of him as he climbed out of his car and warned Caroline not to laugh. He was dressed in heavy desert boots, a khaki jacket festooned with pockets, a knotted handkerchief round his neck, and to top it all (literally), a huge wide-brimmed hat, which only lacked dangling corks.

His rig could have made him an ideal double for Ned Kelly or an early gold-rush forty-niner. Caroline and I were going in jeans and t-shirts.

His first words were, 'We'll go in my car. I've got all the equipment in the boot.'

I wondered just what type of equipment, but didn't ask. I did hope that not too many Costacabana-ites would see us depart. He was quite restricted in his movements in the car, because the wide-brimmed hat remained firmly on his head.

As soon as we arrived at the mine, Max collected bundles of sticks and lit a fire. I wasn't sure of the reason for such pyrotechnics, as the temperature was about 90 degrees, and I could only imagine that it was to keep wild animals away. If this was the rationale, it worked well, as we never saw a single lion, tiger or rabbit throughout the whole day.

The boot of his car contained pickaxes and shovels of various shapes. All that was really needed was a flashlight, a penknife and small hammer. I wouldn't have risked swinging a pickaxe in any of the tunnels. They hadn't been propped or supported for decades, and the roof could have collapsed.

The hamper his wife had put together was something else. She, being French, wasn't lacking in the culinary department. Pâtés, cold meats, salads, fruit, wine (both red and chilled white), correct glasses and napkins with rings—in fact, the works. It was unlikely that Fortnam's could have done better.

During our search, Max did find two rather nice specimens, about the size of a thumbnail. The way he reacted, they might have been either the Koh-i-Noor or the Star of India but the main thing was he was happy and he'd kept us very amused.

About a month later I told him that Caroline and I were taking the yacht to Gib and back.

'Can I come with you? I've never been to Gib,' he pleaded.

'Course you can,' I replied, not thinking.

We were lying in Almeria marina when he joined us. His rig was somewhat startling—jeans and a denim jacket, so new you could have broken them like glass, very expensive and brand-new deck shoes, and also a new pair of binoculars hanging round his neck.

But it was always the lid that created most surprise. A brand new cheese-cutter cap on which there was more gold braid than had graced Nelson at Trafalgar. I'd seen less scrambled egg cover three large slices of toast.

Caroline and I were wearing jeans and t-shirts as usual. We only had a 36-footer—not the Royal Yacht. Unless a favourable wind could be persuaded to treat this headgear as a Frisbee, Gibraltar was going to be in for a big surprise.

We had seen most of southern Spain by road, but only briefly from the air when flying in. I suggested to Caroline one weekend that we hire a light aircraft from the local flying club and fly out over Cabo de Gata, Mojacar and the Sierras.

She said yes, but on one condition—that I keep quiet about it to Max. She went on, 'Otherwise he'll turn up in a leather flying jacket and helmet, a long white silk scarf and goggles!'

I didn't breathe a word.

Credo dieu me pardonnera
(I believe God will pardon me)

- Martin Bengtsson

29

Grandma Bengtsson joined the Previous Millions Club in 1971, at the age of 106 years. Great-aunt Elida had qualified for membership three years previously at 91. Apart from a light dusting, her room remained undisturbed. Lovely Cordelia died in 1970, and her room received the same reverence.

On her writing-desk stood a small oval gilt frame, containing a faded sepia photograph of a fair-haired young man. He'd been killed in action in 1916. Upon whose side he'd fought I'd no idea. It was never discussed.

At this time Vic was abroad somewhere as usual, so Grandma's sister Mia, who lived with her, was now alone. This was to be the demise of my inheritance. By rights the property and all it contained should have been bequeathed to me, as I was the last in the line.

Later the same year my other great-aunt, Louise, came over from Australia with the intention of persuading Mia to return with her to Queensland. I was duly dispatched to meet this frail 95-year-old from the liner *Fairsky* when it docked at Southampton. I gained special permission to pass through immigration in order to meet her at the foot of the gangway. A needless task—she recognised me when only halfway down the gangway (presumably from a recent photo, having seen me only once before when I was about eighteen months old).

'Hi! You must be Mart!' she exclaimed, slapping me on the back with almost enough force to knock me in the dock. For 'frail 95-year-old' substitute 'formidable old bird'.

Once ensconced in Peacehaven she set about organising Mia. Amongst her propaganda was a plethora of coloured photos of family, super houses, her and her late husband's sheep farm where she now resided with a large staff in attendance, and even more super houses. All these selected photos were, of course, taken under cloudless skies in brilliant sunshine. Mia needed little convincing. She immediately decided to go south, travelling light.

This precipitated the grand give-away. As soon as the rumour of the grand divi leaked out, her church-going chums (she was a devout C of E) turned up in droves, and over the following two days they staggered out of the house struggling with all they could manage. Most of the congregation turned up.

The Dresden china and figurines went very quickly. One couple left with two Georgian extending brass standard lamps. I presumed they were going to label them 'his' and 'hers'. One of the clergy departed with a cello under one arm and a French musical bracket clock, appropriately decorated with silver cherubs, under his other arm. This wouldn't have improved the action of the escapement, but nevertheless must have inspired an extra couple of thanksgiving prayers.

It's said, I believe, that God helps those who help themselves. God help those caught helping themselves is also said, but it doesn't matter.

The pair of Louis Quinze wing chairs sailed off indecorously on the roof-rack, along with other items. I was actually repairing a gutter pipe over the gazebo when one pair of vultures arrived in two separate cars, one a shooting brake. They didn't notice me above, and the hen muttered impatiently, 'Do hurry up, there'll be nothing left by the time we get in there.'

I coughed and smiled. They looked up at me—but didn't even appear to be embarrassed or pass the time of day.

Grandma had been a Lutheran, and my having been raised as a Catholic might have gone some way to my disqualification. I would have dearly loved to have had Elida's photographic equipment, and a collection of photographic history taken throughout three-quarters of a century. But all of it vanished like the dinosaurs, including a tripod and easel that probably wound up as coat racks.

I didn't witness the flight of the Broadwood. I couldn't imagine there would be either space or any desperate need for a full-size grand piano in any of the suburban breeding-boxes in Peacehaven. But as it wasn't nailed down, it too disappeared along with more manageable nostalgic possessions. Even the porcelain door-handles and brass finger-plates were removed, but nobody managed to take the bathroom wallpaper or either of the lavatory seats. I did manage to rescue ten paintings. There were not many art lovers among Peacehaven's blessed multitude.

By the second evening, the whole place had been sacked and the locusts had moved on. Mia went to Australia but couldn't stand the Queensland heat. She returned to Peacehaven and died two months later in an old people's home. Her funeral was almost unattended. And, even after such a short absence from the flock, her favourite vicar managed to forget her name during the planting.

With the home now gone, Vic was easily persuaded by some friendly land developers to retire to Spain. They offered him a tiny villa on the beach at Costacabana in return for handing over the deeds of the property and his 25 acres. He could keep the villa until he died. There was also the understanding that if the land were to become available for development he would receive half its value.

He was now 80, needed some warmth and spoke Cuban Spanish, so I didn't discourage him. But I didn't know about the deal.

The land did receive planning permission—17 years and one month later. Strangely, this was a fortnight after Vic had died. Twenty-seven large houses were built there during the following six months.

Nobody would blame you if at this juncture you could detect a slight hint of bitterness creeping in. I could have contested the situation and sought legal redress, but I was advised that although these developers had pulled this stroke on other elderly people in the past, which was fully documented, I would be throwing good money after bad.

I decided instead to trace these crooks, who had become somewhat elusive. California was suggested at one stage. I would make them an offer they couldn't refuse, like they give me half the value of the property, and in return they don't wind up as a statistic or as a stencil pattern for a chalk line on the floor.

I called in a favour from a detective agency who owed me. These crooks were brothers with unusual surnames, so it was well within the scope of the agency to trace them. These bastards robbed everybody and stuck to it.

It took only three weeks for the agency to come up with very precise addresses for each of them. But there was also some bad news as well. They were in two plots in a cemetery near Pasadena. The Prince of Darkness had got at them first.

The saddest part of the revelation was that both the expiries were due to natural causes.

Which reminds me. When I join the departed, I don't want any formal burial. Just a Viking send-off—a quick singe on top of a pile of used motor tyres—and let the wind sprinkle me where my pets are buried.

And please—no spectators. I'd hate to invite the risk of a Mexican wave.

30

By and large, my life has been underscored by if onlys and might have beens. I didn't actually programme the way it turned out, although my genes must have been hard-wired to adventure—and to a lesser degree, lawlessness.

Other factors must have played a small part, but I'm sure the main attribution could be not so much to the women in my life, but to the life in my women.

If only Ms *Jones* hadn't stolen my virginity (mind you, I'm not complaining) I might have stuck to the piano and, as Molly would have wished, had a career in music. If only Eve hadn't provided my release from the bank, I might have remained in that frightful institution and gone slowly potty. If Colombe hadn't died in that dreadful tragedy, I would almost certainly have become wealthy, overweight, and spent the rest of my life in Italy. If Liz hadn't kicked me out of Student Travel, anything might have happened. If only Evelyn, Ewa, Christine, Jackie, Susan by two, my wives and wifelets . . .

I could go on, but I won't. I should thank each of them for their contributions.

Now in my dotage and alone—with absolutely no desire to travel, sail boats or flog guns to anyone—I can now sit back and quietly paint. But I would hate to imagine that my womanising days—and nights—are over. After all, you wouldn't consider taking a vintage car to the dump if it was still performing well, and had recently passed its NCT.

If I do chat up ladies these days, though, I restrict it to 30 seconds or less. Otherwise there's a risk that the call could be traced.

Since my early dabblings with the brush into the methods of old master painters, and the subsequent success of my own efforts, it's been at the back of my mind that I could always forge a living out of art, no matter where my anchor finds its final resting place.

During the past 30 years I've slapped paint on canvas in some quite unusual places. I've kept a sketch-pad at sea, on film sets, and even on spying missions. I don't know why more spies don't include amongst their equipment an easel, a canvas and brushes. They would draw less attention than the semi-covert camera.

While sailing my own vessel or delivering other people's, I used to paint at sea during the passage and display and sell the paintings from the vessel at each port visited. This often led to other commissions, and I think I've done watercolours of just about all the restaurants between and including Marbella and Nice, as well as uncountable yacht portraits.

As well as painting my way along the coastline, Caroline and I decided to start some full-time smuggling.

We were buying J & B Rare out of Gib for 30 bob a bottle, and flogging it in Spain for ten times the price, with a similar mark-up on the returning brandy. The passenger-carrying was a perfect cover for shifting 30 cases per trip. Each time, half a dozen bottles found their way to the Spanish customs, which gave us *carte blanche*.

Of course, all good things come to an end, and the problem arose when the competition started up—when the bars and nightclubs of the Sunshine Strip became saturated with the amber nectar. I had a choice: take up the brush again, or return to the UK.

We were lucky, however. Another Spaghetti Western came in and both Caroline and I got parts in it. The film, *Buddy Goes West*, was a bit of a farce, but we were engaged for ten weeks' work at 1,000 pesetas each per day. I had no stunts to do, but was given a speaking part as the banker. Caroline told everybody this was a misprint in the script.

Very sadly, Vic, my dear old dad, died shortly after this celluloid epic was in the can. He was 97, but still had a paramour called Maria. He'd have been very amused if he'd known the hilarity that his send-off, which was a grand affair, caused.

I drove Maria to where he was at rest in Almeria city—about 15 miles. We'd only been on the road for about five minutes when two large black cars tagged on behind us. Over the years I've developed a habit of checking my driving mirror to make sure I'm not being followed and, if I feel that I am, I lose them.

Today I was sure we were.

I hadn't done any serious business in Costacabana for some time, and didn't have an update on the political or criminal fraternity. I tried to shake off this tail without success. At the outskirts of the city I swerved off the road and onto the rambler. This is a dried river-bed, and can be a short-cut. The black cars did the same.

Maria asked me why I was driving like a maniac, so I told her about our shadow. She laughed, and said not to worry. It was the children.

I didn't think she'd understood me, so I almost ignored her. Of course, when I pulled up to where Vic was, the two black sedans slid quietly in behind me.

Out climbed ten children, each carrying flowers.

Vic was laid out in a magnificent black casket. The children visited one at a time, and after kissing him, each placed a flower in the box. One small boy, who must have known Vic very well, also placed a miniature of brandy and a packet of 20 Ducados cigarettes by his head. I felt a complete prat over my suspicions—which didn't help the enormous lump in my throat.

It took a number of large brandies the following morning to prepare myself for the funeral. It was scorching hot, and in a borrowed double-breasted black suit I was the front pall-bearer along with Ron Baddiley, Vic's friend.

It was very well-attended, including most of the hardmen that I had once worked with. Ron had been a very good friend to Vic and understood his unquenchable sense of humour. So when we reached the graveside which is, by Spanish tradition, a vault in the wall, Ron tapped on the side of Vic's box and in a stage whisper said, 'We're going to pour a bottle of whisky over your grave later Vic, as you requested. But we're going to drink it first.'

With Vic gone, I'd lost the main tie that I'd had with Spain. Caroline and I agreed to return to England, at least for a while. We left the yacht in Puerto Banus, and left.

It was actually the inheritance that Vic had left me that decided it. It consisted of two violins, a cello, a number of paintings and pieces of furniture, but above all a large wooden box, about the size of one and a half tea chests, labelled 'miscellaneous' (and spelt wrongly, incidentally). Its lid was firmly nailed down, and it took me much effort to liberate it, because when Vic nailed anything down, it stayed nailed.

On top of the box there were a number of diagrams of whisky-making equipment and the necessary tools to accommodate the hobby; some early drawings of pre-war aircraft; a ship's bell; an ensign from the *Myzpah* that covered the lower layer. It was, however, beneath these items that the real treasure lay.

Paint. Tubes of it. From the turn of the century. Boxes of watercolour cakes by T. Reeves and Son from the same period. And some even earlier little glass bottles containing dry pigments and an assortment of oils and chemicals. There were sticks of charcoal still in their original cardboard tubes, and hosts of French pastels. There also were a number of superb brushes, palette knives and even some paraphernalia that I wasn't quite familiar with. The best thing of all was there was a lot of it.

This discovery was the conception of a new career. I could now become a very competent forger—this time with impunity, knowing that if any of the paint were tested it would date correctly.

There were tubes of paint from 1842 to 1897. Winsor and Newton introduced the collapsible metal tube in 1842. Also hair brushes, fastened to cane and bound with twine, having been stood in water and shrunk tight, then varnished to hold them secure. There were flat brushes with bristles held by flattened tin and sometimes silver. Cézanne used these. It inspired his new vision, and others followed. There were recipes for some of the early masters, dry pigments, gum arabic, poppy oil and varnish that had been around since the year dot—but still perfectly fluid.

Some of the chalks, charcoals and watercolour blocks were by John Reeves, and the address on the boxes was 6 Whitfield Street. They had actually moved from there in 1901 so it was all prior to that.

All this certainly nourished my enthusiasm. Once Caroline and I were back in England the colours flowed.

We opened a gallery in Langport, Somerset, displayed my 'own work' and sold many of them there. I had an adequate studio where I could perpetrate as many forgeries as I liked, the details of which wouldn't simply fill a chapter—they would furnish a complete book.

At this stage I am not prepared to divulge too many secrets on how to deceive and confound the experts, for one very good reason. I'm still at it.

One day I might write *The Forger's Handbook*. Every auction house and museum should have one, and that'll be my excuse for its production. I've given the kiss of life to 16 plus long-dead painters, some of whom have become much more prolific since their demise. Paul Signac, Paul Cézanne, Georges Braque—all French; Richard Henry Nibbs and Anna Airy—English; Bernard Buffet—another Frenchman; Antonio Jacobsen—American; Althea Proctor—Australian; Eliot Gruner, John William Ashton, Arthur Ernest Streeton and Frederick McCubbin—all Australian; Maurice Utrillo—French; Giorgio Morandi—Italian; and, of course, Emil Nolde—German.

It hasn't been solely for the monetary rewards, and over the time the challenge has lessened. The main joy I receive from this type of work is being able to give two fingers to the art snobs and experts—and I use the term loosely. The biggest thrill, of course, is when the hammer falls at an auction. Some of the connoisseurs I'm sure in any case couldn't tell the difference between a Canaletto, a cannelloni, or a can of worms.

Oils take a bit of time on account of the careful drawing procedure—and cracking them in the right place. But in the past I've done a very quick watercolour, smacked it in a suitable frame, and on the way to the dealer Caroline has held the creation and dried it over the dashboard from the draught from the car heater.

On one occasion when we were in Somerset, Caroline wished to go to Bath in order to buy some swanky boots from a fashionable shop. I had an oil that I'd done some time before and thought I might flog it there. It was dated 1896, of a sailing vessel on a wooden panel.

When we were about to depart I discovered that a knot in the panel had fallen out, leaving a hole. I found the knot, and glued it back in quickly with Araldite.

Upon our arrival at Bath, I covered the painting with a blanket without looking at it first, and carried it into a very upmarket-looking gallery. The proprietor waxed lyrical over it and commented that the artist had been clever enough to create a pink effect where the sun was just visible through the clouds. I turned it round and had to agree that the effect was quite stunning—and bloody surprising as well, thanks to a chemical effect courtesy of Araldite.

He bought it. I've often wondered if the effects spread even further as the sun rose.

A journalist once bet me a tenner that I couldn't fool the *Antiques Roadshow,* a popular programme on TV. I took him on and produced three pictures in just four hours.

The day of the recording of the programme, an eminent valuer was on duty. He passed each of them as turn of the century. Not this century—the one before. I got the tenner from Chris White and he wrote a piece for the *Sunday Express* titled 'The Antiques Rogues Show'.

Before I'd received all the materials from Vic, I made a promise to him that I would carry on with the dodgy art. He thought it was quite a hoot. He said if I didn't he would probably turn in his grave.

I think he's probably lying quite still. It's as easy as stealing candy from a kid.

While I'm on the subject of Vic, I'd better mention that dear old Molly passed away about a year later. Letitia, who was working as a nurse in a Brighton hospital, rang one night to say that Molly had been brought in.

Caroline and I rushed to her bedside and all three of us were with her as she passed away peacefully.

Molly wanted to be cremated and have her ashes scattered across the ocean. I duly complied with the first part of her request, but I didn't yet scatter her ashes. I still have them, and I sometimes address her urn when I feel like talking to her.

I intend to return to Brighton and scatter her ashes as she requested sometime in the future.

Thinking of Vic and Molly always remind me of painting so I'm going to stop this chapter now, as I can feel a Paul Cézanne mood coming on. Now, where are the brushes?

EPILOGUE

Twenty-four hours later, the Cézanne is now out of the way and drying. I've also done a Bernard Buffet, which took barely an hour and a half.

As the vogue now seems to be gravitating towards the frightful modern, I've decided to swallow my pride and concentrate on these. After all, I am a con-artist. But the pictures that I produce do grace some high-class walls, and they must be pleasing to the eye or they wouldn't sell.

Judging by today's standards, most of the artists (and I use the word with tongue in cheek) whose style I copy are the con variety. How the hell can you justify attending an art college, usually at the tax payer's expense, and then pick up the Turner prize of twenty-five grand for a masterpiece consisting of an empty room with a light going on and off? And to produce a tent emblazoned with all the names of the blokes that this creative lady has been poked by is completely asinine.

When you can't hang these on a wall, where is the culture? There simply isn't any. In fact, to my way of thinking, the only trace of it is to be found in a tub of yoghurt.

Poor old Turner. He must be literally turning in his grave. I'm sure they now call him Revolving Joseph.

Purely from the monetary point of view, I intend to knock out the odd (in fact the odder the better) modern splodge once a month and explore the market for suggestions, from Dali's anorexics or Picasso's uni-titted ladies to Kandinsky's doesn't-matter-which-way-you-hang-them-up-type productions.

And there are a few ex-girlfriends' names I could use. I must go out and buy a marquee.

Index

WELCOME TO HELL

AN IRISHMAN'S FIGHT FOR LIFE INSIDE THE BANGKOK HILTON

by Colin Martin

Written from his cell and smuggled out page by page, Colin Martin's autobiography chronicles an innocent man's struggle to survive inside one of the world's most dangerous prisons.

After being swindled out of a fortune, Martin was let down by the hopelessly corrupt Thai police. Forced to rely upon his own resources, he tracked down the man who conned him and, drawn into a fight, accidentally stabbed and killed that man's bodyguard.

Martin was arrested, denied a fair trial, convicted of murder and thrown into prison—where he remained for eight years.

Honest and often disturbing—but told with a surprising humour—*Welcome to Hell* is the remarkable story of how Martin was denied justice again and again.

In his extraordinary account, he describes the swindle, his arrest and vicious torture by police, the unfair trial, and the eight years of brutality and squalor he was forced to endure.